M W
& R

Shaughnessy

Shaughnessy

The Passionate Politics of Shaughnessy Cohen

Susan Delacourt

Macfarlane Walter & Ross
Toronto

Macfarlane Walter & Ross
An Affiliate of McClelland & Stewart Inc.
37A Hazelton Avenue
Toronto, Canada M5R 2E3

Canadian Cataloguing in Publication Data
Delacourt, Susan, 1959–
Shaughnessy : the passionate politics of Shaughnessy Cohen

Includes Index
ISBN 1-55199-046-6

1. Cohen, Shaughnessy, 1948–1998. 2. Canada. Parliament. House of
Commons – Biography. 3. Women legislators – Canada – Biography. I. Title.

FC636.C63D44 2000   328.71'092   C00-930929-2   F1034.3.C63D44 2000

Quote on page 26 from *Fifth Business* by Robertson Davies. Copyright © 1970
Robertson Davies. Reprinted by permission of Penguin Books Canada Limited.

Macfarlane Walter & Ross gratefully acknowledges support for
its publishing program from the Canada Council for the Arts,
the Ontario Arts Council, and the Government of Canada through
the Book Publishing Industry Development Program.

Printed and bound in Canada

"All politics is local,
all politics is personal,
and everything is political."

– *Shaughnessy Cohen*

Contents

Foreword

by the Right Honourable Jean Chrétien

On December 10, 1998, Canadians from coast to coast witnessed a truly rare sight in Canadian politics. The daily business of the House of Commons was put aside so that MPs from all parties could give voice to their grief, shock, and sense of loss at the sudden and stunning death of one of our own: Shaughnessy Cohen.

I will never forget that day. And I will never forget Shaughnessy.

Indeed, the spontaneous outpouring of shared affection and fond memories that flowed from all sides of the House that day stand out in my mind as the most eloquent tribute of all to the irrepressible, irreplaceable Shaughnessy we all knew.

There was no fakery or pretence in Shaughnessy. She held her beliefs deeply and argued them forcefully. She was a fierce partisan. But she never forgot that her opponents were not her enemies. And she forged strong friendships that bridged the divides of region and party.

Shaughnessy was tireless. She returned to her Windsor riding every weekend, listened to the concerns of her constituents, and never failed to give them voice in the caucus. As chair of the

House of Commons Standing Committee on Justice and Human Rights, she was a key player in our government's plans to reform the criminal justice system, especially on what I believe will go down as our greatest legacy in public safety, one of the toughest gun control laws in the world.

But what made Shaughnessy a true original was not how hard she worked, it was the way she did it: with a twinkle in her eye. She had a prodigious appetite for fun. Her debating points were sprinkled liberally with jokes. She loved to trade gossip and delighted in scandalizing us with off-colour anecdotes. And her capacity to party rivalled even that of the Parliamentary Press Gallery – an extraordinary accomplishment, as any MP will tell you.

It was because Shaughnessy was, in so many ways, such a force of nature that the manner of her leaving us was so completely beyond belief. Why coming together in the House on that sad December day was what we all wanted to do. Why our emotions were so freely and spontaneously expressed.

In the end, perhaps that spectacle – played out for the whole nation – was Shaughnessy's last and best gift to us all. For it allowed Canadians a peek behind the theatre and rhetoric of national politics to see their MPs for who we really are: people.

I think she would have liked that.

Preface

In 1993, about six months before the election that brought Jean Chrétien and the Liberals to power in Ottawa, I set out to write a series of articles for the *Globe and Mail* on the education of a rookie politician. Among the possible subjects was Shaughnessy Cohen, a brash newcomer from Windsor and a woman I had known for five years. In the end our friendship disqualified her, and I chose instead a Toronto lawyer named Allan Rock. In the wake of the first piece in the series, and as a result of Rock's impeccable credentials, he was fast-tracked up the Liberal hierarchy to a place where it was folly to be candid with a journalist. As a result, I observed very little of Rock's schooling in the art and practice of politics. But thanks to Shaughnessy and the gift of her generous trust and occasional indiscretion, I was taught volumes about the life of a novice on the Hill. I like to think that we learned from each other; certainly this book is the child of the knowledge and the times we shared.

It is undeniably the biography of a friend. Proceeds from its sale will be donated to the Judy LaMarsh Fund, an organization that offers financial aid to women candidates in the Liberal Party. These facts may prompt some people to raise their eyebrows and question the work's credibility and objectivity. Allow me to tell you about Shaughnessy as a friend and as a female politician. Her brand of friendship came with all the unvarnished truths and frank exchanges that only real friends grant one another. Whether with Anne McLellan, Mary Clancy, or this writer, Shaughnessy never hesitated to offer criticism when it was justified. She would be one of the fiercest critics of this work if it offered a sanitized, semi-fictitious tale of a woman who always did the right thing. Such women and men don't exist in politics, nor will they be found in this book.

Shaughnessy did believe that there were too few women in public life, and she knew from hard experience that lack of money was a major obstacle to their careers. The Judy LaMarsh Fund was established to address that need; the donation of proceeds to its cause is designed to honour Shaughnessy, not to favour any political party or agenda. No one asked for or obtained approval of the contents of this book before it was published, including Prime Minister Jean Chrétien, who agreed to contribute the foreword without knowing how he might be portrayed in later pages.

The president of the Judy LaMarsh Fund, Marian Maloney, is a formidable woman whose history with Shaughnessy spanned the legal and political worlds they both inhabited. Marian has been a steadfast supporter of this project since we first discussed the idea in Windsor, on one of the saddest days we can remember. She is the first among many people I want to thank for making this book possible.

Shaughnessy's husband, Jerry Cohen, along with daughter Dena, allowed me to dredge up memories that were still painful as well as to sift through precious mementoes for material. Thank you, Jerry and Dena.

Shaughnessy's parents, sisters, brothers, nieces, and nephews were unfailingly generous with their time and assistance. The Murray family is an amazing collection of bright, funny, disarming people;

my affection and respect for them is immense. In true Murray fashion, though, I must single out a favourite, Shaughnessy's sister Judi Miller, with whom I have enjoyed a long friendship. This book could not have been written without her kindness and patience.

Mary Clancy and Roger Gallaway were not just sources for this enterprise but steadfast allies as well. Mary possesses a bottomless well of hilarious stories and intelligent insights, which she has drawn on many times for my benefit through the years. As for Roger, I relied on him in all the ways Shaughnessy did: to provide much-needed comic relief, to be a supportive sidekick, and to make the difficult possible. Roger and his assistants, Tim Weil and Jon-Paul Hanley, shared their office with me when I needed space to gather and organize material on the Hill. Time spent in that little corner of the Confederation Building was itself an education in the life of a member of Parliament.

Beyond these essential helpmates were people who had no obvious reason to contribute other than the fact that they are kind and giving. I include in this group the librarians at the *Windsor Star*, Denise Chuk and Ute Hertel, who treated me to the same kind of above-and-beyond aid that they gave to Paul Martin Sr. when he came to do research in the newspaper's files. Also, Percy Hatfield and Jerry Head at CBC Windsor, who, through the wonders of videotape archives, let me see my friend laugh again.

Commons Speaker Gib Parent, his assistant Heather Bradley, and Parliamentary Press Gallery manager John Waterfield made sure I had access to the Hill and its research resources. David Ho, a law student at the University of Windsor, plowed through the files of an organizationally challenged lawyer/politician and helped me follow Shaughn's legal career. Yvette Soulliere at the Law Society of Upper Canada came to the rescue when I needed hard facts.

Shaughn would be proud of the help I received from a number of young women: Molly Roberts, one of Shaughnessy's nieces, came to Ottawa to be my able assistant; Sandra Leffler, now working for Health Minister Allan Rock, answered repeated requests for details at the editing stage; Farah Mohamed, Kate

Archer, and Christina Smith organized the March 1999 tribute on Parliament Hill that helped finance my research.

I have many words to thank Jan Walter, the publisher and editor of this book, and Barbara Czarnecki, its copy editor. But I suspect they would have a way to make those words even better, all the while respecting the integrity of the effort.

Janet Smith, the head of the federal government's Task Force on an Inclusive Public Service, gave me strength in all kinds of ways and I owe her a deep debt of gratitude for believing in me.

Closer to home, I thank my dear partner, friend, and inspiration, Don Lenihan. He not only tolerated the experience of living with someone who found herself tackling a writing assignment unlike any other, he offered a supportive empathy that saw it through. We've talked a lot about the difference. He knows what I mean.

My parents, John and Vera Delacourt, as well as my brother, John Delacourt, and his partner, Tamara Cosby, also know how much I relied upon them. Through their example, I know how to spot extraordinary people when I see them.

That brings me finally to Shaughnessy. This book is my thanks to a wonderful, joyful, and talented woman who left behind more than perhaps even she could have imagined. When Paul Martin heard that this book was in preparation, he remarked that the story of Shaughnessy's life would be worth reading for the same reason that the wartime correspondence between soldiers and their wives is more fascinating than the dispatches from the front. It's those letters – not the official war histories – that reveal most about the fabric and texture of the times.

Shaughnessy was a stalwart political soldier, to be sure, who could have penned many letters home about the battles fought and the campaigns waged in her years in Ottawa and Windsor. But her passion was for the daily drama of politics – the rivalries and the loyalties, the personal and the human – behind the scenes of public life. If this book achieves what Martin envisioned, as I hope it does, one of Shaughnessy's gifts will be a glimpse of the real world of Canadian politics.

A Week in December

On Monday, December 7, 1998, Shaughnessy Cohen, the Liberal member of Parliament for Windsor–St. Clair, was making final preparations for a very important event. Of course, everything that this mischievous, fun-loving, 50-year-old woman did was billed as "very important." Working the phones, she was contacting the key journalists in Ottawa to confirm their attendance at a briefing scheduled for her office later that evening.

"I'm calling it a briefing. Let's just say that," she told Bill Walker, the bureau chief for the *Toronto Star*. "But you better get here early or all the booze will be gone."

It was, in fact, a party. To describe the occasion as a "briefing" was yet another joke Shaughnessy played on those who actually believed her self-important declarations. Shaughn and her closest caucus pal, Sarnia-Lambton MP Roger Gallaway, would host an event they dubbed "The Can-Am Canteen" in Shaughnessy's and Roger's offices that Monday night. The "Can-Am" title was chosen because they represented border ridings and celebrated their constituencies' close ties with the United States. The "canteen" part? Well, that was another reminder of a perpetual Cohen-Gallaway gag, played at their own expense. Self-admitted "large" MPs, they didn't deny their appetites.

Shaughnessy Cohen was a large woman. Though she stood only about five-foot-five, her weight hovered around and sometimes well above 200 pounds in the years after she was first elected in 1993. When people described her as "larger than life," they were not just referring to her effervescent personality. She wasn't pleased that her size made her the brunt of fat jokes, but she dealt with it by telling disarming fat jokes about herself. Moreover, she was surrounded by large people, and the collective self-deprecation would quickly develop into a comedy routine. "We're big, we're back, and we're loud," she'd bellow, as a punctuation mark to the hilarity between herself and her large friends. There was, of course, a method behind this madcap routine. Shaughnessy couldn't be humiliated if she punctured her own dignity first.

December in the nation's capital is a predictable blur of schmoozefests and cocktail parties, perfect opportunities for the not so powerful to mingle with the powerful. Political aides, journalists, and politicians seem permanently attired in their best going-out clothes as every evening they hurry from their offices to yet another social event. Fun, yes, but it's work too. Deals are made, ambitions stoked, and egos stroked in the glow of holiday party candles.

This December, Shaughnessy and her fellow Liberals were wrapping up a fall session that had seen tumultuous debate over Prime Minister Jean Chrétien's security arrangements at the 1997 summit of Asia Pacific Economic Co-operation countries in Vancouver. Simmering in the background was the closely watched issue of bank mergers. Four of Canada's big banks had announced merger plans in 1997, setting off a public outcry against the banks' power, and Liberal MPs, including Shaughnessy, were being inundated with voters' demands that the government disallow the deals. Finance Minister Paul Martin was due to make his decision public before year's end, and speculation about his strategy fuelled the conversation at countless Christmas parties.

Shaughnessy Cohen thrived in this atmosphere and intended to spend the week at full party throttle. Her Monday-night "briefing" was the kickoff event for a string of social engagements that would include two big Liberal Party functions and a smattering of receptions all over town. Indeed, Shaughnessy was double-booked the night of her own party – she intended to leave early to attend a Christmas dinner at the residence of the American ambassador, Gordon Giffin, and his wife, Patti. Shaughnessy was one of the few non-cabinet Liberals invited to the Americans' holiday celebrations at their imposing stone house perched at the peak of Rockcliffe, overlooking the Ottawa River. Perhaps even more significant, Giffin had confirmed his attendance at Cohen and Gallaway's Can-Am Canteen.

Cross-border good cheer was certainly the theme of the affair. Roger, a big, balding former mayor from the Sarnia-area community of Point Edward, was Shaughnessy's favourite co-conspirator in such escapades. His huge, booming laugh and quick one-liners could reduce her to giggles in an instant. He had spent the weekend gathering up posters and U.S. memorabilia from his Sarnia friends, and the two MPs passed a good part of the day plastering the walls of their offices with their finds. Shaughn and Roger had spacious quarters, each divided into large offices for themselves and separate areas for two or three assistants, in the Confederation Building, a nine-storey limestone building that sits on an angle facing Wellington Street, just a five-minute walk downhill from the West Block on Parliament Hill. A stairway separated Shaughn's office in Room 461 from Roger's in Room 361.

The Can-Am Canteen would take over both offices, plus the corridors and stairwell between. The whole area was decorated in tribute to Canada-U.S. friendship; the menu was a banquet of chicken wings and other bar food, catered by Ottawa's Lone Star Café. Shaughnessy was not there to welcome the earliest arrivals: she was stuck in the House of Commons along with MPs from all parties, voting on various bills they wanted to deal with before the long winter break. Gordon Giffin was in Shaughnessy's office already, keeping an eye on the parliamentary TV channel to determine when his host might get to her own party. In her absence, he found himself acting as greeter. "Hello, thanks for coming," Giffin repeated, shaking hands with a growing crowd of guests at the entrance to her office.

When Shaughnessy and Roger were finally released from their House duties, they hurried over to the Confederation Building. Shaughnessy told Roger that she'd talked to her office and things were under control. "I'm very, very important," she laughed. "I've got the U.S. ambassador greeting people at the door for me."

Music was blaring from the speakers when they arrived, and the place was filling up with well-wishers and dignitaries, MPs and political aides, all juggling drinks and chicken wings. Roger, an accomplished piano player, had made the musical selection for that night. The voices of the Montreal Jubilation Gospel Choir raised the noise level along with everybody's spirits. Smoke filled the rooms, in direct violation of Parliament's no-smoking policy.

Progressive Conservative MP Peter MacKay, a handsome young lawyer turned rookie politician and the son of former cabinet minister Elmer MacKay, walked into the room.

"Here's my favourite Tory!" Shaughnessy called out, guiding MacKay to the bar and then to her bookshelves, to admire her photographs. The centrepiece of the display was a picture taken just a couple of weeks earlier in the prime minister's office when the pop singer Neil Diamond, a soft-rock icon of Shaughnessy's generation, had paid a visit to Ottawa. As with every male celebrity Shaughn encountered, she had flirted shamelessly with him, quoting his own lyrics: "You are the sun. I am the moon. You are the words. I am the tune. Play me!" Shaughnessy had purred as she was introduced to Diamond.

Almost every visitor to the Can-Am Canteen was dragged over to admire the photo. "You heard what I said to him, didn't you?" she'd ask. Partway through the festivities, though, the picture disappeared. Shaughnessy frowned, glanced around the room looking for it, then decided that someone must have taken it down to examine it more closely. It would turn up.

At around 8 p.m., while the party was still under way, Shaughnessy, accompanied by former New Brunswick MP Paul Zed, set off for the American ambassador's residence. When they walked in the door, Giffin couldn't wait to tease her.

"So you invite me to your Christmas party, I go out of my way just because it's you — and you don't show up!" he chided her. "And then I discover the reason you don't show up is because you're voting on legislation that for the first time puts a prohibition on foreign officials. I've just shown up in Canada as a foreign official and *now* you choose to prohibit bribery!"

The party began, as all diplomatic functions do, with formal cocktails and pleasantries. Jane Stewart, then the Indian affairs minister, was there. So was the *Globe and Mail* columnist Jeffrey Simpson. Shaughn waded into the room with her trademark zeal. Outfitted in a red suit with a sequined black top underneath, she came prepared with an outrageous icebreaker. As she wandered from group to group, bidding hello, she flashed open her jacket: "How do you like my sparkly tits?" she asked. She could deliver this type of line with such a broad grin that it was almost impossible to be offended. The unmistakable whoops of laughter signalled to the room that Shaughnessy had arrived.

The ambassador served decidedly better cuisine than the chicken wings Shaughnessy had abandoned back at the Can-Am Canteen. His guests were treated to maple-lacquered roast salmon, goat cheese soufflé, seared veal medallions, and a hazelnut and Chambord ganache tower. Shaughnessy's table was a mix of the stiff and the relaxed — the French ambassador was there, as was Maryscott "Scotty" Greenwood, the fun-loving but politically astute young woman who served as chief of staff at the embassy. Greenwood alternated between total immersion in Shaughnessy's stories and nervous concern about the reactions of her more restrained tablemates. With dinner over, however, the music went up, the less energetic guests went home, and Shaughnessy and friends proceeded to make a night of it.

One tangle of guests lingered around the dining room, where Patti Giffin led a line-dancing lesson. Shaughnessy and Scotty were in the library with the ambassador, talking baseball and politics. The wine was still flowing, and every now and then, Shaughnessy would make a foray into the other room to dance a bit, but she kept returning to the library, where the fun was more her style – all talk. By 1:30 a.m., Giffin was reluctantly sending hints that it was time to go. Shaughnessy looked as though she could stay all night, even if she did seem tired.

On Tuesday, despite the late-night revels in the ambassador's library, Shaughnessy was up at 4:30 a.m. She had always had problems sleeping and she'd been having more lately. She called Mary Clancy, Canada's consul general in Boston, early in the morning, as was her custom, to describe how she had been "queen of the world" at the Giffins' function the night before. Mary, an inseparable friend to Shaughnessy when she was the MP for Halifax, was almost like a sister. When they served together in Parliament from 1993 to 1997, they shared clothes, secrets, friends, and tea in the evenings. Mary had one parliamentary term under her belt when Shaughn arrived in Ottawa and she had shown her friend the political ropes. Shaughn, in turn, taught Mary how to lighten up, how to be self-deprecating about her size and her vulnerabilities. After Mary's defeat in the election of 1997, Shaughn remained in almost daily phone contact with her friend, even though she was 500 kilometres and a country away.

Early-morning phone calls were part of Shaughnessy's repertoire. Among most of her friends, it was understood that if the phone rang before 7 a.m., it was either a family emergency or Shaughnessy, "just checking in" before her day began. She would often pick up the phone as she watched her political pals on morning TV news shows, analyzing their performances as they were aired. Her criticism could be withering or inspiring, but she would be just as hard on herself.

Early into her tenure at the Boston consulate, Mary made the mistake of having an assistant telephone Shaughnessy and ask the MP to "please hold for the consul general."

Shaughnessy accepted the call sweetly and then plotted her revenge. Several days later, while the Liberal caucus was meeting, Mary received a phone call. The voice at the other end was familiar: "Mrs. Cohen would love to talk to you, but she's very important. Could you please hold for the member of Parliament for Windsor–St. Clair?" Mary suddenly recognized Finance Minister Paul Martin. She was then subjected to a round of famous voices, such as Foreign Affairs Minister Lloyd Axworthy and Industry Minister John Manley, asking her to hold the line to speak to the very important Shaughnessy Cohen.

After talking to Mary, Shaughnessy dressed in preparation for a doctor's appointment. Her eyes had been red and irritated. She joked that she had "pink eye," but Sheila Finestone, an MP from Montreal and one of her closest friends on the Hill, was disturbed. Finestone took Shaughnessy to see her son, a doctor at Ottawa's Civic Hospital whose specialty was delivering babies. He took a look at Shaughn's eyes and prescribed a mild antibiotic. When Shaughnessy got to Parliament Hill later than usual, Roger asked where she had been. "Oh, I went to have my eyes checked by a gynecologist," she said.

At noon on Tuesday, Shaughn sat down with the heads of all the major Commons committees, who form what's called the liaison committee on Parliament Hill. This group of two dozen members manages the $2 million spent each year on committee work: the costs of travel, staff, translation, publication, and research for parliamentary committee reports. The Finance Committee and its budget consultations eat up almost a quarter of this fund; the other committee chairs have to fight among themselves for the balance. As head of the Justice Committee, Shaughnessy was constantly arguing that her work required a major share of the resources. At this meeting, she was more dogged than ever, arguing that the Justice Committee would probably be the repository of the flood of private members' bills expected in the Commons following a loosening of restrictions on that type of legislation.

"So this wonderful change to private members' business means that our committees need more resources. We need a hell of a lot more than $2 million for us to get through this stuff, because some of this private members' stuff is absolutely wingy... And that's putting it as bluntly and kindly as I care to do it," she said.

Shaughnessy spent the rest of the day in the House. The scheduled social event that evening was the Liberal caucus Christmas party, a more exclusive gathering than Wednesday's Liberal Party of Canada bash, which routinely draws more than 3,000 people to Ottawa's Congress Centre.

Shaughnessy didn't much enjoy the massive Liberal Party get-together or any of the grand-scale functions that MPs must attend. She preferred smaller, more intimate gatherings. She was more likely to enjoy the big events if she collected a band of fellow fun-lovers and held her own breakaway functions apart from the mob. She gave the appearance of someone at ease and happy in a big crowd, but if you looked for her after 10 p.m., you would be more likely to find her at home with her tea and the news.

This wasn't the only dissonance between Shaughnessy's party-girl reputation and the "real" Shaughnessy. The image of this MP, focused so much on her reckless sense of humour and her love of the social limelight, belied her intense concentration on work and political concerns. Underneath all the camaraderie with fellow politicians was the calculation that friendly relations could open doors. It was similar to the calculation she employed in her relations with journalists. What few people saw was her almost instinctive strategizing and a rock-hard determination to achieve her political objectives – a determination hidden behind a mask of bonhomie and backslapping. The Liberal caucus party was another opportunity to blend the professional and personal for Shaughnessy.

The caucus was gathering at the Sala San Marco, in Ottawa's Little Italy district, about a 15-minute cab ride from Parliament Hill. It's a huge, ornately decorated hall that has seen more than its share of big Italian weddings over the years. Leading a small delegation of MPs and eschewing a cab, Shaughnessy jumped on one of the little green shuttle buses that operate exclusively on the Hill and demanded to be taken to Preston Street. The bus driver, one of the countless people Shaughnessy had managed to charm in her five years in Ottawa, laughingly agreed and trundled his political passengers over to the hall.

Shaughnessy marched into the party and right over to the table of Paul Martin. Heir apparent to the prime minister's job and the architect of the Liberals' sound economic platform, Martin was the man with whom almost every Liberal wanted to be seen, the man who was being pressed constantly to pay attention to others. Shaughnessy Cohen, the inheritor of the Windsor seat long held by Paul Martin Sr., and a hardworking supporter of Paul Martin Jr.'s leadership bid in 1990, enjoyed a standing, embossed invitation into his inner circle. At the Tuesday-night Christmas party, Shaughn was among those at Martin's table, along with Roger Gallaway and Health Minister Allan Rock, the other main leadership contender, and his wife, Debbie Hanscom.

Shaughnessy, an unaccomplished dancer, to say the least, dragged everyone onto the floor. She shouted for more Motown, prancing and pointing her fingers into the air along with the music, backup-singer style. At her table, a parade of acolytes and Liberal heavy hitters cruised by for a word, keen to catch the ear of Martin if only for a moment or two.

Martin was clearly distracted that night. The deadline for a decision on the bank mergers was looming, and Martin's choice could have far-reaching implications for his aspirations to lead the party. If he went any farther in pleasing big business – as he had done by settling the deficit issue – he would risk losing the Liberals' left-leaning, more populist flank. Shaughnessy, though a devoted ally of Martin's, understood that left flank. Windsor is a union town, and Shaughnessy's biggest threat came from the New Democratic Party. Her instincts ran towards whatever would be described in Canada now as the "left," and she often spoke seriously about social justice and the social contract among Canadians. Added to this was her obsession with the local auto industry. The banks were hoping to find an entry into the car-leasing business. The auto manufacturers, all three with big operations in Windsor, did not want the banks intruding on this lucrative turf.

Shaughnessy and Paul Martin were enjoying themselves, but business was not far from their minds. At about 9 p.m. Martin announced that he had to leave. "You're not going anywhere," Shaughnessy told him as he rose.

"C'mon, Shaughnessy. I have a huge decision to make and I've got reading to do," Martin said.

"You're talking about the banks, aren't you? Sit down. We're going to share a bottle of wine, and I'm going to tell you what you're going to do," Shaughnessy declared, and summoned a bottle of red to the table. This was not a request. It was an order. And the finance minister complied, even if it meant that he'd listen while Shaughnessy drank.

On Wednesday, December 9, at around 6 a.m., Shaughnessy was already awake and on the phone again with Mary. Shaughnessy simply couldn't wait to tell her what she'd missed at the caucus party. (Consuls general, no matter how deep their partisan pedigree, are not allowed to attend political functions.) Emphasizing her monopoly of Martin gave Shaughnessy particular pleasure: the two women competed fiercely to be Paul's "favourite."

"Go away, you horrible child," Mary said when she picked up the phone. "I was out late last night and I'm not going into the office until 10, so I can sleep in today."

No one got rid of Shaughnessy that easily – not even Mary. "Hang up," she ordered Mary, "put your feet on the floor, let the dog out, and call me back." Shaughn then gave Mary a detailed, hilarious account of the evening's events, beginning with the hijack of the shuttle bus. Their conversation drifted to the state of Shaughnessy's health. She said she had cancelled gallbladder surgery scheduled for later that month because she was too busy. Her story, she decided, would be that she needed to put some space between

Christmas and the operation so that she would receive two rounds of gifts. She talked about Dr. Finestone's prescription for her eye problem. Mary chided her for cancelling the gallbladder operation.

Roger Gallaway was at Shaughnessy's apartment early, waiting outside for her at about 7:45 a.m. They were off to the series of smaller caucus meetings that precede the weekly gathering of all Liberal MPs. That morning, the southwestern Ontario caucus was meeting, followed by the larger Ontario caucus. As usual, the talk at these meetings revolved around how the various regions were responding to the major issues on the government's agenda – this week, the banks were on everyone's mind – and the local concerns that MPs wanted to put before the national caucus. Shaughnessy was into full Windsor-booster mode that day, lecturing her colleagues on the need for Canadian content regulation in whisky production. Windsor was home to two distilleries, Hiram Walker's and Seagram's, and Shaughnessy had a long-standing complaint about the way their products were being imitated by foreign competitors.

In late morning she took time out to record the standard televised holiday greeting to her constituents in Windsor. Folding her hands demurely, training her piercing blue eyes on the camera, she stood by the towering Christmas tree in the Centre Block's Hall of Honour and wished everyone back home a happy and safe holiday season.

At lunchtime, Shaughnessy headed to the weekly meeting of the Liberal women's caucus, which is held in a room off the Parliamentary restaurant. Though she was conducting her usual round of business – on this day, still babbling about whisky – she was also upset. A fellow MP, Nancy Karetak-Lindell, had learned that morning that her husband had died, and she had flown back to her home in the Arctic. Shaughnessy talked of trying to get to the funeral and worried about what could be done to help the Nunavut MP.

As the 2:15 p.m. opening of Question Period drew near, Shaughn made her way down to the government members' lobby next to the floor of the House. She ran into Tony Valeri, the MP for the Niagara-area riding of Stoney Creek.

"I've got this goddamn headache," she told Valeri. "It's probably a hangover." Settling into her place in the chamber, she said to Simcoe North MP Paul De Villers: "This is my last Question Period." Wait a minute, De Villers said – there was also a sitting scheduled for Thursday. "Not for me," she said. "I'm going home."

Shaughnessy nipped into the lobby to telephone her husband, Jerry Cohen, a psychology professor at the University of Windsor. Even at long distance, Jerry was the centre of Shaughnessy's world. He was her best audience, her most loyal supporter, her strongest critic when needed. Though the two lived almost totally separate lives during the week, they would constantly seek each other's advice and support by telephone. On this day, Shaughn wanted to tell Jerry about the death of Nancy's husband. She had been worried by Jerry's reaction to another friend's death a few weeks earlier and was keeping a close eye on his emotional well-being.

"Hi!" she said. "I'm just calling to make sure my husband is still alive!"

She made her way back to the chamber and sat down near Bob Nault, the MP from Kenora–Rainy River, just in time for the usual procedural housekeeping that followed Question Period. Like all MPs, maybe even a bit more than others, Shaughn tended to roam from her seat during routine business, to chat and gossip. MPs must sit in their own seats if they want to be recognized by the Speaker or to vote, but they often move around the House at other times. Nault was in the chamber because he was the focus of a privilege complaint. Bill Casey, a Tory MP from Nova Scotia, argued that Nault had tried to intimidate him a couple of days earlier in the Commons. Shaughnessy had said to Nault: "Don't worry, Bob, I'll sit with you and back you up!" He didn't need much backing. The Speaker dismissed the complaint.

Nault left his seat to go for a cigarette. As he slipped behind the curtains, Sheila Finestone made her way over and sat down with Shaughnessy. The two had travelled to the North a few months earlier and met Nancy Karetak-Lindell's husband. They spoke about the shock of his death and how their friend would be taking it. They paid scant attention as Randy White, a Reform MP, stood up to berate the Liberals for leaks of committee reports. Shaughnessy scoffed at Reform. "They are never going to form a government unless they start to understand foreign affairs, you know," she said. Then Sheila pulled out a piece of paper and put it in front of Shaughnessy. It was a copy of a petition she intended to present to her own government, to be signed by a small group of Liberal senators and MPs.

"Same-sex relationships deserve nothing less than full equality. If the government wants to recognize their equality, it should do so openly," the letter said. In strongly worded language, Finestone's letter urged the Chrétien government to be courageous in the face of "family values rhetoric" that masked anti-gay sentiment.

"Sure, I'll sign that," Shaughnessy said and scribbled her signature on the page. As she rose to move on to another seat, another chat, she handed the pen back to Sheila Finestone. Then she suddenly said, "Oh," and collapsed to the floor. Roger, sitting at the other end of the chamber, waiting to release a Commons-Senate committee report on child custody and access, was mildly annoyed. "What now?" he thought. Horrified, he realized the fallen comrade was his friend Shaughnessy – and that she hadn't just tripped. The Commons proceedings were halted.

Blood foamed from Shaughnessy's nose and mouth. Tory MP André Bachand and Liberal MP Peter Adams ran to her. Finestone rushed to the lobby and called an ambulance while Reform MP Grant Hill, a doctor, performed mouth-to-mouth resuscitation on Shaughnessy. Friends joked later that Shaughnessy went into cardiac arrest at that moment simply because that was easier than explaining why she had allowed Grant Hill to give her mouth-to-mouth resuscitation. Or because she had to do something to upstage Roger and his controversial report. There was no question, regardless, that she had turned the Commons on its ear. While the House dissolved in bewilderment, the media pack outside erupted in the throes of news panic.

Within nine minutes of her collapse, Shaughnessy was whisked through the foyer on a stretcher. Her eyes were open; blood covered her face. Even bystanders could see that it didn't look good – her considerable body already seemed lifeless. Journalists scrambled to get close to the spectacle, while politicians and aides tried to keep them at bay. It was not a pretty sight, especially for her colleagues who wanted to shield this private, life-shattering moment from the prying eyes of the TV cameras. They were unsuccessful: cameras caught the picture of Shaughn being carried out of the House, as her friend and roommate, Anne McLellan, the minister of justice, ran alongside.

While this melee was erupting on Parliament Hill, members of Shaughnessy's family were being contacted. Jerry was at his laboratory at the University of Windsor, tied up on the phone. Somewhat impatiently, he accepted the call from Ottawa. Vancouver Centre MP Hedy Fry, another medical doctor, told Jerry what had happened. Shaughn would need to see him if and when she awoke, Fry explained. He was to get on a plane immediately. Dazed, unsure what awaited him at the end of his trip, Jerry headed for the airport.

Those huddled around Shaughnessy at the hospital knew how serious the situation was but were desperately trying to keep a lid on the information. Doctors immediately recognized what had happened: an undiagnosed brain aneurysm had suddenly burst. Although some people live through the rupture of a blood vessel in the brain, this was a severe incident. Liberal MP Carolyn Bennett, a doctor from Toronto, was in the crowd that had rushed to the hospital, and she delicately tried to tell the anxious group that it would be kinder if Shaughnessy didn't survive. Just by observing the external symptoms, Bennett knew that Shaughn's brain was massively damaged.

No one wanted Shaughn's husband and family to find out from news sources that she was near death. Those fears were well founded. Her imminent demise was a topic of public conversation within an hour or so of the episode. As Jerry settled into his seat for the flight to Ottawa, he overheard two other passengers talking.

"Hey, did you hear about this Shaughnessy Cohen guy who just collapsed in the Commons? They say he might be dead," one was saying to the other.

As soon as the plane was airborne, Jerry got up and located the two people.

"Excuse me," he said. "I just heard you talking about Shaughnessy Cohen. She's my wife. Have you heard anything else on the news about how she's doing?" The two just stared at him, shaking their heads. Jerry didn't really want to know the answer anyway. Not yet.

A radio bulletin had alerted Shaughnessy's sister Pat Murray in Ridgetown, in southwestern Ontario, to Shaughnessy's situation. She got on the phone to another sister, Judi Miller, who runs the hardware store in nearby Thamesville, Shaughnessy's hometown. Immediately, Judi leaped into her role as communications coordinator for the huge Murray family. While trying to maintain calm and offer comfort to their parents, Bruce and Betty, who also lived in Thamesville, Judi called all the other Murray siblings; there were five sisters and three brothers altogether. Most of the Murray family gathered at the parental home and waited to hear whether they should go to Shaughnessy's bedside.

In Boston, Mary Clancy had just returned from a late lunch when Gerry Byrne, a Newfoundland MP, got her on the phone. He hadn't been in the House, but his TV was on, and he told Mary what he'd seen. He didn't want her to find out from the news.

Mary thanked him, then sat still at her desk for about three minutes. "She's dead," she thought. "A gallbladder problem doesn't make you fall down." She collected herself and got to work, trying in vain to reach Anne McLellan through her ministerial office and by cellphone. In the meantime, calls were flooding into the consulate from Liberal MPs telling her to get to Ottawa quickly. Finally, Mary was patched through to Anne.

"Mary, it's not good," Anne told her old college roommate. In tears, Anne told Mary that the life-support machines were being kept on until Jerry arrived from Windsor.

"I'm on my way," Mary said.

At about 8 p.m., Jerry landed in Ottawa. Deputy Prime Minister Herb Gray's senior assistant, Garry Fortune, collected him from the airport. Jerry's daughter Dena would arrive from Vancouver in a couple of hours. Dena didn't know a lot of the details, but she feared the worst.

When Jerry walked into the hospital, he had to wade through a crowd of some 25 politicians who were milling around Shaughnessy's room and nearby waiting areas. Paul Martin was there; Jane Stewart too. Burlington MP Paddy Torsney was on hand, still trying to reach all Shaughn's friends by cellphone. The doctors brought Jerry into the room where Shaughnessy lay. Her heart had stopped more than half a dozen times since her collapse.

Jerry asked for a moment alone with his wife. He kissed her and said goodbye, then ordered the life-support machines to be turned off. The devastated band of Liberals at the hospital cracked open a bottle of scotch that Torsney had smuggled in and wept as they toasted their friend. Jerry, who by now was accompanied by Shaughn's old friend from Windsor, Brad Robitaille, was whisked off to the home of Herb Gray. Dena was brought there too when she got to Ottawa later that night.

Over at the Liberals' Christmas party at the Congress Centre, small knots of people gathered to whisper the news: Shaughnessy was gone. Roger Gallaway showed up, zombie-like, to play the piano as scheduled with the True Grit Band, a group of Liberal MPs who entertain at party gatherings. Friends of Shaughnessy's were pulled aside by grim-faced colleagues who had come from the hospital with the bad news. MPs, staffers, aides, and journalists were shaking their heads, incredulous. Finally, an announcement was made. Most of the MPs and party brass disappeared, going home or to friends' apartments to absorb the shock. Other Liberals, especially those who had flown in for the occasion of the festivities, were only vaguely aware of this MP from Windsor and they carried on dancing. Life goes on.

The next day in Ottawa was a sombre one. A caucus meeting had been scheduled to wrap up business before the break, but business wasn't on anyone's mind. The prime minister had agreed, in unprecedented fashion, to allow CTV cameras to follow him around for "a day in the life" of Jean Chrétien. Unfortunately for CTV, this was no ordinary day in the life of Parliament. Shaughnessy Cohen's death had stolen the show, in more ways than one.

At the caucus meeting, Liberal members of Parliament clung to one another and cried; then they made their way to the House of Commons at 10 a.m. Less than 24 hours after she had been buzzing about this same chamber, giggling and plotting as usual, Shaughnessy was commemorated by her parliamentary colleagues.

Jean Chrétien spoke first. Beside him, Heritage Minister Sheila Copps sat wiping a steady stream of tears from her eyes. MPs on both sides of the aisle bowed their heads as the prime minister spoke.

"It is amazing the deep sorrow I felt last night when I learned of her passing and when I saw my colleagues crying. A sister had left us," Chrétien said. He praised Shaughnessy for her partisanship, her quick wit, and her commitment to Liberal causes. "I have to tell members that in many ways Canada is a better place because Shaughnessy Cohen has been with us."

Over in the Reform benches, Deborah Grey had been designated to speak, but she was too devastated. The task fell to Randy White, who had been speaking the day before when Shaughnessy collapsed.

"I liked Shaughnessy's style," he said. "I liked her energy. I admired her tenacity. I respected her forceful advocacy for the causes she believed in and the constituents she represented. I also appreciated her kindness and wonderful sense of humour. That was the amazing thing about this woman from Windsor. She was a seemingly impossible combination of vigorous partisanship and of open-minded friendship. Those of us on this side of the House should know because we have been on the receiving end of both. There will never be another quite like her."

Up in the gallery, in the spot reserved for guests of the prime minister, were Jerry and Dena. Beside them was Mary Clancy, who sat up attentively to hear the next speaker. It was Alexa McDonough, the New Democratic Party leader who had defeated Mary in her Halifax seat in June 1997. Kindly, eloquently, McDonough used her speech in the chamber to make public note of Mary's grieving.

"Everybody talks about Shaughnessy Cohen's stories," she said. "I had an opportunity this morning to speak with Mary Clancy, who was a dear, dear friend of Shaughnessy and one who really thinks of herself as a sister. I said to Mary: 'If you had an opportunity today to tell some of Shaughnessy's stories, what would you say?' Mary said, 'Most of them are not repeatable, at least not here in this House, at least not on this day.'

"But I think Mary spoke for all of us when she said, 'Shaughnessy was the most joyous human being that I have ever known.' That is why she is going to be greatly missed in this place."

In Thamesville, Shaughnessy's parents and siblings were gathered at the family home, huddled in front of the television, witnessing complete strangers mourning the loss of their daughter and sister. Ottawa had never felt so far away. But then Elsie Wayne, speaking for the Progressive Conservative Party, rose to pay her tribute to a woman, she said, who was "different" in this Commons – a woman whose humour and love of her job were infectious.

Addressing the family, she said, "You are in our prayers and she is in our prayers. You will continue to be in our prayers from here on out. On behalf of my colleagues, our condolences to all of you. Thank you for sharing Shaughnessy with us."

Back in Shaughnessy's office, still littered with Can-Am Canteen memorabilia, her staff members and friends were fielding the hundreds of calls coming into the office. Deborah Grey stopped by, her eyes red from weeping, to offer a note of condolence to the people who worked with Shaughnessy. It was placed among all the other notes and cards that were piling up on the desks.

Beneath this pile, though, sat a plain white envelope that had arrived the day before, in the hours before Shaughnessy died. Inside the envelope was a ransom note for the Neil Diamond picture, lifted during the Can-Am Canteen as a prank by Paddy Torsney and her assistant, Farah Mohamed.

Over the next couple of days, Shaughnessy's death remained front-page news, with reporters and analysts almost apologetic for their high-profile treatment of the tragedy. The *National Post* reporter Paul Wells tried to explain: "You should know that there are reasons why Ms. Cohen's death is getting so much ink and TV time. MPs die every now and then and usually the obits are perfunctory. This one's different. Part of it, of course, is the horrible spectacle of her collapse on the very floor of the House of Commons... And part of it is a bias we might as well admit. Journalists liked Ms. Cohen, relied on her for gossip, came to expect only the finest dish and the best jokes from her. The adversarial relationship between scribe and subject was shot to hell whenever Ms. Cohen hovered into our sights."

On December 10, Shaughnessy's body was flown back to Windsor on a Hercules jet. "Shaughnessy Comes Home," read the headline in the *Windsor Star*. Her final journey was being accorded all the pomp and circumstance due a hero or a national leader.

On December 12 at the St. Anne Roman Catholic Church in Tecumseh, near Windsor, hundreds of people flooded into the pews. The RCMP provided an honour guard and Canada Customs agents, at their request, also served as a colour party. At the front of the church rested Shaughnessy's coffin, draped in the Canadian flag that was flying from the Peace Tower on the day she died.

In the front row, on the left-hand side of the church, sat Prime Minister Jean Chrétien, Deputy Prime Minister Herb Gray, Commons Speaker Gilbert Parent, and Finance Minister Paul Martin. The rows behind them were filled with most members of the cabinet, dozens of MPs, and hundreds of people whom Shaughnessy called friends. An overflow crowd watched the funeral on TV monitors in another room.

As speaker after speaker paid tribute to her, it was Shaughnessy's sister Cathy Roberts, with the Murray family's trademark directness, who put this parade in the proper perspective: "Shaughn would have loved this bunch up front paying homage to her, which is probably how it should have been all along."

She was just a 50-year-old MP, a second-term backbencher, little known outside the world of Ottawa. And yet hundreds of people wanted to say goodbye to her. Maybe it was true, after all. Maybe Shaughnessy Cohen was very important.

2

Leader of the Pack

Is it possible that people are born to be communicators? The woman who later called herself "Radio Shaughnessy" – as much for her indiscretion as for her penchant for sharing information – was the granddaughter of a man who helped establish the formidable communications network known as Canadian Press.

Thomas Murray, born in Scotland but raised in Toronto, was one of Canada's leading experts in Morse code, the dot-dash language used to transmit messages over the telegraph in the early part of the century. After service as a telegraph operator during the First World War, he got together with an Englishman named J.F.B. Livesay, who had a dream of establishing a telegraph news network across Canada. Tom, fresh from his electrical engineering course at International Correspondence Schools, became the technologically adept Canadian on a British-led team that travelled coast to coast, installing the teletype machines that would link all the nation's newspapers.

At the newly established Canadian Press, Tom Murray took

the job of traffic superintendent, which plunged him from the telegraph business into the newspaper business. Tom was installed at the *London Free Press* as the regional bureau chief for Canadian Press. He moved his wife, Emily, and his only child, Robert Bruce Murray, then 12 years old, to London and quickly became part of the city's media community. The Murray home was filled with newspapers and gossip from the newspaper business, stories straight out of movies like *The Front Page* or *His Girl Friday*. Newspapering then was a man's business, best suited to the thick-skinned souls who could handle hard drinking, rough language, and the cynicism born of seeing too much for too little pay.

Occasionally the walls of this male-dominated world were breached by an outsider. Not long after Tom Murray arrived in the newsroom, a young woman named Isobel Plante joined the *Free Press* after three years of on-the-job journalistic training at the *Brantford Expositor*. Plante knew she was regarded as an intruder. She got her first job in 1940 when the editor at the Brantford paper unenthusiastically declared that he might as well hire her, since all the "fellas" had signed up for military service. In Brantford, Plante had not been allowed to cover the police beat, even when no male reporter was available. It just wasn't done for women to cover such unseemly affairs as crime and punishment.

The *Free Press*, where she landed in 1943, was a feminist paradise by comparison. Plante's first assignment was to cover developments at the Supreme Court of Ontario's sessions in London. She immersed herself in the work and in the paper's social scene. In this world, Tom Murray was a much-loved character. He had a drinker's nose, "all red and ribbled," Plante recalled, and his flamboyant humour was legendary throughout the newsroom.

While Plante was finding her place at the paper, Tom's son, Bruce, was discovering new worlds of his own. Canada had been at war since September 1939, and the conscription debate was just beginning to boil. Bruce was just 16 when he decided to sign up for navy service in 1941. His initial training was in London and in Nova Scotia, at the Cornwallis base. Then he was dispatched to various training ships, HMCS *Hamilton* among them. At 17 years of age, he was selected as an officer candidate, attending King's College in Halifax. At 19, he won promotion as a sub-lieutenant and was posted to St. John's, Newfoundland.

At the Hotel Newfoundland in St. John's, Canada had set up a unit known as the XDO, the External Defence Office, which was in charge of monitoring the harbour. Bruce was stationed there before heading out to sea on HMCS *Dawson*, to patrol the oceans looking for enemy submarines. Though his unit saw some combat, attacking a few submarines here and there, most of Bruce's war years were taken up with training, routine, and discipline. In 1944, he was made a full lieutenant, becoming one of the youngest of that rank in the Royal Canadian Navy. He left the service in October 1945, shortly after the end of the war.

Like many men who went to war early, Bruce quickly learned to put the experience behind him and get on with his life. He didn't form long-lasting bonds with the men he went to sea with: he didn't want to. The war was one chapter of his life; he was eager to begin the next. Bruce decided that his future lay at the pharmacy where he had worked occasionally while on leave. He secured himself a full-time job at the Wilton Pharmacy on Waterloo Street in London, where he had been delivering parcels since he was 12.

Behind the soda fountain, in his pharmacy whites, Bruce cut a handsome figure. Tall, lean, efficient, and aloof, he seemed unapproachable. He was already a young man of strong opinions and serious ambition, and you had to look closely to see that mischievous sparkle in his eyes. Betty Brennan and her friends were among those who wanted to get a closer look. They were constantly finding reasons to visit Wilton Pharmacy to observe this apparently unavailable young man. "He doesn't go out with girls," Betty was warned by one of her pals. "I'll bet you can't get him to ask you on a date."

Betty was no shrinking violet. She was the daughter of William Brennan, a local manufacturer's agent in London who lived well and cared well for his family. Betty had a fur coat and the carriage of a debutante. Her glossy, shoulder-length brown hair was cut in the fashion of the day. She could match Bruce Murray's quiet wit with her own playful spirit. She sashayed into that pharmacy and made it her mission to get a date with this man. Bruce, as it turned out, was an easy mark. He asked her out.

Their first date was a dance at the London Armoury in October 1945, where Betty was delighted to be the escort of one of the RCN's youngest and most dashing lieutenants. A short courtship followed during which, Betty said, Bruce was "too cheap" to entertain her anywhere but in the Brennan home, where he came regularly for dinner.

They were married on July 30, 1946, and almost immediately moved to Toronto, where Bruce took a pharmacy degree at the University of Toronto on his serviceman's pension. This provided them with free tuition for Bruce and a monthly income of about $80 a month − not a lot of money back then. Hamburger was 10 cents a pound, and Betty stretched their grocery budget by buying caseloads of tomato soup and using it as a cheap base for everything from casseroles to stews. To help out the newlyweds, the Brennans bought them a $9,000 home in the Toronto neighbourhood of Leaside. Though they were supposed to pay $35 a month in rent to her parents, Betty found it almost impossible to live on the meagre pension and the rent payments were erratic. Her father often passed through Toronto on business and would slip her some money to pay for groceries. He also bought his daughter dozens of tropical fish when she complained of being lonely and homesick in Toronto. Sooner or later, she knew she'd return to southwestern Ontario, and she did. In mid-1947, Betty became pregnant, and she went back to her home in London to have the baby.

Elizabeth Shaughnessy Murray was born on February 11, 1948, at London's St. Joseph Hospital. Her middle name, Shaughnessy, was her grandmother Brennan's maiden name. Though Bruce's father's roots were Scottish, his first-born was handed an Irish name that her parents hoped would carry her far in the world.

Betty and Bruce soon realized something interesting about their new daughter: there was a significant discrepancy between her verbal development and her physical dexterity. Little Shaughnessy could talk, in full sentences, long before she could walk. They couldn't decide whether this meant she was precociously verbal or merely a very late walker.

Bruce would watch as Shaughnessy was held by friends or family. Eventually, they would try to put her down on the floor, where it was assumed that she would toddle over to another set of welcoming arms. One of their friends was the first to feel Shaughnessy's outspokenness.

"Don't put me down. I can't walk yet," the infant Shaughnessy warned the adult. Perhaps not believing her, the friend put her down. Shaughnessy sank to the floor. "I told you not to put me down. I can't walk yet," she said.

Indulged, coddled, and cuddled, Shaughnessy enjoyed the run of the Murray home. She was the first grandchild for the Murrays or the Brennans and was thoroughly spoiled. She posed willingly for the usual round of baby pictures, tilting her head coyly at the camera. At 10 months, she sat quietly as her mother read to her, already naming the animals and objects in her picture books. She was enormously fond of words and chatter, even while still a baby in everyone's arms, and she had everyone's full attention. There is an old expression the family used to describe Shaughnessy and the air of entitlement that seemed to surround her: "She took her piece right out of the middle."

It came as a shock to her to discover, in 1950, that her mother had gone into hospital to have another child, four days after her own second birthday. Shaughn, just entering her terrible twos, realized quickly that a competitor was moving in on her territory, and she threatened to pinch this interloper if her parents brought the new baby – a sister – home from the hospital. Apparently unmoved by their toddler's threats, Betty and Bruce brought Cathy home anyway, and in time the two girls became friends and allies.

As his family grew, so too did Bruce's ambitions. Though he

was made manager of the Wilton Pharmacy in 1948, he wasn't content to work for someone else. He dreamed of opening his own pharmacy, and by 1951 he was ready to make his move. In the small town of Thamesville he began building the pharmacy that would carry his name and the home where he would raise his growing brood. A year later, with house and store in place, Betty moved from London to join him. Shaughn and Cathy were still tots and a third child was on the way.

Thamesville, population 1,000, lies midway between London and Windsor. It was the birthplace of the Canadian literary icon Robertson Davies, who used Thamesville as the inspiration for his fictional small town Deptford. In his 1970 novel *Fifth Business*, the most celebrated of Davies's Deptford Trilogy, the town was described this way.

> It was called Deptford and lay on the Thames River about fifteen miles east of Pittstown, our county town and nearest big place. We had an official population of about five hundred, and the surrounding farms probably brought the district up to eight hundred souls. We had five churches: the Anglican, poor but believed to have some mysterious social supremacy; the Presbyterian, solvent and thought – chiefly by itself – to be intellectual; the Methodist, insolvent and fervent; the Baptist, insolvent and saved; the Roman Catholic, mysterious to most of us but clearly solvent, as it was frequently and, so we thought, quite needlessly repainted. We supported one lawyer, who was also the magistrate, and one banker in a private bank, as such things still existed at that time . . . We were serious people, missing nothing in our community and feeling ourselves in no way inferior to larger places.

Shaughnessy's Thamesville was not that different from the town where Davies had lived and worked at his father's newspaper. Like many southern Ontario towns where the trains used to stop, Thamesville was virtually frozen when Canadian National cut its passenger rail lines in the 1960s. To visit it today is to step back into another, quieter era in southwestern Ontario: no big-box stores ring the community; no monster garages dominate the residential streetscapes. Thamesville's London Road boasts the familiar small-town restaurant with Arborite tables and hot-chicken sandwiches on the lunch menu. It has a dime store, where people can sit at the back among the video rentals, enjoy a smoke, and scratch instant lottery tickets. Thamesville also has a busy Home Hardware store, crowded with everything from Rubbermaid to stereo equipment to fertilizer, owned today by Shaughnessy's sister Judi Miller. The major factory in town, then and now, is Bulldog Steel Wool, housed in a long, low, red-brick building close to the Thamesville water tower.

The Murray Pharmacy sits on the same London Road site that it occupied in 1951, its stark, medicinal green-and-white signage proclaiming the serious health merchandise sold in the store. Bruce Murray is still behind the counter, dispensing medication for all the ailments that afflict small-town citizens. The only feature of the decor unrelated to business is a row of photographs at the cash, featuring Bruce's grandchildren and his daughter Shaughnessy.

In its early years, the Murray Pharmacy was like other drugstores of the time — it dispensed pharmaceuticals behind its pristine white counter and refreshments at its soda fountain. The good citizens of Thamesville would gather there, sitting inside at the soda-fountain counter or, in good weather, outside on chairs overlooking the street in front of the shop. Bruce was on duty almost all the time, except during hunting season, when he would put an ad in the paper, complete with illustrations, explaining that another druggist would be on hand to serve customers. He also shut down the business, as was the practice of retailers in Ontario, on Wednesday afternoons and Sundays. Even when most businesses in the province and the country expanded their hours and 24-hour drugstores popped up on every corner, Bruce kept to this old-fashioned retailers' schedule. There was nothing that wouldn't

keep, even in the drug-dispensing business, on a Wednesday afternoon or a Sunday in Thamesville.

Bruce Murray had built the family house – a sprawling bungalow – on Anne Street, a wide, tree-lined street just a few blocks
from the pharmacy. Anne Street was then at the very edge of tiny
Thamesville, and the new neighbourhood was surrounded by fields
and creeks where children could spend their summer afternoons.
On those lazy days, the only sounds in the quiet town would be the
train whistle, the song of birds, and the shouts of laughing children
cycling or playing in the yards.

Shaughnessy was one of those high-spirited youngsters. Margaret
Ellen Kelley, who worked at the pharmacy and lived on the street
behind the Murrays, remembered the arrival of Bruce's family in
town. She recalled being impressed by Shaughnessy as a smart,
sharp, and highly social child who would regularly visit the Kelleys.
She could be charming and disarming, always curious and always
armed with a plan or scheme.

Cathy, growing up in Shaughnessy's shadow, regarded her
older sister as fearless. While Cathy would fret and brood over any
small incident in their lives – especially those that were bound to
get them in trouble – Shaughnessy would brazen it out. The two
girls were expected to cut the broad lawn at the back of the house.
To navigate that 600 square yards of grass, they had to be careful to
avoid a sewer-pipe opening that would knock off the lawnmower
blade. On one occasion, whether on purpose or by accident,
Shaughnessy ran the mower right over the metal cap. The mower
blade broke and flew like a Frisbee across the lawn. While Cathy
looked on, dreading her father's reaction, Shaughnessy marched right
into the house and confessed her carelessness. Bruce was angry, but
Shaughnessy merely shrugged.

"I don't have to cut the lawn any more, do I?" she said to her
sisters.

Until she was 13, Shaughnessy lived the life of an average
adolescent in small-town Ontario. She attended public school,
played with friends, and hung out at her dad's drugstore. To a

family of three daughters (Judi had arrived in July 1952) the Murrays added a burgeoning canine family as well. Bruce and Betty, life-long dog lovers, bred Irish setters. But there were other breeds too. Cathy's dog was Bob, a greyhound. Katie, the beagle, was Judi's dog. Humphrey, the bulldog, became the pet of Patty, the fourth daughter, born in 1956 when Shaughnessy was eight years old. Shaughnessy wouldn't have her own dog until long after she left Thamesville. As a child, she was just too preoccupied with the world to be trusted with the routine tasks of pet care. Nor did she do much housework.

"Hell, you'll be forced to do it soon enough," Betty told her daughters, freeing them from any chores Bruce might have attempted to give them.

Aided and encouraged by Betty, the Murray girls developed strong-willed and independent temperaments. When Bruce went hunting, Betty would declare a holiday and allow all the girls to take time off school. On such occasions, Betty would resemble an indulgent babysitter more than a serious mother. She and her daughters would lie around, watch TV or listen to music, and eat junk food. The whole day was one long party.

Though Shaughn seemed Bruce's daughter in many ways, especially in the barbed wit that lurked behind those eyes, Betty's influence on Shaughnessy can't be underestimated. Dubbed "Noodles" in later years by her grandchildren, Betty was a fearless, fast talker, prone to salty language and instant character assessments. She was impressed by titles and ranks but not cowed by them, and she would walk up to complete strangers and demand to know how much they had paid for some possession or another.

Her five daughters carried stories of her far and wide. The best may be the one about the death of Diana, Princess of Wales, in 1997. Betty phoned all the girls to complain loudly about the presence of Luciano Pavarotti at the funeral. Using rather intemperate phrases to describe his physique, she asked her daughters how the Italian tenor had the nerve to show his face. It was only after some moments of her sputtering fury that Cathy, Judi, and the rest realized that

Noodles had spent the entire week misunderstanding and mis-hearing the newscasts: when reporters said paparazzi had killed the princess, she thought it was Pavarotti who had chased Diana into that Paris tunnel.

Betty bestowed upon her daughters her own eclectic taste in reading and entertainment. She read biographies and pulp fiction and was a loyal fan of TV soap operas and fantasy shows. Shaughnessy, mastering literacy skills early in life, was also an avid reader. By her early teens, she was devouring *Northanger Abbey* and *Cue for Treason* and loving them. She began then to nurse a dream of writing mystery novels.

Shaughnessy was the undisputed leader of the all-girl clan that Bruce and Betty had produced. She happily led her sisters as they tore through the house or trampolined on the beds. She was the instigator of food fights at the table. At dinner one night, she asked her sisters whether they had heard that egg rinses were good for their hair. When Judi asked how that worked, Shaughnessy pur-posefully walked round the table and cracked two eggs on her sister's head. Together, Cathy and Shaughnessy once bound and gagged Judi, then 12, and forced her to listen to all the lurid details of the facts of life.

"One game she loved to play was trying to trap us into admit-ting something we did when we were little so she could squeal on us. She had a great memory and could out-talk most of us," Judi said. "She would also tell us off if we needed it. She wouldn't take any crap."

Shaughnessy and her childhood friend Donna Haggith got into the kinds of trouble that young girls usually find for them-selves. They went into the pharmacy, lifted some chocolate bars, and set up a lemonade stand to sell their wares. Once caught, they got their "hides tanned" for their efforts, Haggith said. On another occasion, the two girls picked all the flowers along Anne Street and then sold them for a nickel to unsuspecting neighbours. Donna Haggith became a schoolteacher in the 1960s and lost contact with her childhood friend more than 30 years ago. She could still recall her, though: "She had a far superior intelligence but never threw it in our faces."

Bruce prized and cultivated this intelligence among his daughters. His sternest lectures revolved around the value of education. He especially urged them to know their history as he knew his. Bruce was a prodigious reader who beamed with pride when he saw his daughters absorbing any reading material they could find – even the backs of cereal boxes. He was not going to raise a bunch of girls to become housewives. He encouraged them to find careers and callings.

When his oldest daughter turned 13, Bruce decided that she should attend boarding school. His reasons for dispatching Shaughnessy to a new and strange place were strategic and ambitious.

"The chances of a child in public school making it to university were one in 20, maybe one in 30," he said. "The chances of a child in boarding school making it to university were much greater. I wanted my daughters to go to university." Shaughnessy was sent to Mount St. Joseph Academy in London, an hour's drive from her Thamesville home. The boarding school years were formative ones for Shaughnessy. She didn't achieve impressive marks, but she was a social success. The nuns regarded her as clever though undisciplined. If she was homesick or ill at ease at Mount St. Joseph, she didn't reveal it to her friends.

Here, by coincidence, Isobel Plante entered the picture again. In 1953, after 13 years in the newspaper world and still carrying painful memories of the war, Plante was seized with the eternal question: Is that all there is? She decided to become a nun. Sister Mary Isobel earned her honours degree at the University of Western Ontario with a combined major in English and French. She became a teacher and was assigned to Mount St. Joseph.

A teacher with exacting standards (60 percent from Sister Mary Isobel was equal to 70 percent from other teachers), this journalist turned educator wanted her young charges to learn that knowledge came through attentiveness to the world around them. She assigned Shaughnessy and her classmates the task of keeping journals of their daily observations. Shaughnessy took to the exercise with a combination of duty, curiosity, and sentimentality. Her first journal entry, dated September 16, 1962, was a predictably prosaic commentary on her surroundings at "the Mount," as the girls called it.

"Today I noticed a beautiful rainbow in the sky after the rain. I also noticed that the curtain rod in one of the dorms has fallen. Cynthia and S. M. Catherine tried to repair it. Ci isn't a very good repair man. Today I also noticed that the blonde spot in my hair is turning orange. My sister's homesickness seems to be blowing over."

This was Shaughn's second year at boarding school, but it was Cathy's first. When Cathy arrived, she found Shaughn completely at ease with the nuns and her fellow students. Cathy, on the other hand, was devastated to be so far away from home and the warm embrace of the Murray family. Shaughn managed her sister's grief – but it was more as a counsellor than as an overprotective sibling.

As Cathy recalled later: "She always kept an eye on me, but not in the same way you would expect. She just sort of 'advised' me as opposed to getting into all of the emotional stuff. I know she really had a problem understanding why I disliked school so much, because she rolled right along with it. She had a circle of friends, the nuns respected her, and I think she just had this enormous confidence in herself."

Betty wrote to her daughters frequently. Her beautifully handwritten letters conveyed matter-of-fact love and care. She'd encourage them to bring home friends on their monthly visits to Thamesville. Sometimes her letters were written on the back of a drawing or a design that Patty had scribbled on the good writing paper.

Betty's parents, whom Shaughn called Grandene and Daddy Bill, lived in London, and the two girls were allowed to visit them every Sunday. Daddy Bill, who had an impressive home in the well-to-do Broughdale district, would pick them up at school in the early afternoon. Before they left, Grandene would take them aside and give them each ten dollars and tell them not to say anything to their grandfather; then Daddy Bill would do the same.

Shaughnessy's journals recorded highlights of these visits, along with the details of her adolescent enthusiasms and preoccupations – not least her frequent experimentation with hair colour. Both girls lifted henna rinse from their dad's drugstore and brought it back to the boarding school residence. October 23, 1962: "Today I observed that my hair is going orange again. I don't know what I'm going to do with it."

But the journal also revealed the ways in which Shaughnessy was being exposed to deeper moral questions, learning tolerance and respect for diversity from the school's own example as well as from its lessons. On September 20, 1962, Shaughn wrote about her pleasure in the sound of the French language, an unusual sentiment in a 14-year-old girl from insular, small-town Ontario. In fact, the students of Mount St. Joseph were encouraged to appreciate the French fact in Canada, and during her final year, Shaughn and her classmates descended on Quebec City for a school trip.

Though the school was Catholic, it was attended by non-Catholics too. This was a time when parents would still disown sons or daughters who married outside their faith or even into another church. Shaughn's journal entry for November 7, 1962, noted the mood at the school as the Catholics prepared for a religious retreat while the Protestants were allowed to go home. She wrote: "I saw that many Catholics envied the non-Catholics because they were going home. I don't feel that this is a very healthy attitude." She had come to view her classmates as individuals rather than as members of one church or another.

Mount St. Joseph tried to educate its students in mind and spirit. Charity and compassion were rewarded virtues. Empathy was highly prized, especially for those less fortunate. The nuns expected their students to absorb spiritual questions and make the answers a part of their lives. They put up "quotes to note" on the blackboard, such as "Life is too short to be little." And above all, Sister Mary Isobel wanted her students to observe, observe, observe – whether at school or out of school. "We were trying to teach them to be alert to the world around them, to notice things," she said.

Some of Shaughnessy's most astute observations were made when she was out exploring the world on her own. There she turned her attention to others. Saturday, October 27, 1962: "Today I saw that I got on the wrong Richmond St. bus. I went all the way out to Baseline Road but it was fun. I saw a poor man who was crippled. He had a little girl with him. I guess it was his grand-daughter. I also saw a lady with her two children, one boy and one girl. The boy was dressed as a girl, however, for a Hallowe'en party. He sure fooled me and the girl had her costume in a large bag. They got off downtown. A little old lady got to the door of the bus at one of the terminal points and because of the cool weather the door was closed. She was banging away and the bus driver was gabbing to someone else so he didn't hear her."

Had this been a real diary and not a journal intended to be read by the nuns, Shaughnessy might have written about more intimate matters: her various crushes or the time that Morris Vale, her first boyfriend, kissed her by the back fence and Bruce, working on the roof of the house, caught them and gave Shaugh-nesssy hell. At about the same time, Bruce got fed up with his daughters dyeing their hair with henna. He made Shaughnessy wash hers back to its natural shade.

"You know, I can remember her being pissed off at him, but I cannot remember her crying or carrying on over it," Cathy said. "She always recovered really fast from that kind of thing. You know – 'Oh well,' and get on with the next event."

Shaughnessy was no angel, and whether she led her sister into temptation or they goaded each other to action, both had a remarkable ability to get into trouble. Shaughn and Cathy could attract disapproval even when they were innocent. It might have been the sparkle in their eyes, inherited from both parents. Or it might have had something to do with the fact that the girls were already smoking. Shaughnessy was 14 when she started buying Rothman's; Cathy was 12. At a time when smoking seemed harm-less, Betty was happy to have her girls join her in the tobacco habit. Cathy and Shaughn had been given permission to choose the decor of their bedroom, and they settled on an outrageous black-on-white design of naked women. Red broadloom and a big brass bed completed the brothel theme. In this den of iniquity, the girls and their mother would smoke and giggle and tell secrets – well out of sight of Bruce, who believed his wife had quit smoking and who was paying her a few dollars a week as a reward. For most of the Murray girls, the smoking habit would be hard to reverse. Shaughn, though, would eventually quit in her 20s and become a rather firm anti-smoker, despite the fact that she always seemed to be surrounded by ashtrays.

Smoking got Shaughn and Cathy suspended on one occasion. Betty and Bruce were telephoned and told to come and pick up their daughters, because they had been caught sneaking off to have cigarettes. But suspension was for high crimes. The more common punishment was to be "campussed" – a public shaming in the form of notices on the school bulletin board and punishment through isolation. Campussed girls were not allowed to leave the premises, even for family visits. Judging from Shaughn's journals, this was not an uncommon occurrence for her.

October 13, 1962: "I was campussed. I observed how slowly I print. I wish we could write the rules." Two days later, she was in trouble again. "Today just wasn't my day. I got campussed for not having my science homework done." So accustomed was Shaughn to being in the nuns' bad books, in fact, that a day without incident was noteworthy. On October 26, 1962, she wrote: "The campus list went up today and I'm not on it. Well, what do you know!"

Another frequent punishment employed by the nuns was to force the girls to do housecleaning around the school. (This may explain why housework was not one of Shaughn's priorities in later life.) At a staff meeting one Saturday, the sisters conspired to contain Shaughnessy and her pals – the Happy Gang, as the teachers called them – with a simple strategy: keep them busy.

"If they're busy, they can't get into trouble," Sister Mary Isobel reasoned.

The Happy Gang was busted for no crime at all. Shaughnessy

was philosophical. Her journal notes: "Cathy, Ci, Ann and I were called out of study today because we weren't working as hard as we should. The only thing is, we were studying. Oh well, that makes up for the times we haven't been caught. Anyway, Ann had to clean the coke room, Ci the rec room and I had to do the ping pong room and help Ci. Cathy had to clean the sink, floor and toilet in the little bathroom."

It wasn't all hair dye and discipline, though. Shaughnessy did take time out to learn, and while her marks were far from stellar, she was singled out for honours from time to time. The nuns were impressed by her capacity for leadership, and she was steered towards the yearbook committee. In later grades, Shaughn went on to serve as student council president, and in her final year at the Mount, she took 11 subjects instead of the required 10, and went off campus, to South Collegiate, to take additional science courses.

Almost reluctantly, she accepted an award for Level Two music theory when she was 14. As her diary revealed, it wasn't the honour that daunted her but the public presentation.

"Today I noticed that I wasn't really scared to go up onto the stage to receive my award," she wrote on November 13, 1962. A short time later, she was asked to appear in the school's annual Christmas play. "Five days until the play," she wrote on December 4. "I wonder why S. M. Isobel picked me." Evidently, though, the theatricals went off without a hitch. Reporting on December 9: "I enjoyed being in the play so much. All of my family loved it. They thought it was even better than last year's." As it turned out, she was developing a taste for public performance.

3

Windsor

Shaughnessy graduated from Mount St. Joseph in 1966 with the comfortably average marks that had become her habit. It was understood that university would follow, though as yet she had no grand plan for her life, only eager anticipation of the next big adventure. With grades that fell below the entrance requirements of the University of Western Ontario and most of the other major institutions in the province, Shaughnessy was happy with acceptance by the University of Windsor.

She lived first on campus in the girls' dormitory near the Detroit River – Electa Hall – and slipped into that milieu as easily as she had adjusted to boarding school. In subsequent years, she lived off campus in noisy, disorderly student houses with other young women. Her ebullient personality masked an aversion to studying. Had she applied herself, friends and family believed, she would have shone academically; she had a remarkable ability to retain information. Shaughnessy could breeze through most of her courses and more than once boasted about the A's she received on tests for which she'd barely studied. She took all her exams orally, preferring to talk about what she knew rather than write it.

This was to be Shaughn's strength and weakness throughout her life. Smart, clever, quick on her feet, she didn't have to try hard. Her parents often worried that she was lazy, since she'd loaf or socialize instead of tackling homework or housework or sports. She devoted her energies to people, to making them laugh, to organizing good times. Confident and outgoing, she was a natural leader who attracted friends wherever she went. She was, in other words, a politician in the making.

An early dedication to English literature gradually gave way to an interest in sociology and psychology. Eventually she did a double major in these subjects, supplementing the regular program with courses in the summer. The material was a natural fit with her enthusiasms – people and group dynamics. As well, she was particularly fond of a young professor, Dr. Jerome Cohen, who taught her undergraduate psychology.

Jerry Cohen was a dark-haired, moustachioed academic, intensely devoted to his research in behavioural psychology. An American who had grown up on Long Island, he did his undergraduate work at Michigan State University and obtained his Ph.D. in psychology from Wayne State University in 1964. He spoke with a strong Long Island accent and fervently embraced both Zionism and the radical left of the American political spectrum. As a teenager, he told his parents he was going to a Jewish boys' club every Friday when in reality he was hanging out with a crowd of Trotskyites at a local bookstore. At university, he sat on the steering committee of the Student Non-violent Coordinating Committee and marched proudly in anti–Vietnam War protests.

The same year he obtained his doctorate, he married, and soon he was the father of two daughters: Cheryl, born in 1965, and Dena, born in 1967. But the marriage had ended shortly after he took a teaching position at Windsor in 1968. When he met Shaughnessy, Jerry was living on his own in a dim, dish-littered bachelor apartment, with hard-won visitation rights with the girls in Michigan.

One evening in the fall of 1969, a group of psychology students and professors gathered at Windsor's Dominion House tavern. Shaughnessy, by now a graduate student in sociology, decided to crash the party. She spotted Jerry Cohen at the bar and made a beeline for him.

"I was in your class last year," she reminded him. Jerry, an academic whose observation skills were honed in the laboratory, not in the study hall, could not recall her. His undergraduate psychology class was a large one and Shaughnessy's attendance record was not perfect.

"My dad took a course from you too," she said, recalling that Bruce Murray had taken a number of university courses over the years. Now this name Jerry knew. "I clearly remembered him as one of the most opinionated people I had ever met," Jerry said.

Shaughnessy was all twinkle and flatter, at the same time trying to impress Jerry with her graduate work on the American sociologist Talcott Parsons, a specialist in functionalism – the theory that stresses the interdependence of all of society's behaviour patterns and institutions. Good material for her later political life, maybe, but hardly fodder for romantic conversation.

Jerry wasn't listening to the substance of her comments; he was charmed by the presentation. Shaughnessy was a shapely young woman whose freckled face lit up when she smiled. Her laugh was contagious. She kept asking Jerry if she was talking too much and he simply shook his head, marvelling at the sound of her voice, "like a babbling brook." After an hour or so of conversation, he asked if she wanted to get out of the "DH," as it was called, and maybe find a cup of coffee someplace. Shaughnessy hardly needed coffee; she had been keeping herself awake with caffeine pills so that she could, as usual, complete an assignment at the last minute. Nonetheless, she accepted and the two ended up back at Jerry's place. Not much happened – the combined effects of the beer, the caffeine, and too many late nights caught up with her. Within minutes of arriving at Jerry's tiny apartment, Shaughnessy fell asleep. It was Jerry's first clue that this funny, bold young woman had two speeds: full throttle and complete stop.

In the morning, Shaughnessy was mortified. She apologized for her bad manners in falling asleep and assured Jerry that she was a good Catholic girl who didn't just meet men in bars and go home with them to spend the night.

Jerry was quick to arrange another, more formal date with Shaughnessy. He told her: "You've already slept with me, we might as well go out together." Laughing, she accepted his invitation to a movie. It was *M*A*S*H*, the 1970 anti-war comedy-drama. Their first really serious date, though, was an evening of theatre at Wayne State University, then dinner in Detroit's Greektown. Again, Shaughnessy babbled and chattered, stopping only to ask Jerry whether she was talking too much.

Not long into the courtship, Shaughnessy decided it was time to see whether Jerry met with the Murray family's approval. One weekend Shaughnessy, Jerry, Dena, and Cheryl packed themselves into the car and headed to Thamesville for dinner. The girls were just two and four years old. Jerry was adamant that the visit be brief; he had to return his young daughters to their mother in Michigan at the agreed-upon hour or risk yet another argument with his ex-wife, Carole.

Shaughnessy, in typical fashion, had taken great delight in telling her parents that she was dating a Jewish man. Rather than fearing their reactions at this first meeting, she confronted the situation with shock humour. When Betty asked what she should serve a Jewish man, Shaughnessy had a quick answer: pork. Jerry was served a very un-kosher dinner – crown roast of pork – and took it as notice that the Murray family was not bending its tastes to please anyone, not even a man with whom their eldest daughter had become quite serious.

The Jewish issue was never far from the surface in his relations with the Murrays. Like most Catholic families, they were close to the local priest, Father Charles McManus, who would often be at the house when they gathered for dinners on the weekend. On one occasion, Shaughnessy and Jerry were visiting on a Sunday and fell into a heated conversation in the den. Though they were trying to keep their voices down, the others heard Jerry exclaim in exasperation: "Jesus Christ, Shaughn!"

Father McManus smiled and nodded to the eavesdropping Murrays. "I think Jerry's coming around to our way of thinking after all," he said.

Jerry had worked on a kibbutz in Israel in the summer of 1969 and told Shaughnessy that fall that he intended to return the following summer, perhaps even to stay on and teach in Israel. Shaughnessy liked the idealism behind the trip, but she was worried by what his summer absence meant for their relationship. By now, Shaughnessy and Jerry were spending most days and evenings together. They had gone to Chicago to meet Jerry's father and stepmother. Lois Cohen, who observed her Jewish faith strictly, greeted Jerry's new girlfriend with the declaration, "Shaughnessy? That's not a Jewish name!" Murray Cohen, who had worked and attended church with a Catholic family when he was a teenager during the Depression, was less concerned about the religious mismatch. He was instantly taken with Shaughnessy.

Despite Shaughnessy's reservations, in the summer of 1970 Jerry set off for the Ashod Yaakov Ichud kibbutz in Israel, to spend a few months planting trees and tending livestock on the farm. He wrote frequently to Shaughnessy, with whom he had left his car and his heart back in Windsor. Shaughnessy wrote just as often, relating events around town, gossip from the university, and amusing stories about her family. Finally, Jerry realized that he could not bear to be away from her – not this summer, not ever. He proposed marriage in a letter; she replied immediately, with an enthusiastic yes.

Jerry and Shaughnessy were married at a senior citizens' hall in Windsor on December 18, 1971, in a rather unorthodox ceremony. They couldn't be married in the Catholic church because Jerry was divorced. They couldn't be married according to Jewish faith because Shaughnessy refused to convert. So they managed to find a rabbi of somewhat relaxed views and surreptitiously borrowed a *chuppah* – the canopy that hangs above the couple in Jewish wedding ceremonies – from a local synagogue. The first sight that greeted guests as they entered the hall was a huge, elaborately decorated Christmas tree.

The Murrays were there, of course, as were Murray and Lois Cohen. A small contingent of Bruce and Betty's friends were also invited. The photos depict typical 1970s wedding fashion: the bride's long hair organized into a complicated do of stiff curls on her head; the groom outfitted in wide lapels and beaming smile.

Shaughnessy only half realized what she was doing, as she later told friends. It hit her the day after the wedding, as the two set out to drive to New Orleans on their honeymoon. Well into the trip, Shaughnessy gazed over at Jerry and thought: "So, Elizabeth Shaughnessy Murray Cohen, you've married a Jewish divorcee, six years older than you, with two kids! Now you've really done it!"

A few months before they married, they had decided to buy a house. In Amherstburg, a half-hour drive from Windsor, they found a modest, 24-by-16-foot cottage on River Road. It was just one room, but they intended to expand it, by building either bigger or higher. They dreamed of turning its tiny deck, which looked out on the Detroit River, into an expansive, party-worthy platform. They bought the house immediately and Jerry moved in right away, drawing up plans for the renovation he expected to do himself. They returned from their honeymoon and began work on a 30-by-16 foot addition.

Shaughnessy bought decorating magazines and cookbooks and threw herself into domesticity. She developed a repertoire of recipes to serve up to Jerry each night: vegetarian lasagna, pastitsio (Greek noodles with lamb and rosemary), Beef Wellington, and lots of meat-and-potato dishes.

Jerry, meanwhile, was absorbed by house construction and the maze of municipal red tape attached to the enterprise. His involvement in these intricacies soon earned him an invitation to sit on the local Public Utilities Commission and membership in the Essex Region Conservation Association Foundation.

Almost every weekend they travelled to Detroit to pick up Dena and Cheryl. Shaughnessy always got along better with Dena, whom she described as "a cool kid," than with Jerry's older daughter. Shaughn was an exuberant if sometimes scattered force in their lives now that she was "Dad's new wife." She could draw them into whirlwinds of busy activity and elaborate plans but would also deliver sharp verbal smacks if she thought they were being disrespectful to their father. The tension between Jerry and Carole was like an uninvited guest in the room in the early days of Shaughn's marriage, but she staunchly stood by Jerry in the battles and soothed his temper when it overheated.

Shaughnessy, like any new wife, soon set about fixing all of her husband's annoying little habits. One of her serious peeves concerned Jerry's pickiness about food and his claims to a wide range of allergies. Having inherited Bruce's buck-up, no-nonsense attitude to human frailty, Shaughn believed allergies were all in the head. She was particularly annoyed that Jerry believed he was allergic to apples — no one is allergic to fruit, she said.

One day, Shaughnessy came home with a bushel basket of freshly picked apples. When Jerry arrived, he found Shaughnessy sitting with the bushel between her knees and the car keys jingling in her hand.

"Eat one of these apples," Shaughnessy commanded.

"I can't eat apples. I'm allergic," Jerry said.

"You're not allergic to apples. You don't like apples. I'm not going to keep hearing this," she said.

"But — ," Jerry said.

"I'm not taking no for an answer," Shaughnessy said. "You're going to eat one of these apples. If you have an allergic reaction, I've got the car keys right here and I'll drive you directly to the hospital."

Jerry obediently took a bite of the apple. Nothing happened. No rash, no choking, no wheezing.

After a few moments, Shaughnessy smiled and said, "See? From now on, you won't say you're allergic to apples. You'll just say you don't like them."

Jerry had a few peeves of his own. He was a firm anti-smoker, and Shaughnessy soon abandoned her pack a day of Rothman's, taking up jujubes instead. After she quit, she never lapsed, becoming a zealous reformed addict. Shaughnessy didn't allow smoking in her home, but she would always say that the ban was in deference to Jerry.

Jerry also resented Shaughnessy's blithe indifference to such details as paying parking tickets. More than once, a sheepish policeman – whom Shaughn inevitably knew – would show up at the door with apologetic requests for tickets to be paid. Similarly, Shaughn was lax about phoning home when she knew she'd be out late. Not long after they were married, Jerry arrived home from the university expecting Shaughnessy to be there before him. There was no note and no call. As the hours ticked by, Jerry started to worry and considered calling the police. Finally, well after midnight, Shaughnessy rolled in. She'd been out with friends, she said, and simply lost track of time.

Jerry was furious; he even challenged her about whether she was cheating on him. It was the angriest he had ever been with her. From that day forward, Shaughnessy always called when she expected to be late. She didn't shorten her evenings, but Jerry could count on hearing from her, usually pleading with him to join her. More often than not, Jerry declined. "We were just different that way," he said. "But that was fine. She did her thing and I did mine." Her thing was being out with friends or talking to them on the phone; his thing was quiet nights at home, preparing for classes, reading novels, or watching TV.

Shaughnessy had begun teaching sociology at St. Clair College in Windsor and Chatham in 1971 – a job she loved – while completing her master's degree in sociology. Laurie, the fifth and last of the Murray girls, born in 1963, frequently came to visit Shaughnessy at her classes and would sometimes be installed with crayons and paper beside her big sister's desk. If Laurie thought the students weren't paying close enough attention to Shaughnessy, she would loudly shush them.

Her family, though still in Thamesville, was a constant fixture in Shaughnessy's life. She would see them regularly when the Murrays travelled to Detroit for bargain shopping across the border. Sneaking stateside purchases past Canada Customs was a sort of national sport for residents in the area. Thin Canadians would cross the Detroit River and come back a few hours later, suddenly hefty under layers of brand-new garments. During these shopping trips, the Murrays often dropped in on Shaughn and Jerry in Amherstburg.

The family had moved to a larger, more stately home in rural Thamesville in 1968. The town had expanded around the Anne Street bungalow and the Murray clan, then still growing, installed itself in expansive new quarters in the country, where they had a swimming pool and 144 acres of land. But as the girls started to leave home, for boarding school or university, Betty began to get lonely. Cathy and Shaughn were at university, Judi at nursing school. Betty loved the noise of young children around the house; she would put sneakers in the clothes dryer to mimic the sound of kids' feet running down the halls. The home was just too quiet.

The Murrays began to entertain the idea of adopting one of the children who appeared in the newspaper's "Today's Child" column, the highly successful feature from the Children's Aid Society that tried to find loving homes for older foster children. They were especially drawn to children from other cultures and nationalities. It was just a small step from dreaming about new Murray children to making it happen. Betty and Bruce called up the Children's Aid Society regularly to inquire about the children they saw in the paper. Inevitably they were told that the kids were already adopted.

Then, in 1969, they got a call. Twin aboriginal boys, 22 months old, needed a good home. Accompanied by 17-year-old Judi, Betty made the trip to the Children's Aid office in North Bay. It was love at first sight. The twins, with jet-black hair and deep brown eyes, ran towards Betty and Judi with open arms. Named Bill and Tom Murray, they won Betty's heart.

A few months later, Children's Aid called about another aboriginal boy, Richard, age 10. "Well, send him over and we'll have a look at him," Bruce said in characteristically blunt fashion.

Another child walked into their home and charmed them. Holding out his hand, Richard came right up to Bruce and said, "Hello, Dad." With that bold gesture, he became a Murray on the spot. In later life he would follow Bruce in his career, opening up his own drugstore in nearby Ridgetown.

Were the Murrays just lucky in their experience of aboriginal adoption? In the 1980s and 1990s, cases of native adoptions gone badly awry prompted social scientists and child care agencies to reconsider the idea of raising aboriginal children so far away from their own cultures. Shaughnessy's family, however, did not experience such heartbreak. The success of the Murray adoptions lay in their determination to maintain the connections between their adopted children and their roots. Faithfully, but with great trepidation, Betty would take her sons on annual pilgrimages to northern Ontario so they could stay in touch with their native relatives. She would fret for days before the journey, worrying that the boys might decide they didn't want her as their mother after all.

Shaughnessy was away at university when the boys came to Thamesville. When they were young, she was a blur of laughter in motion that swept through the house from time to time. It wasn't until they were older that they came to know her better and experienced her concerted campaigns to make sure they were aware of their native heritage. Richard in particular felt these efforts were unnecessary, but Shaughnessy didn't let up. Periodically, through the mail, Richard would receive dispatches from Shaughnessy, imploring him to read this or that article to better understand and appreciate where he came from.

Those close to Shaughnessy were well aware of her fierce, protective devotion to the Murray clan. "You could slight her but not her mom or dad or brothers or sisters," Jerry said. "Do that and you were an enemy for life." At least one guest was banished from the Amherstburg house after making a snide comment about

Betty that Shaughn overheard. Loyalty was no small issue to her.

The five girls of the Murray family all had their own characters, though someone observed that if you blended the personalities of Cathy, Judi, Patty, and Laurie, you would end up with the entire character that was Shaughnessy. Cathy was the warm, emotional side; Judi, the tough, no-nonsense element; Patty, the gentle wit; and Laurie, the animal lover with scattered energies.

Shaughn's marriage was the second in the Murray family. Cathy married Robbie Roberts in 1969, had two children, and set up house in Newmarket, Ontario, where her husband ran a museum. Six months after Shaughn married, Judi wed Warren Miller, a farmer from Thamesville, and quickly started the family that would include four children. Patty and Laurie were still too young to contemplate marriage when their older sisters wed, but they would eventually have their own children too. Only Shaughnessy among the sisters remained childless. The reasons she offered ranged from "It hurts" (to give birth) to the assertion that Jerry's daughters were kids enough for them.

Shaughnessy doted on the nieces and nephews as they arrived. Christmas was her favourite family holiday: it gave her an excuse to shower the clan with gifts and remind the youngsters that she was their favourite aunt. It was also an opportunity to torture her siblings with a highly satisfying prank. It became her habit on Christmas morning to get up as early as 4 a.m. and phone the kids. She would whip the children into a frenzy by telling them Santa had arrived and then smugly return to bed, leaving the sleep-deprived parents to try to calm their Christmas-crazed offspring.

By 1973 Shaughnessy was finishing her post-graduate work in sociology and preparing her thesis, "The Segregation of Women in the Labour Force of Ontario – 1921 to 1961." Trying to figure out what to do next with her life, she sent out two applications: to the doctoral program at Wayne State University and to the University of Windsor law school. She would put her future in the hands of fate and become either an academic or a lawyer, depending on which institution accepted her.

But both schools were prepared to admit her. Indeed, Wayne State, only a 30-minute commute away from Windsor, offered a scholarship. Jerry liked the idea of a husband-and-wife academic team. He believed that Shaughnessy was too reticent about her intelligence; a doctorate beside her name would leave no doubt. They would have the same vacations and the same hours and move in similar circles. Her father, however, was intent on Shaughnessy becoming a lawyer. "A profession! That's what you need," Bruce would tell his oldest daughter.

Among Shaughnessy's friends at the time was a Michigan lawyer named Carrie Flaherty. Shaughn went to Flaherty and sounded her out. Flaherty suggested she come to court one day and observe the proceedings. At the time, Flaherty was acting as defence lawyer in a high-profile case. The media were all over the courtroom, and Shaughnessy watched in awe as Flaherty stepped adeptly into the limelight and danced through reporters' questions. When she got home that night, Shaughnessy told Jerry: "I've decided. I watched Carrie today and that's what I want to do."

Shaughn entered first year at the University of Windsor law school in 1974 with about 180 other would-be lawyers. The group was split up into three sections, alphabetically. Thanks to her name change, Shaughn was in the same section as a politically ambitious student named Brian Ducharme.

Ducharme was a fast-talking, self-assured man who could match Shaughnessy in verbal dexterity. Though she hadn't studied politics, she was impressed by the circles in which Brian travelled. Politicians were still somewhat lofty figures in the 1970s, especially in Liberal-laced Windsor, and Shaughnessy was transfixed by the inside knowledge that her friend Brian, quickly dubbed "Beanie," seemed to possess.

Brian had interrupted his education in 1972 to go to Ottawa, where he served as executive assistant to Eugene Whelan, MP for Essex-Windsor and the new minister of agriculture in Pierre Trudeau's cabinet. Whelan was a genuine character whose signature accessory was a huge green Stetson. He prided himself on being one of the people, especially the rural people, and he talked with a farmer's plain-spoken drawl. He was no country bumpkin, though. Whelan played politics for keeps and watched his Windsor Liberal stronghold closely. Ducharme's job was to help him do just that.

Ducharme stayed with Whelan two years, immersing himself in the heady atmosphere of federal politics and enjoying all the perks a young aide could grab in those days. But after the election of 1974, Ducharme chose to return to Windsor and law school. He kept his ties with Whelan, though, working part-time as a "special adviser" while pursuing his studies. It was through this connection of Ducharme's that Shaughnessy got her first close look at Liberal politics in Windsor, especially as it was played by the tangled web of lawyers, politicians, and community leaders in the city.

For a city of its size, Windsor played an unusually large role in national politics throughout the 1960s, 1970s, and early 1980s. The dean of the Liberal establishment in Windsor was Paul Martin Sr., who represented Windsor-Walkerville (earlier Essex East) for 33 years in the Commons and served as health minister and external affairs minister in the Liberal governments of W.L. Mackenzie King, Louis St. Laurent, and Lester Pearson. Martin, who ran three times for the leadership of the party before going on to serve in the Senate and as Canada's high commissioner to Britain, kept Windsor on the map. If there was money available – and the country seemed to be swimming in it for most of his time in office – Martin would ensure that Windsor got its share for everything from job programs to new building projects. No matter how senior his stature or how high his rank in Ottawa and the world, Paul Martin Sr. could be counted on to ask, when faced with a thorny domestic issue: "What does it mean to Windsor?"

Martin Sr. faded from the scene after his leadership loss to Trudeau in 1968, but no fewer than three ministers from Windsor eventually rose up to succeed him in speaking for the city at the cabinet table. Windsor West (earlier Essex West) had Herb Gray, the solidly loyal Liberal who had sat in the Commons since 1962.

Gray's personal style was decidedly conservative but his politics were left-leaning. He served in Trudeau's cabinets in the early 1970s and again in the 1980s, making his mark as an economic nationalist. Windsor-Walkerville had Mark MacGuigan, the brilliant former dean of the University of Windsor law school. Succeeding Martin Sr. in 1968, he was destined for a portfolio, becoming secretary of state for external affairs in 1980 and justice minister in 1982. Eugene Whelan in Essex-Windsor (earlier Essex South) completed the triad. While these three formed a united chorus for Windsor in Ottawa, back home they displayed seething competition and territorial chauvinism. A joke of the 1980s had it that the tiny Windsor airport sported three gates because each cabinet minister wanted to boast of one.

Ducharme was in Whelan's camp, and that, to borrow from Windsor's rather unimaginative city slogan, was the place to be. Eugene Whelan was the cabinet minister in charge of the southwestern Ontario region and wielded the heaviest clout over everything from grants to patronage appointments. Whelan employed Ducharme in the search for appropriate judicial appointments. It was Ducharme's job to consult with lawyers around town to find good candidates for the bench.

Like all would-be political players, Brian Ducharme and Shaughnessy delighted in gossip and discussed all kinds of things they probably shouldn't have. "Of course, she wanted to know who was being consulted and who was likely to become a judge," Ducharme said. "I didn't know exactly, but based on my discussions with Gene, I had an idea of who he might name."

Lesson number one in politics: knowledge is power. And prior knowledge is even greater power. Shaughnessy began to see that possession of any whispered information about judicial appointments, any well-informed gossip, could make one a force to be reckoned with in Windsor's legal world. And how does one get gossip and prior information? Through connections, of course. For Shaughnessy, Ducharme's role was a case study in the power of a network in politics. Ducharme and Shaughnessy were becoming a network in themselves, with the young woman learning at the feet of the young man who had already worked in Ottawa and was currently playing the local political game with considerable expertise.

Shaughnessy finished her law courses in 1977. She hadn't achieved any particular academic distinction and there was no flurry of offers to take her on as an articling student. Thanks to Ducharme and his wide circle of legal contacts, however, she didn't have to worry that she would be unemployed. Her first position was with McTague Clark, a well-respected downtown Windsor firm. There she completed her articles and was hired after being admitted to the bar in 1979.

Shaughnessy, though almost consumed by her new life in the law, was also trying to find a role for herself in community service. In part, this was a reflection of Shaughnessy's nascent ambitions on the political level and the upward social trajectory she had planned for herself in Windsor. But it was also rooted in her upbringing and Bruce and Betty's examples of community and church involvement. Shaughnessy simply knew that a full life included some community or charity work.

In 1977, Brian Ducharme urged Shaughnessy to get involved with a fledgling women's shelter near the University of Windsor; at the time it had enough room for only nine women and children. Called Hiatus House, it was run by the determined, American-born daughter of a Presbyterian minister, Donna Miller. Ducharme was already on the board there, and he suspected that Shaughnessy and Miller would work brilliantly together.

Miller first encountered Shaughnessy when the young law student was asked to chair a panel discussion sponsored by Hiatus House on legal issues surrounding battered women's shelters. Miller was impressed with Shaughnessy's skills in the chair. Though Shaughnessy was just 29 years old, she conducted herself like a professional, radiating authority and leadership — but always with a sense of humour.

"She defined things differently than the average person," said

Miller. "When she was working she was playing, and when she was playing she was working. The two were not separate for her... Your average lawyer would say that Shaughn was never in work-hard mode. That's because she played at everything she did, no matter how serious it was. There's something to be learned there."

When Shaughnessy became more involved in Hiatus House, Miller knew that she wasn't motivated by any personal experience of domestic abuse. As a strong woman herself, Miller recognized that the issue draws those to whom it has happened and others who fundamentally cannot imagine why it is happening. Shaughnessy was one of the latter.

During the time that Shaughnessy was active as a board member at Hiatus House, it grew from its modest beginnings to a modern, 42-bed complex near the river's edge. Shaughnessy was on the board from 1981 to 1984 when Jean Chrétien, as justice minister, helped the shelter establish a legal support system for complainants. Her involvement predated the time when the debate over wife abuse entered mainstream commentary, before docudramas and education campaigns made it a crime that could be discussed in the open. Hiatus House grew along with that public acknowledgment; women's shelters would be funded, after all, only if the public at large admitted that abuse was actually happening.

"She was involved when it was not necessarily the fashion-able thing for a young lawyer to do," Miller said. "And she stuck with it."

Much of Shaughnessy's early experience as a chairperson and as a public debater was gained in her days at Hiatus House. She was repeatedly asked to make the shelter's presentations to the United Way, for instance, because Miller found her quick on her feet and able to articulate the underlying issues when people challenged the work of Hiatus House.

Miller knew that Shaughnessy wasn't always on the side of the victims. As she developed her practice as a defence lawyer, Shaughnessy could find herself defending a man whose wife might well have been one of the shelter's clients. These cases would be consigned to the off-limits zone of conversation between Miller and Shaughnessy.

—   —

In the summer of 1977, Jerry was offered a teaching job in Sydney, Nova Scotia. It was just a summer position, but a welcome opportunity for Shaughn and Jerry to take the girls on a working vacation and see some of the rest of Canada. He bought a new car, a yellow Volkswagen Rabbit, and the four drove from Ontario to the house they were renting in Cape Breton. Dena was 10 and Cheryl was 12. They did all the usual "touristy" things, Dena recalled, and the summer flew by.

Shaughnessy was able to manage this trip financially by handling some part-time law-related work in Halifax. Naturally, she soon developed a circle of friends there too. One day she was invited to have lunch with two Liberal women in town, Mary Clancy and Dale Godsoe. Mary was a lawyer, just getting her practice under way. Dale Godsoe was the wife of Gerry Godsoe, a high-profile Liberal lawyer in Halifax.

The three women agreed to meet at an upscale restaurant, Fat Frank's. Within minutes of the introductions, Mary and Shaughnessy were swapping stories about Liberal politics and players, most notably about Prime Minister Pierre Trudeau and those who might wish to succeed him, including John Turner.

This was, as Mary remembered it, the debut of the Shaughn-and-Mary road show. "We literally met and knew we'd be friends for life. It wasn't even discussed. It just was," Mary said. "They threw us out of the restaurant when the dinner crowd arrived and Shaughnessy had to catch a plane to Sydney." Thereafter, the two women talked about once a month – long phone sessions that would weave in and out of subjects ranging from their law practices to their clothing purchases.

As the summer holiday wound down, Dena and Cheryl faced the prospect of returning to California, where their mother then lived. Dena didn't want to go back, so she confronted Shaughn and Jerry directly: could she live with them? Shaughn and Jerry sat stunned and slack-jawed. So intense was their exchange of glances that Dena felt she had to quickly apologize for asking.

But Jerry said at once that it was fine with him. He would have to work things out with Dena's mother, but if Carole agreed, Dena could stay. Shaughnessy would tearily confess later to Cathy that she feared what she was getting into; she hadn't counted on being a mother to an almost teenaged daughter when she married Jerry. She was also worried that Dena's mother would reconsider any agreement to let her daughter live so far away and that this would prove heartbreaking to Jerry. So Shaughnessy insisted that a document be drawn up for Carole to sign, consenting to Dena's change of address.

"No such document was really needed, but Shaughn reasoned that this legal sleight-of-hand might dissuade Carole from changing her mind," Jerry said. "We lived on pins and needles for the first couple of years - especially when Dena went to California to visit her mom during the summer. Shaughn was as anxious as I was, waiting at the airport for Dena to come back home." There were echoes of Betty, Shaughn's mother, who was always nervous too that the natural parents of her adopted boys would want to take them away.

Shaughnessy wanted to win the affection of the new child in her house, but she was also determined to be a firm hand and strong example to Dena. "I may not have produced Dena, but I directed her," Shaughnessy always boasted. As circumstances would have it, though, Shaughnessy was not in Amherstburg by the time Dena arrived to live with them in 1978. She was back in London, living with her Aunt Betty and Uncle Bill Brennan while taking her bar admission course.

When she returned to Amherstburg, Shaughnessy's life was transformed. She found herself a new mother and a new lawyer at the same time, juggling home and career concerns with little or no preparation. Dena would be planted in Shaughn's law office after school, told to do her homework while Shaughnessy finished off her day's work. Then the two of them would head home, where Shaughnessy made dinner, rescuing Dena and Jerry from the fish sticks or frozen foods they would eat if no one was there to cook for them.

The process of becoming a family, with all its demanding routines and daily dramas, was far from easy. Dena had walked into a home where two people were busily trying to establish their careers, while she simultaneously required but shunned a lot of parental attention and guidance. Shaughnessy was confronted with the inherent conflicts and guilt of a working mom.

— —

Windsor learned early that there was money to be made in giving Americans what they couldn't have in their own country. It started with the bootleggers during Prohibition, when Hiram Walker's set up shop on the banks of the Detroit River, and continued through to the 1980s, when Windsor became the home of Canada's first privately run casino. It was the Windsor lawyer Pat Ducharme who was instrumental in helping stretch the legal limits to allow the proliferation of nude-dancing establishments in the city in the 1980s. Indeed, Windsor always seemed to be sitting at the edge, not just of the country but of the law. Brian Ducharme's firm, for instance, became the first in Canada to launch television advertising, testing the traditional view that such self-promotion was beneath the legal profession.

None of Windsor's racy businesses, though, survived entirely on American patronage. Thanks to the arrival of the auto manufacturers in Windsor at the turn of the century – which came about because American carmakers needed a toehold in the market of the British empire – many of Windsor's citizens became regular wage earners. At the weekend, with money in their pockets and a need to blow off the fatigue of their repetitive work on the assembly lines, these Windsorites would be looking for a good time. Windsor became a blue-collar entertainment mecca, as it remains today.

With an economy fuelled in part by alcohol, gambling, and other diversions, Windsor started to experience its share of the criminal activity and social problems that accompany such activities. An extensive community service network didn't arrive in Windsor by accident – alcoholism and violence were sad facts of life in the city as well.

One volunteer job would probably have been enough for Shaughnessy, but she soon found her way to another good cause: Brentwood, a recovery home for alcoholic men in Windsor, founded by the deeply spiritual but irreverent priest Father Paul Charbonneau.

Paul Charbonneau had grown up an angry young man in blue-collar Windsor, raised in an alcoholic family. Small but athletic, he had no fear and was always getting into scrapes in the neighbourhood. Though these early years might have led him down a more dangerous path, his vocation saved him. After schooling at the seminary in London, Ontario, he moved through parishes in Sarnia and Windsor, also working overseas immediately after the Second World War as a chaplain with the troops stationed in Germany. He finally came home to Windsor, where he became a community leader in caring for alcoholics, renowned for taking his ministry beyond the confines of the cathedral and out into the streets and homes of the city.

"In my visits in parishes, I could spot right away when a guy was an alcoholic," he said. "It was the look in the kids' eyes, the wife's fear, the look in her eyes. The heart would have gone out of the home. People were just existing. There wasn't any joy."

When Charbonneau came across such a home, he would plunk himself down and ask, "Look. I'd like to meet your husband. Do you mind if I hang around and talk to him when he gets home?" Often the women were afraid of the confrontation that Charbonneau threatened to provoke. Or they would be embarrassed that the family's secret was about to be exposed.

Invariably, the husband would return home three sheets to the wind. In the manner of drunks, he could be abusive or self-pitying, or wildly bouncing between the two. Charbonneau was of the tough-love school on dealing with drunks: no new-age therapy or soft-pedalled, not-your-fault rhetoric from him. Honesty was the best approach, he said, even when it hurt.

"Listen," he'd say to these men. "You're a fucking drunk. You're ruining your family's life."

Charbonneau became involved with Alcoholics Anonymous and spent endless sleepless nights with a committed core of people who were dedicated to helping alcoholics beat their addiction. They decided that a full-time residence was needed, to give 24-hour care, support, and monitoring of recovering alcoholics. Their program started in 1963 when seven of them pooled $50 each and took over an empty restaurant on Windsor's Wyandotte Street, turning it into a streetfront support centre. A year later, more money was pooled from local churches and charities, and the group was able to buy a building where alcoholic men could also be housed. For 10 years, this project grew, expanding its aid to feed the men's families and offer counselling.

The boom times for Windsor's car companies were also boom times for alcohol addiction. "They were coming from the factories, especially from the big three," Charbonneau said. "We would have a minimum of 25 men from Chrysler, 18 to 20 from Ford, 12 to 15 from GM, just from those three plants, all at the same time." They were being sent to Brentwood by their unions and by word of mouth among other recovered alcoholics. Sixty men were squeezed into housing facilities designed for 20, and the stronger folks were consigned to outpatient status.

In the 1980s, Brentwood moved into an old hotel that had long been boarded up. In its glory days, it had been the Elmwood, a glamorous 1940s nightclub that featured entertainers such as Sammy Davis Jr., Bing Crosby, and Milton Berle. It had closed in the 1960s, when the nightclub scene moved to Las Vegas. To finance its efforts to help men recover from the vice of alcoholism, Brentwood tapped into another Windsor addiction – gambling – and held lotteries and bingo games to raise revenue.

Shaughnessy joined the board in 1982, referred by a close friend, Don Tait, a lawyer and long-time supporter of Brentwood. She was always late for the board meetings, but once there, she sat quietly, listening. She was often asked to take on a case for one of Brentwood's residents, for little money or none at all. When Brentwood initiated a program for alcoholic women, Shaughnessy was there, just talking to the women and offering a supportive shoulder. "She didn't mind coming just to talk," Charbonneau said.

Fortunately, the up-close contact with suffering humanity at Brentwood and Hiatus House fused well with Shaughnessy's legal work. Her case file was filled with divorce and custody suits in which alcohol often played a destructive role. She was catching a glimpse of how the other half lived, of family lives far removed from the peaceable world she had known in Thamesville. Cases came her way in which women and children had fled violence and threats and sought refuge at Hiatus House; she was tough in her questioning of the husbands. She acted as an advocate for three children in one case where a woman and a man (not her husband) had participated in sexually abusing the children, who had already suffered similar abuse at the hands of their father.

Her courtroom style was becoming known. Unafraid of strong language, she had been reproached on more than one occasion for her raw rhetoric. Judge Ken Ouellette, the husband of Shaughnessy's good friend Doreen Ouellette, had even taken her aside and advised her to clean up her act. The rough-hewn language had to go, he told her.

In 1983, Brian Ducharme became judicial affairs adviser to Mark MacGuigan, the minister of justice. Ducharme arranged to divide his time between law and politics: he worked three days in Ottawa and three days in Windsor at Wellman Bonn Wilkki Cohen

Ducharme, a firm he and Shaughnessy and some law school class-mates had established the previous year. Shaughnessy was delighted to be a full partner, and the new arrangement would give her and Ducharme the flexibility to pursue their sidelines.

Every week when Ducharme returned from Ottawa, he regaled his friends and associates with inside stories of political life in the capital. Very soon, Shaughnessy was hooked.

4

The Political Bug

Shaughnessy, like most Liberals who came of political age in the 1970s, was an unabashed admirer of Pierre Elliott Trudeau and a passionate believer in his "Just Society." In her work as a lawyer and community activist, she consciously made that idealistic slogan her personal goal, and if she was asked where on the Liberal spectrum she felt most at home, she would proudly declare: the left.

Trudeau's policies had positioned the federal Liberals well to the left of the party's historic centre. Throughout the nearly two decades that Trudeau dominated national politics, Liberalism was confidently expansive (and expensive, conservatives might also say) in its view of government's role in society. The Liberals promoted multiculturalism, for instance, and Windsor exemplified it, from the well-established Italian community around Erie Street to the Sikh and Indian families just beginning to make their homes in Windsor's suburbs. Shaughnessy regarded cultural diversity as a strength and a benefit, and she was proud of her Jewish-Catholic marriage. Her very name served as a billboard for her convictions about tolerance.

Two other factors drew Shaughnessy to the Liberal Party: her religion and her family. In the middle decades of the 20th century, the Liberals were the party of choice for Roman Catholics. Moreover, though Shaughnessy's father, Bruce, was not a Liberal — he believed that a citizen's duty was to vote against the party in power, and he always did — Betty came from a Liberal home. The Irish Catholic Brennans were strong partisans, and Betty's brother, Bill, had married Betty Wintermeyer, whose brother, John, was leader of the Liberal Party of Ontario from 1958 to 1963.

After his famous walk in the snow on February 29, 1984, Trudeau made his bows from the federal scene, and the next chapter in the party's history was dominated by others. In the following decade, there would be a significant reshaping of the party's ideology while it weathered two crushing federal election defeats, two bruising leadership battles, and the rise and fall of its Ontario counterpart. Nonetheless, the federal elections of 1984, 1988, and 1993 would offer opportunities for young Liberals like Shaughnessy Cohen to become involved with the party. The leadership contests of 1984 and 1990 would attract ethnic voters, sometimes controversially, to the party membership. And the ascent of David Peterson's Liberals on the provincial scene in 1985 would give some of these new Liberals a taste of the power that was being denied them at the federal level.

It was an ideal time for a tyro to sign on, and Shaughnessy did. She had already become the Liberal riding association president in Eugene Whelan's Essex-Windsor constituency in 1983. There was, of course, an element of strategy involved. Her friend Ducharme had his eye on Whelan's seat, should it become vacant, and it would help his chances immeasurably if an ally controlled the membership of the riding association. The membership of the riding association, after all, decided who would be the candidate.

The man who seemed destined to take over from Pierre Trudeau was John Turner, the silver-haired, blue-eyed Bay Street lawyer who had been a dashing, much-admired finance minister during the early days of the Trudeau government. But after repeated disputes with Trudeau, Turner bolted from the cabinet in 1975 and bided his time among Toronto's towers, waiting for his old foe to leave the field. Turner's coronation was not assured, however. Jean Chrétien, the self-styled "little guy from Shawinigan," the loyal Quebecker who had helped patriate the Constitution as justice minister in the early 1980s, was mounting an emotionally stirring and serious challenge to Turner's ambitions. Don Johnston, a Montreal lawyer and a relatively low-profile cabinet minister, was picking up support from young Liberals.

As the Liberal leadership race heated up in the spring of 1984, Windsor became a divided town. Two candidates from the city — Agriculture Minister Eugene Whelan and Justice Minister Mark MacGuigan — entered the lists, and local Liberals had to choose sides. Whelan's campaign attracted many of the newer party members, as well as a strong rural constituency; MacGuigan inherited the establishment Liberals who had long supported Paul Martin Sr. The fractiousness only worsened when Herb Gray, the stalwart president of the Treasury Board, threw his lot in with John Turner.

Shaughnessy and Brian Ducharme found themselves in a dilemma. Brian worked for Mark MacGuigan, but Shaughnessy was Whelan's riding president. Both were fond of MacGuigan, the former dean of the law school they had attended, but both served on the executive of Whelan's riding association and Ducharme wanted to win that seat some day. There was no question that whatever their choice, they would choose together. "We were one. Whatever I did, she did, and whatever she did, I did," Brian said. Together, they decided that loyalty to Whelan had to outweigh their affection for MacGuigan.

It was not a decision that bought them any particular glory. Whelan's campaign was a plodding affair, virtually ignored by the mainstream media. While John Turner and Jean Chrétien blitzed the country scooping up delegates for the June convention, and Don Johnston orchestrated an upbeat, "go ahead and jump" leadership crusade, Whelan trailed as a comic also-ran, basing his campaign almost exclusively on issues related to agriculture. "Why is there gold flake on the windows of the bank when people don't have enough cornflakes on the table?" was one of his more enduring slogans. Whelan had chosen to unveil this rhetorical flourish at a debate between the candidates in Toronto. Unknown to him, the gold-leafed windows he referred to were those of the Royal Bank tower, where Turner had worked as a lawyer for McMillan Binch since 1976. "God damn you, Gene, my office is in that building!" Turner told Whelan as they exited the meeting. It was an inadvertent slight, but a telling incident: Turner and Whelan were not going to have a happy future together.

By the time Whelan arrived at the convention in Ottawa in June, Turner still enjoyed the position of front-runner. Whelan had just 63 delegates promising him their first-ballot votes. Two of those delegates were Shaughnessy and Brian Ducharme.

"It's hard going to a leadership convention with a guy you know can't win," Ducharme said. "Gene thought at the time he was the best-known politician in the world. I don't think Ronald Reagan would have agreed with that."

On the first ballot, Whelan collected just 84 votes and stood dead last. Turner, though far out in front, didn't have the majority of ballots cast. There would be at least one more vote. As the last-place finisher, Whelan had to drop off the ballot and release his delegates to other camps. He was under terrific pressure from Chrétien and Turner to endorse one or the other, a move that would signal where the momentum was in this race.

Herb Gray, on behalf of his candidate, Turner, paid a call. He approached Ducharme and Shaughnessy and chatted to them about coming over to the side that was obviously going to win. Then André Ouellet, the senior Quebec minister in the Trudeau cabinet, was sent to make an appeal. Ouellet talked about how Turner was the steady hand that the party needed; how he, as a Quebecker, respected Turner's view of the country; and how important it was to be on the winning side of leadership contests.

Whelan was furious at these pressure tactics from the Turner camp. As he wrote in his 1986 memoir, *Whelan*: "They pressed pretty hard on the people that were sitting with us. They threatened them with being shut out of the party if they didn't come over and join Turner... It was a lot more vicious than anything I saw or heard in 1968."

No matter how flattered they might have been by the Turner camp's attention, Shaughnessy and Ducharme knew that they would do whatever their candidate asked. Future considerations commanded their fealty to the MP for Essex-Windsor.

They traipsed outside the sweltering convention centre in Ottawa's Lansdowne Park and over to the small trailer where Whelan was considering his next move. They had no idea what their candidate would do; there had been no discussion of whom to endorse because Whelan genuinely expected to win. Chrétien was on the phone, pleading for his support. On the first ballot, Turner had 1,593 votes, Chrétien 1,067. The sentimental favourite still believed that if every other leadership contender came to him, if an "anybody but Turner" movement took hold, he could knock out the lawyer from Bay Street.

It was time, in convention parlance, to walk the floor. Trailing his most loyal supporters behind him – including Shaughnessy and Ducharme – Whelan marched over to Chrétien's camp. But their gesture wasn't enough. With 1,862 votes, Turner scored a decisive victory on the second ballot; Chrétien trailed second with 1,368 votes. Presiding over the final act of the convention, Iona Campagnolo would say that Chrétien "came first in our hearts."

Neither her first nor her second choice as leader had won, but Shaughnessy was anything but disheartened. The action, the tension, the media barrage – it was high drama and she loved it. As she walked across the convention floor with Brian on their way to Chrétien's section, she confessed her boldest ambition: "I want to be a candidate some day," she said. Not for leadership – simple elected office would suit her just fine.

Once the convention was over, the bad blood started to surface. When John Turner announced his new cabinet at the end of June,

Eugene Whelan was not in it. Whelan described in his autobiography how Turner had delivered the news to him: smiling, cigar in hand, while the ousted agriculture minister pleaded with him to keep his job.

Ducharme, in the meantime, was winding up his job at Justice and decided to talk to none other than the "Rainmaker" himself, Senator Keith Davey, about the lay of the Liberal land in Windsor. Davey was one of Trudeau's long-time advisers and a power broker in the party. His knowledge of the media, which had propelled him to the head of a royal commission on the future of newspapers in Canada in the 1970s, established him as one of the country's top communications gurus.

Davey confided in Ducharme that Whelan was not likely to stand for re-election. Trudeau was in the midst of a final patronage push, plugging literally hundreds of Liberals into cushy patronage posts, and Davey thought that Whelan had earned a safe sinecure in the Senate. Ducharme was delighted with the idea – it would mean an opening in Essex-Windsor and a chance for him to run. His friend Shaughnessy was equally delighted – she imagined herself as the executive assistant to cabinet minister Brian Ducharme. She dreamed of having influence over those highly desirable judicial appointments.

As it happened, Whelan didn't want to be a senator, and he had told Trudeau as much even before getting his walking papers from Turner. Whelan hoped to stay close to the world he knew best: agriculture. He wanted to be the ambassador to the United Nations Food and Agricultural Organization in Rome. There was a financial incentive too: with his MP's pension and the UN position, he could make more money than he could as a senator.

But Whelan had not given Ducharme the nod by the time Turner called an election on July 9, and he was not amused by Ducharme's evident eagerness to replace him. Ducharme announced his candidacy immediately. The local CBC broadcast the story, showing an earnest young man promising to make job creation his number one priority. The camera panned to Ducharme's supporters in the riding association, notably "his friend and law partner Shaughnessy Cohen," beaming behind her big-framed glasses. But the big green Stetson cast a shadow over Ducharme's announcement. Noting that Ducharme had once been the campaign manager for Eugene Whelan, the CBC reported that the former minister's support was curiously absent. When asked who he would back to succeed him, Whelan damned his former assistant with faint praise, saying he was just happy at the prospect of a spirited contest. "I'm taking no sides whatsoever on who seeks the nomination," Whelan told the CBC. "We knew that several were watching what I was going to do and I think that's great if there's competition." Whelan's appointment as FAO ambassador was announced two days later.

Ducharme won the nomination easily, but the election was another matter. Nineteen eighty-four was not the year to be running as a Liberal. Like 241 other Liberal candidates across Canada, Ducharme was bluntly told that the nation had had enough of the "natural governing party." He was soundly defeated in Essex-Windsor by New Democrat Steven Langdon, and in Ottawa Brian Mulroney became prime minister. That was Ducharme's first and last run at federal politics. The dreams of going to Ottawa now belonged solely to Shaughnessy.

The next couple of years presented Shaughnessy with an opportunity to observe the bare-knuckle contests that are fought within political parties at the local level, campaigns that can be nastier than those waged against other parties. After the defeat of 1984, Shaughnessy had to fight to retain control of the Essex-Windsor riding association. Though Whelan was gone, his supporters and loyalists remained uneasy about the Ducharme-Cohen alliance. Ducharme believed that he, as the duly nominated candidate in 1984, had earned the right to speak for the riding. The former agriculture minister and his supporters didn't think that a failed election effort entitled Ducharme to be the kingpin in Whelan's heartland. Beyond the riding, bitterness lingered about the way Whelan had been treated by Turner, and Chrétien's former supporters grumbled that Turner should face a leadership review because he had lost the 1984 election. The grassroots of the party were crackling with continuing rivalry.

Shaughnessy loved the fray, but such battles required organization, and this was not her strength. She was never an efficient administrator, in political work or in legal work. In the 1987 provincial campaign, for example, she was entrusted with the precious list of homeowners who had agreed to post Liberal signs. The list somehow ended up in the pile of junk in the trunk of her car, where it was destroyed by battery acid. But her friends knew that detail was not Shaughnessy's strong suit – she was a big-picture, meet-the-people kind of campaigner. If she was kept busy at the work of personal contact, she'd be a tremendous asset. The lists and the files and the phone numbers would have to be managed by more adept hands.

Enter Brad Robitaille, a bearded, soft-spoken Windsor lawyer, who proved to have remarkable organizational skills – exactly what Ducharme and Shaughn lacked. The three lawyers banded together and played Liberal politics as a territorial sport, fending off challenges to their management of the Essex-Windsor riding association by keeping their own friends on the executive. These were "meaningless skirmishes" in the larger Liberal battle, Robitaille said, but they were instructive. Shaughnessy learned how to work the back channels of politics, cultivating contacts and mobilizing them when the time was right.

Shaughnessy's home life was particularly conducive to her political dalliance in the mid-1980s. Jerry kept his distance, unsure whether politics was a long-term commitment for her or just a passing fancy. He was immersed in his own career, huddled in his lab doing behaviour and cognition experiments with laboratory rats. ("He's a good rat man," colleagues said admiringly.) Dena was away by then at boarding school, after finding life at the local public school far too dismal. Shaughnessy, a boarding school graduate, was keen for Dena to have a private-school education. They settled on Alma College, about an hour's drive from Windsor, where Dena took Grade 12 and 13 courses.

"I was thinking of far, far away, like the Swiss Alps," Dena said. "But they didn't have the money for that, nor were my grades good enough for an exclusive school." Still, she believed Shaughn was right to put her into a school where she could pay more attention to her studies. Dena lived at Alma College during the school terms from 1984 to 1986, returning home on the weekends. Shaughn, freed of the responsibility of raising a teenaged daughter, became even more intensely involved in Windsor politics.

As Shaughnessy's political aspirations solidified, her circle of friends expanded too. One of her more eclectic networks revolved around a ladies'-lunch set that included a half-dozen of Windsor's most interesting women.

Jane Boyd, a Conservative candidate in the 1985 Ontario election, was in this group. So was Carol Derbyshire, executive director of the Hospice in Windsor, whose position required that she remain apolitical. Karen Hall, then a reporter with the *Windsor Star*, had first met Shaughnessy a year or two before but came to know her better at the lunches, usually held at Plunkett's restaurant on Pitt Street in downtown Windsor or at the Chatham Street Grill. They were lively affairs – the maître d' often stashed the group at one of the more remote tables in the establishment so they wouldn't disturb other diners. Shaughnessy was invariably the noisiest of them all, her stories often accompanied by stand-up performances.

Karen Hall knew she would get along with Shaughnessy as soon as she met her. It was the early 1980s, and Hall was out walking in downtown Windsor, dressed in a loud floral suit. A petite woman who paid close attention to her appearance, Hall rued this fashion mistake almost as soon as she got it home from the store. "It looked like Grandma's drapes, do you know what I mean?" she said. But to get some wear out of it, she had donned the outfit that summer morning. As she made her way to her destination, she saw the dreaded ensemble drifting towards her in a much larger size. It was Shaughnessy. She stopped, looked at Hall's suit, looked at her own, and said, "We've got to talk."

Talk they did, and for years thereafter. Despite their differences and the impenetrable walls that are supposed to be erected in cross-party friendships or journalist-politician relations, the group became allies and intense supporters of one another. Carol Derbyshire thought their bond was forged through community involvement: all of the women spent a great deal of time on social policy projects in Windsor. "We had a lot of the same values," Derbyshire said. "We had a responsibility to do things in the community, and we weren't the kind of people content to do a nine-to-five job ... We were all connectors."

In those years, Jane Boyd was being wooed to run in various elections, but after 1985 she refused. She told the *Windsor Star* that women were simply "too straight" for politics. "Our nature is that we're conciliators and peacemakers. We like to lay our cards on the table and reach a point of consensus. Men do that and then walk away and stab you in the back," Boyd said.

The issue of a women's style of politics was naturally one of the topics on the agenda at the ladies' lunches. Shaughnessy was aware that she would be held to a different standard than the men; the male-dominated legal profession had taught her that. Men would be unlikely to caution their male pals against the use of profanity.

Shaughnessy was also acquiring strong women friends beyond Windsor. Mary Clancy was one of those; the author Margaret Atwood was another. Atwood came into Shaughn and Jerry's lives through one of their friends at the university, Mary Lee Stevenson. Stevenson's hobby was birdwatching and the Windsor area, so close to Point Pelee National Park and Pelee Island, Canada's southernmost inhabited zone, is a mecca for birders.

One night, when Stevenson was at a dinner with Shaughn and Jerry, she mentioned that she and her friend Margaret Atwood were hoping to head to Pelee Island to do some bird watching. *The* Margaret Atwood was interested in Pelee Island? It happened that Shaughnessy and Jerry owned a place on the island. Several years earlier, they had visited on a day trip and immediately fallen in love with the place. It's only a 30-kilometre trek around the perimeter of the island, which is mainly residential with a few touristy outposts – a couple of restaurants and bed-and-breakfasts, a bakery, a pheasant farm, acres of grapes that make the famous Pelee Island wine, and a little quarry on the northern tip.

Near that tip, Shaughnessy and Jerry had found a small, run-down farmhouse for sale. On an impulse, they decided to buy it. They hoped to renovate eventually or rebuild a more modern cottage, but this "falling-down mice hotel," as Atwood called it, would do for now. Shaughn and Jerry were delighted with their getaway home and started planning summer weekends and holidays around it.

They offered their retreat at once to Mary Lee and her author friend and hosted Atwood and her husband, Graeme Gibson, on several occasions. A typical evening with Shaughnessy and Jerry, said Atwood, was "very talkative. Sometimes we'd go over to their place and there'd be a lot of talking, laughing, eating, and drinking. That was basically the pattern. Shaughnessy was very big on jokes, on gossip, on her opinions, and on the state of the world."

Soon Atwood and Gibson realized they couldn't continue to stay at Shaughn and Jerry's and began to look around for a place of their own on the island. They found a secluded property, nestled among the trees, where they had privacy and proximity to some of the best birdwatching in Canada. Shaughnessy acted as their lawyer and handled the cottage purchase quietly and discreetly. And she devoured every Margaret Atwood novel that appeared. "Can I be a character in one of your novels some day, Peggy?" Shaughnessy would ask. "Make me thin, though. And taller. You can call me the tall, thin, Shaughnessy Cohen."

Pelee Island was Shaughnessy's idyll. Her favourite friends on the island were the Kirkendalls – John, a Michigan judge, and Carolyn, his wife – and "the boys," Barry Wayman and Tom Brown, who were building a spectacular beach house at the northeast tip of the island. Over the years, this Pelee gang became yet another branch of Shaughnessy's extended family. She would spend days down at the Kirkendalls' beach cabana or evenings over decadent meals with Wayman and Brown.

In 1987, David Peterson and the Ontario Liberals seemed well positioned to secure a majority government for themselves. They had perched precariously but generally successfully at the helm at Queen's Park during the previous two years, thanks to a minority-government accord with Bob Rae and the New Democrats. With the polls looking favourable, Peterson snappy in his red tie, and a breezy summer campaign ahead, it was a great time to be a Liberal candidate.

The provincial riding of Windsor-Walkerville was held by the long-serving Bernie Newman, who was 73 years old as this election rolled around. Brian Ducharme had been expecting for some time that Newman would decide not to seek another term. There were rumours that the veteran politician was not as sharp as he used to be, that he had actually found himself in Kingston while driving from his hometown to Queen's Park – so distracted, it was said, that he overshot his destination by a good 300 kilometres.

After the bruising federal defeat in 1984 and the subsequent battles with Whelan's forces, Ducharme had turned to provincial politics. He began to organize an attempt to win the Liberal nomination, assisted by his loyal deputy, Shaughnessy. They had started selling memberships in Windsor-Walkerville in early 1987.

But much to Ducharme's subsequent embarrassment, Bernie Newman had no intention of resigning. The word spread that Ducharme and his cohort were trying to unseat the Windsor warhorse. "I became the guy who was trying to push poor Bernie Newman, and it didn't look good," Ducharme said. Once again, unseemly haste was the charge.

As it turned out, Bernie Newman ultimately did retire, and Windsor councillor Mike Ray threw his hat into the ring. All those people annoyed with Ducharme's rumoured attempt to oust Newman – including Whelan, his daughter Susan, and their supporters – sided with Mike Ray. (Eugene Whelan had returned to his home turf; Mulroney had withdrawn him from the FAO post after only a few months.) The battle between these two camps was a preview of a larger war that would erupt at the next Liberal leadership convention. Whelan's troops were rehearsing for the fight on behalf of Jean Chrétien; Shaughnessy's group was honing the skills it would need to campaign for Paul Martin Jr.

The August 5, 1987, nomination meeting, held just a few days after David Peterson had called the election, was a barely controlled mob scene. Shaughnessy had volunteered for the nastiest mission in the Ducharme campaign to stop Mike Ray. Wearing her lawyer's hat, she was going to challenge every one of the memberships sold for the Ray nomination. According to the rules, she was entitled to do this in one of two ways: she could question the address cited on the form, or she could demand to know whether the membership was paid up in full.

The result was chaos. About 2,000 people filled the Caboto Club, a huge dance and dinner hall in the city, only to find Shaughnessy reining the proceedings to a dead halt. As the *Windsor Star* reported: "The tactic, which enraged Ray supporters, forced party members to stand in line for up to three hours in stifling hallways, then line up again to prove their identity, address and membership to the party... Dozens of other elderly supporters of Ray gave up and left the meeting without voting... At least one Ray supporter left the Caboto Club in tears after standing in line for hours before being denied a vote. Others left vowing they would never vote Liberal again after their eligibility was challenged."

Brad Robitaille remembers that Shaughnessy was pushed and shoved a number of times by angry Ray delegates. If she was afraid, she didn't show it. She even challenged the membership of Bernie Newman Jr., the former MP's son. "He lives outside the riding," she snapped.

The effort was in vain. Brian Ducharme lost the nomination by almost 200 votes and Mike Ray, in turn, lost the seat to the New Democrats.

If nothing else, the Ray-Ducharme skirmish taught Shaughnessy another lesson about political confrontation and the skills required to secure her own eventual nomination and election victory. She would need her Liberal friends, and lots of them.

Unfortunately, the antics of the Ducharme squad that night cost her some of those potential allies. Politics could be an unforgiving business.

No one knew what awaited the Liberals in the federal election of 1988. John Turner was warming up for an anti-free-trade campaign, against what he described as the sell-off of Canada by the Conservatives under Brian Mulroney. But Turner's potential as prime minister looked shaky, even though the Tories had been plagued by scandal since the earliest days of their mandate, with a record number of cabinet resignations over everything from tainted tuna to strip-bar visits by ministers. The election was everyone's to lose – or to win.

Shaughnessy's Amherstburg residence was in Essex-Windsor, but she didn't think she'd have much of a chance in Whelan country. Instead she set her sights on the seat held by New Democrat Howard McCurdy, in Paul Martin Sr.'s old riding; formerly Windsor-Walkerville, it had just been renamed Windsor–Lake St. Clair. (The Cohens bought a small house there and briefly considered making it their principal residence, to demonstrate Shaughnessy's commitment to her potential constituents, but in the end they rented it out.) Martin's legacy represented a challenge in itself: before she could take on the New Democrats, she would have to fight her own party for the nomination.

Paul Martin Sr. did not like Shaughnessy. Her politics were of the rough-and-tumble sort that didn't sit well with the genteel traditionalists around Martin. These people preferred the more dignified intellectual appeal of a Mark MacGuigan, Martin's successor in the riding. (MacGuigan himself had been appointed to the bench.)

"Who's going to work for that lady lawyer?" Martin asked one day, when he was pressed yet again to consider Shaughnessy as the candidate. He snorted when someone mentioned the name of a long-time Liberal in the riding who was promoting Shaughnessy's candidacy. "She can't go door to door," Martin said of this supporter. "She's too fat." Rumours swirled that Martin's camp was looking hard for an establishment candidate to go for the nomination, but in the end, Shaughnessy's only rivals for the seat were a local radio host, Al Pervin, who pulled out before the vote, and Anderson Township reeve Greg Stewart. Still, she had to fight to be taken seriously.

When Shaughnessy started circulating the word that she wanted to be a candidate, her lunch group was there to offer counsel on everything from policy to deportment. Boyd and Derbyshire were advised to speak to Shaughnessy about the etiquette of public life. Dick Walker, a Conservative who had worked with Shaughnessy in a law firm, thought his friend and former associate could use some friendly advice.

"Talk to her about her swearing," Walker told Boyd and Derbyshire. "Tell her she has to clean up her language." As well, he said that Shaughnessy needed a not so gentle reminder of the basic courtesies. "She was notorious for not returning phone calls," Derbyshire said.

They chose Brigantino's restaurant for the intervention, sitting tensely through lunch, waiting for the moment to raise these delicate issues with their friend. Shaughnessy was oblivious to their discomfort and bubbled with enthusiasm. "She was already gone," Boyd recalled. "She *was* the candidate, in her mind."

Finally they mustered their courage and put matters on the table. "Yes, yes, I should return phone calls," she agreed hastily. When chided about her language yet again, Shaughn twinkled: "What the fuck do you mean by that?"

Boyd feared that for all her hard-won experience as a backroom worker, Shaughnessy wasn't fully prepared for duty as a candidate. Windsor's political landscape was dominated by men. Shaughnessy was the only prospective female candidate for federal office in the three Windsor ridings, among all the parties. In fact, the numbers showed that women who had served in public office were leaving – a phenomenon that continues to this day. While men "moved on," often to lucrative prestige appointments in recognition of the time they served, women tended to flee, returning to former careers and simply abandoning public service altogether.

Shaughnessy was disturbed by this trend, saying that women who left were setting an unfortunate example for other women who wanted to be politicians. "They made a signal to other women – when there's too much heat you go back to the kitchen," she told Gord Henderson of the *Windsor Star*.

Nor was she about to be discouraged by Paul Martin Sr.'s obvious antipathy. Too bad about him, Shaughnessy decided. She was encouraged in this approach by Ron Doherty, a bright-eyed, ebullient Liberal who had relocated to Windsor from the Niagara region, as part of a career move with CN Railways. He fell under Shaughnessy's charismatic spell at their first meeting and vowed to help her get elected. She immediately established a warm relationship with Doherty's wife and children and delighted them with her outrageous humour.

Doherty had done volunteer work for the party in the past, and when he met Shaughnessy, he was convinced that she was going places. He particularly admired her reaction to Martin. Shaughnessy told Doherty: "I'm not going to worry about the 12 Liberals in Windsor who don't like me. I'm going to find myself a whole new group of Liberals and get support from them."

Shaughnessy didn't patent this strategy, of course. Ever since John Turner had become leader in 1984, big recruitment campaigns to attract new party members had become standard practice. But it was new to Windsor, where a succession of powerful ministers had kept a tight lid on their organizations. Shaughnessy decided that if she couldn't charm her way to the top of the current Liberal cadre, she would just create one of her own. Her work and her volunteer commitments had given her plenty of connections in the riding. Thus began the endless solicitation of friends and family – anyone Shaughn and Jerry knew in Windsor's academic, legal, and community service worlds. Brad Robitaille kept the lists and strictly monitored follow-up on these new members. With Shaughn's social skills, Jerry's devotion, friends' loyalty, and Robitaille's organizing talents, the nomination victory seemed assured.

On the night of the vote, Shaughnessy rehearsed her speech in the bathtub. She wound up her address and pulled the plug – the draining water sounded just like applause to her ears. That's a good sign, she thought.

About 500 people turned up at the Caboto Club to choose the Liberal candidate for Windsor–Lake St. Clair. Greg Stewart was Shaughn's only challenger, but she took nothing for granted going into the meeting. Shaughnessy gave an inspired speech, in which she reached out to the establishment Liberals in the riding as well as to the new members she had helped to recruit. She appealed to the two groups to introduce themselves to each other and work together to help her win the riding with a united effort. She endorsed her leader's opposition to free trade and unhesitatingly voiced her personal opposition to abortion. It worked. Shaughnessy won the nomination. As the victory was announced, she ran the length of the room and vowed to make Liberals proud in the next election.

True to her goal, Shaughnessy had expanded the Liberal network in town, mostly through the force of her own personality. Once Mulroney made the election call in September 1988, the first Shaughnessy Cohen campaign was under way. Her chief opponents were the incumbent, New Democrat Howard McCurdy, and the Conservatives' Bruck Easton, a local lawyer. Her campaign manager was a Windsor lawyer and former football player from the University of Western Ontario, Brian Fortune, whose brother, Garry, was heavily involved in provincial politics and a close friend to Ducharme, Robitaille, and Doherty. Garry had been quietly working the local scene as an organizer over the past few years. The Fortune brothers were happy to be caught up in the Cohen election effort; here was a candidate who seemed to have a limitless capacity for raucous good fun. Her other workers were a diverse group, to say the least: lots of young people, mainly women, many older veterans of campaigns past, and, in what made for a few strange moments, some interesting characters encountered in the courtroom.

One day Shaughnessy and Norma Coleman, a supporter who had worked in the office of Premier David Peterson, were outside the campaign office, supervising the hanging of a banner over the window. Norma was barking out orders to the volunteer on the ladder.

"No, no! Higher! No, lower! A little to the left!"

Shaughnessy had a mysterious smile on her face.

"You know how I met this guy?" she asked. "I put him in jail! He's out on parole now," Shaughnessy said, describing in detail the man's violent crime and how she had made sure he was put behind bars.

The parolee/campaign worker turned on his ladder and said to Norma, "How's that?"

"Perfect," said Norma.

Shaughnessy's views on abortion had surprised those who didn't see the deeply thoughtful woman beyond the rough-talking lady-lawyer facade. It was more than her Catholic schooling; Shaughnessy had given serious thought to the notion that all life was precious. Throughout the Windsor campaign, the abortion issue was raised frequently. At an all-candidates' debate at F.J. Brennan High School, described as "rambunctious" by the *Windsor Star*, Shaughnessy was called upon again to defend her views.

"Though her party has not yet defined its position on the issue," the *Star* story reported, "Cohen assured the students that Liberal leader John Turner has 'personally, to me, and publicly made it very clear that whatever happens in the House of Commons... we will be free to vote our conscience.'"

But in another newspaper report, Shaughnessy's carefully crafted position on abortion was blown away by an offhand conversation between a *Toronto Star* reporter and John Turner's chief aide, Peter Connolly. Connolly told reporter David Vienneau that the Liberals were about to announce a pro-choice platform.

Shaughnessy read the story and blew a gasket. But before doing anything hasty, she recalled the lessons of Ducharme versus Whelan: remember your regional boss. Pay attention to the local hierarchy.

Herb Gray was now the boss. Over the previous four years, with the other prominent Windsor Liberals retired, Gray had become the senior statesman — not just of the area but of the Liberal Party. Shaughnessy dutifully filed her complaint with him.

Turner had come to depend on Gray to keep a tight rein on the caucus while he tended to the overt and covert challenges to his leadership. Though he seemed staid and dull and his stern, bespectacled countenance rarely registered any emotion — Gray Herb was one of his nicknames — people close to him knew that he possessed a delightfully dry sense of humour, a sophisticated knowledge of rock music, and impressive media savvy. He understood precisely when and where to generate headlines for the Liberals while they sat on the opposition benches. All of this, combined with his more than 20 years in the House, made Herb Gray a significant ally for Shaughnessy. Gray was also fond of her, believing that the party needed high spirits such as hers to re-energize the Liberal benches.

Shaughnessy telephoned Gray herself and demanded to know why John Turner's assistants were freelancing on party policy in the volatile atmosphere of an election campaign. Gray, in turn, phoned headquarters and reported the unease of his local candidate. Point taken. Turner himself was anti-abortion. Connolly was warned against musing aloud with reporters on policy matters as sensitive as abortion.

That episode was possibly the least of Turner's problems at the time, however. In the midst of a campaign in which the Liberal leader had soared in the polls after his spirited anti-free-trade tirade in the debates, an incredible story was broadcast one night on the CBC-TV news. Turner, it was reported, was being asked to step down in mid-campaign by key Liberal insiders who believed the party would stand a better chance with another leader (read: Jean Chrétien). Seasoned Ottawa pundits were inclined to dismiss the story — no one, not even the besieged Liberals, could be that stupid, it was said. But the CBC story was true. Turner and Connolly, though dismissing the story at first with carefully neutral remarks, subsequently confirmed that the Liberal leader had been asked to resign.

That debacle, combined with massive negative advertising by the Tories, deflated any momentum that Turner might have gained from the debate. Liberals on the ground, such as Shaughnessy and her team, knew that their chances were diminished. But candidates have to believe that they will win; it's what gets them out of bed every morning and out knocking on doors. They must hold to the conviction, however ridiculous or far-fetched, that victory is possible.

In the final three weeks of the campaign, Shaughnessy's advisers pulled Jerry aside. "Shaughn has to do that early-morning campaigning at the factory gates," they told him. "We don't think she should be driving back and forth from Amherstburg every night. We're going to keep her in a hotel here."

In fact, Shaughnessy hated doing factory-gate campaigning, although it is a mainstay of any candidate's repertoire. Film footage from the 1988 campaign explains her attitude: her nose red, lips chapped, her beige trenchcoat flapping around her, Shaughnessy looked miserable and humiliated as she tried to hand leaflets to union workers who barely wanted to make eye contact. A Liberal campaigning against a New Democrat in Windsor, especially one as popular as Howard McCurdy, was hardly likely to find a welcome in that terrain.

There was another reason for taking Shaughn away from her husband at this point in the campaign: Jerry was a worrier. "Shaughn was the motivator, I was the demotivator," he joked. As his wife's prospects worsened, Jerry openly fretted. Shaughnessy's team feared that his negativity would rub off on her.

Even as inevitable defeat loomed, Shaughnessy looked for a silver lining of some sort. She fixed her sights on a respectable Liberal turnout in 1988, and by and large, she won it. Though the voters of Windsor–Lake St. Clair sent McCurdy back to Parliament, he won with 18,915 votes, compared with 16,192 for Shaughnessy. She had bettered the Liberals' 1984 vote share by more than 5,000 votes.

Shaughnessy was not surprised to have lost. Supporters at her headquarters were naturally dejected – especially Jerry, who had worried himself into a state that night. They shook their heads as the results were posted on the board, groaning, sometimes booing, as Shaughn's bid faded in front of their eyes.

Shaughn told the crowd that they had given the local Tories and New Democrats a run for their money and that they hadn't done badly for a team made up of plenty of people new to politics. That's the price of making the party broader, she told her friends. It was going to take some practice to get this winning thing right. And she was up to it, turning her attention almost immediately to the next election.

The *Windsor Star* reported that Shaughnessy was initially over-whelmed, but that "her self-pity was shortlived. She thrust her hands defiantly into the pockets of her red dress and gave notice she would be back in four years." Shaughnessy offered the *Star* reporter an accurate forecast of her game plan. "Next time I hope to get an early nomination and do a lot of canvassing and a lot of hard work and in the meantime I will try to keep my profile up. Hopefully, name recognition will help."

Shaughn's sister Cathy was on hand to console and comfort if necessary. Once again, just as in boarding school, the older sister was the more resilient. "I remember feeling bad for her and think-ing I would be in bed for a month brooding over a loss so public as that," Cathy said. She was stunned when Shaughnessy described the experience as "great fun."

Shaughnessy was prepared for the loss, but not its after-effects. Political campaigns provide an incredible high. You are surrounded by friends. You're busy all the time. You're getting tons of attention, and if you're a level-headed person, you don't even mind when the attention is negative. The prospect of the next four or five long years until the next adrenalin rush was too much to ask of Shaughnessy Cohen. She would need another outlet for her political passions.

Camera-ready: At age eight, Shaughnessy was already at ease before the camera lens. Her younger sisters Judi (centre) and Cathy were always slightly in awe of their confident, outgoing sibling.

Ticket to the future: Shaughnessy was sent to a girls' boarding school because Bruce and Betty Murray wanted the best education possible for their daughters. Graduation from Mount St. Joseph Academy in London, Ontario, was the first step on the road to a master's degree in sociology.

Untraditional bride: A Jewish-Catholic union, conducted under a traditional *chuppah* by a rabbi and held in a hall graced by a Christmas tree. So began the 27-year marriage of Shaughnessy and Jerry Cohen, shown here with Jerry's brother, Neil, far left; his father, Murray Cohen; and his stepmother, Lois.

A family: "I didn't produce Dena, but I directed her," Shaughnessy said of her role in raising Jerry's daughter from his first marriage.

The favourite: Paul Martin didn't win the 1990 leadership race or become prime minister in 1992, as his campaign buttons predicted and his father, Paul Sr., seen just behind his left shoulder, desired so fervently. But Martin would always remain Shaughn's favourite.

Friends and allies: Shaughnessy loved to introduce her Ottawa friends to her Windsor friends. Here, Shaughnessy and Sheila Finestone (centre), then secretary of state for the status of women, pay a call on Donna Miller at the Hiatus House women's shelter in Windsor, to which Shaughn devoted so much of her volunteer time over the years.

Political pals: Brian Ducharme introduced Shaughnessy to the world of politics when they sat beside each other in law school in the 1970s. Shaughn eventually won the electoral prize that eluded Ducharme.

Passion greets reason: Shaughnessy didn't meet former prime minister Pierre Trudeau until after she became an MP in 1993, but it was his 1984 resignation that set off the chain of events in Windsor that drew her into active Liberal politics.

We're big, we're back, and we're loud: Shaughnessy and Roger Gallaway, the MP for Sarnia-Lambton, should have been rivals in the ego-heavy world of Liberal caucus politics. Instead, they were allies, co-conspirators, and a reliable comedy team within Liberal ranks. (Mike Scandiffio/ *The Hill Times*)

The mentor: Shaughnessy always believed that what was good for Herb Gray, a three-decade veteran of the House of Commons and Liberal boss of Windsor, was good for her too. When Gray needed Shaughnessy at his side, she was there.

In the land of large women: Shaughnessy and Mary Clancy, friends since the 1970s and inseparable as fellow MPs, could be counted upon to make even the most sedate affairs – including this 1995 garden party at 24 Sussex Drive – outrageous.

Roommate and neighbour: Female politicians form deeper friendships than men do, according to Anne McLellan, shown here with Shaughnessy and Essex-Windsor MP Susan Whelan. Shaughn's relationship with Whelan was marked by bitter rivalry in Windsor through the 1980s, but by warmth and affection after they were both elected. (Janet Wilson/*The Hill Times*)

Free advice: As justice minister and later as health minister, Allan Rock was coached by Shaughnessy in the delicate art of caucus persuasion and media spin. In June 1998, she accompanied him to the Hospice in Windsor, where her ladies'-lunch pal Carol Derbyshire (left) served as director.

Intimations of mortality: It was a sombre discussion on the Challenger jet as Shaughnessy and John Manley flew to the funeral of Chrysler Canada president Yves Landry in March 1998. Their conversation about life's fragility prompted Shaughnessy to cancel her Ottawa appointments for the rest of the week and remain in Windsor to be with Jerry. (Jean-Marc Carisse/**PMO**)

The Boss: Prime Minister Jean Chrétien loved some MPs because they could get things done and others because they could make him laugh. Alfonso Gagliano (left), a key Quebec organizer and minister in Chrétien's government, surpassed his expectations in the first department; Shaughnessy and Roger Gallaway did so in both. (Jean-Marc Carisse/PMO)

Holding court: Shaughnessy's favourite seat in the House was a floral couch in the Commons lobby. Here she huddled with pals, plotted strategy against her foes, and summoned cabinet ministers to account for themselves. Listening to Ottawa MP Marlene Catterall, Shaughnessy is all business.

5

Hitch Your Wagon

Political activism might not yet have earned Shaughnessy a second career, but there were already important spinoff benefits for her legal career. Thanks to countless events that called for speeches and presentations, she returned to the courtroom with increased confidence. Thanks to the victory of the provincial Liberals in 1985 after four decades in opposition at Queen's Park, she was given appointments to a number of interesting boards.

In 1986, for instance, Shaughnessy had been appointed vice-chairwoman of the Health Protection Appeal Board of Ontario. This panel heard appeals against orders from medical officers of health in the province. Restaurants that had been closed down on health grounds, for instance, could go before this board to argue their case. Shaughnessy joked that she knew every dining establishment in Ontario to avoid.

The board met about 15 times a year and Shaughnessy eventually ascended to the chair in 1987, adding extra responsibilities to what was intended as a part-time position. Add to this her continuing work at Hiatus House and Brentwood, and Shaughnessy was becoming a very busy person.

Being busy suited her socially, but not financially. After the partnership with Ducharme broke up amicably in 1985, Shaughnessy worked as an associate at some big Windsor firms, where she enjoyed the prestige but had trouble taking on enough cases to keep up with the high overhead costs. She was never at her best with housekeeping details, and now she was neglecting matters such as billings and accounts payable. During the time she was a partner in Ducharme's firm, he walked into her messy office one day, looked down at the floor, and found a $700 cheque – payable to a client – lying there.

"Shaughnessy!" he demanded. "What's this cheque for? Who gets it? Where's it supposed to go?"

In fact, as her legal colleagues noticed, Shaughnessy was beginning to see politics as her first profession and law as something she did on the side. "She lived it and breathed it and took time off to practise law," her friend Brad Robitaille said.

One of Windsor's top lawyers was Harvey Strosberg, a self-assured legal hotshot with a tough-talking demeanour. Strosberg described Shaughnessy as lacking the administrative discipline to be a good civil lawyer. Criminal law is legal work on the fly: lawyers might be handed a case in the morning and called upon to assemble arguments for the judge as early as that afternoon. Civil law is more of a back-and-forth paper chase, full of detail and long-range strategy. Shaughnessy was more comfortable testing her legal abilities on her feet. Unfortunately, criminal work is far less lucrative than civil. Clients who pursue a civil-law action usually have the money to pay for high-priced legal help; accused criminals and victims generally do not.

"If you're going to assess who's a good lawyer by who makes a lot of money, she failed miserably," Strosberg said. In his few dealings with her, mostly on divorce cases, Strosberg found Shaughnessy's habits enormously frustrating. She would agree to send something on in 30 days; the date would come and go; she'd ask for an extension, fail to meet that deadline, and then go silent. Many days, sometimes weeks later, Shaughnessy would phone and charm her way out of trouble.

"She had a huge weakness in her ability to get anything done in a timely fashion on the civil side," Strosberg said. "The problem was that she was so endearing that you could forgive her anything. It was very hard to get angry with her. She'd call you up and she'd say, 'I know I should have had it in 30 days ago, but I'm just so busy!'"

When Shaughnessy giggled at her own failings, Strosberg would find himself laughing too. "It didn't matter how angry you were. You were always cajoled into giving her another extension."

Ironically, she was far more punctual in her unpaid work. The staff at Brentwood and Hiatus House knew they could rely on her to deliver when she promised legal services pro bono and were always slightly amazed that she had the time to do such things.

Sooner or later, with her energies diverted elsewhere, Shaughnessy was bound to run into trouble. The legal profession and its Ontario governing body, the Law Society of Upper Canada, take a dim view of organizationally challenged lawyers. Meeting deadlines, keeping accurate records, maintaining proper billing systems are all essential parts of a lawyer's life. For Shaughnessy, they were annoying distractions. What couldn't be delayed was simply ignored.

That attitude usually proves unsustainable in any business, and this is especially true for lawyers. Around the time Shaughnessy was consumed by her first run for office, she missed a deadline for filing an action in a personal injury case. Not only were she and her firm, Wilson Walker Hochberg Slopen, going to be sued, Shaughnessy was also facing disciplinary measures at the Law Society.

Complaints about lawyers to the Law Society are not uncommon. Even in the late 1990s, when complaints were declining, the Law Society received about 5,000 a year – meaning that at any one time approximately 15 percent of the profession in Ontario was under complaint. It's a long, complicated road from complaint to discipline in the legal world. The first step is a formal letter from

the person or group complaining about a lawyer's work. The
lawyer involved has to retrace every step in the handling of the case
– hence the need for good recordkeeping – and respond to the
complaint. Only in about 5 percent of the cases does the Law
Society decide there's a need to take the next step, a disciplinary
hearing. Shaughnessy found herself among those 5 percent.

She could no longer deflect or ignore her difficulties, though
she could and would keep Jerry in the dark about them. "It was
probably better that I didn't know," Jerry said. "We were sloppy
financially, but all I would do is worry about it."

Dena, in fact, was the most organized member of the household in Amherstburg. Though she was just a student, studying
communication and visual arts at the University of Windsor at that
time, she made more of an effort than her father or stepmother to
stay on top of the family's finances. On countless occasions,
Shaughn or Jerry would dispatch Dena to the bank in Windsor
between her classes to top up their savings account before cheques
bounced, or to pay some long-overdue utility bill. "A few times
our phone line was disconnected because they forgot to pay the
bills, and hydro was shut off for the same reason at least once,"
Dena said. Jerry and Shaughn often vowed to get their affairs in
order but just as often put it off. In legal matters, procrastination
was no solution.

To deal with the hearing at the Law Society, Shaughnessy was
advised to seek out Don Brown, a lawyer with the high-powered
firm of Blake Cassels & Graydon in Toronto. Brown, almost ten
years older than Shaughn, was an imposing figure, with a shock of
grey hair and a loud, hearty laugh. The graduate of the University
of Manitoba and Osgoode Hall had a master's degree in law from
Harvard University. He was a senior partner at Blake's, and an
accomplished author of legal texts, including a definitive volume
on labour arbitration. At the time Shaughn met him, he was also
lecturing in civil appeals and judicial review at the University of
Toronto law school. Brown was well seasoned in dealings with the
Law Society of Upper Canada.

Shaughnessy visited Brown in his offices. Gone was the bravado, the buffoonery, and that famous facade of noisy self-confidence. Instead, a mortified woman sat before Don Brown and told him she had no excuse for screwing up like this. She was just too pre-occupied with politics.

Brown, who had his own sentimental streak, fused with hard-nosed legal dexterity, immediately tried to set Shaughnessy at ease. "We'll handle this," he said, and the two set about preparing her defence for the panel of three Law Society benchers who would hear the complaint. In the end, their discipline amounted to a rep-rimand, which, thanks to Brown's efforts, was not publicized. Shaughnessy was told that if she aspired to become a legislator, she should try to set a better example as a lawyer. Meekly, she agreed. That was the extent of her punishment.

Shaughnessy was immensely grateful to Brown, and they became great friends. Both were Liberals, though Brown was at the periphery of the party. Shaughnessy talked up her fabulous lawyer friend all over Windsor and Ontario, and sent business on to him. Brown, in turn, invited Shaughnessy into his powerful legal circle in Toronto and gave her a place at the Blake's table at the Confederation Dinner, an annual Liberal Party fundraiser.

It was at this tony affair that Shaughnessy was observed by Marian Maloney, wife of Judge William Maloney. Marian had heard her husband describe Shaughnessy as a sharp-tongued, funny young woman with a healthy streak of irreverence. "It was impos-sible not to like Shaughnessy, as soon as you met her," Marian said. Shaughnessy was the type of young woman she believed the Liberals needed.

Marian Maloney was one of the most loyal and hard-working volunteers behind the scenes in the federal Liberal Party and a big booster of women's participation. When the party set up a special fund to encourage and help finance the campaigns of women candidates in the mid-1980s, Maloney was involved and later took charge. The fund was named in honour of another sharp-tongued and bright female star in the party, Judy LaMarsh, who had died of cancer in 1980. LaMarsh was the Liberals' first female cabinet minister.

The annual Confederation Dinner was an opportunity for Shaughnessy to catch up with Mary Clancy who, unlike Shaughn, had been elected in 1988. Through Mary's eyes, Shaughn was learning what it meant to be a member of Parliament in Ottawa, and the prospect was deliciously tantalizing. Mary was having the time of her life, serving as women's issues critic and getting to know the major Liberal players outside her Maritime home. In later years, after Shaughnessy was elected, she would still sit at the Blake's table at the Confederation Dinner and feed that old enthusiasm by introducing new political rookies around the room. She would perform for others the role that Mary and Marian had for her, regaling neophytes with stories of life in Ottawa.

Once the unpleasantness with the Law Society was behind her, Shaughnessy left Wilson Walker and set herself up as a sole practitioner, aiming to take on only as much business as she could handle responsibly. Don Brown understood Shaughnessy's weaknesses as a civil lawyer but had no question about her talents on the criminal side, whether she was working for the defence or the prosecution. "She was bright. She was quick. She had a great understanding of personal peccadilloes and shortcomings," Brown said. "She was funny. She could be aggressive. She was glib. She was a showman. All of these qualities are essential to being a good cross-examiner in criminal cases, where all the issues involve human frailties."

Brown also saw her in action at the Health Protection Appeal Board, where he served as legal counsel, largely because Shaughnessy, the chair, wanted him there. "As chair of the board, she was, believe it or not, serious, dignified, and a presence that demanded respect," he remembered. But Shaughnessy could easily don the mantle of officiousness or aggression if her work demanded it. Even friends could become foes when that work clock was ticking.

Brian Ducharme recalled an occasion when he found himself on the opposite side of the courtroom from Shaughnessy. He was defending a man who had been accused of leaving the scene of an accident to avoid a drinking-and-driving charge. Ducharme's only hope was to mount a defence based on identity – the man accused of the crime was not actually the man who caused the accident. What he hoped to prove was that the police had nabbed the wrong man. Fortunately for Ducharme, the accident had taken place on a cold winter night and his client had been wearing a heavy parka with a fur hood. Witnesses couldn't positively identify the perpetrator of the accident, because his face was obscured by the hood.

"So I told him to bring the fur coat to court, and he put it on when he was on the witness stand," Ducharme said. "Sure enough, the fur covered his face."

Shaughnessy, the Crown prosecutor, stood up and protested. Ducharme, she charged, was indulging in dramatics, using "Matlock-like" tactics.

"She'd said this in open court!" Ducharme said. "I was offended! But she wouldn't give in." The Matlock style didn't succeed as it did on TV. Shaughnessy easily proved that the cops had the right man, and she simply smiled in satisfaction when her friend lost his case and his client was convicted.

As she became increasingly expert at criminal prosecution, friends urged Shaughnessy to consider a career as a full-time Crown attorney. She would have a salary with benefits, and vacations. A fine idea, she thought, but there was a problem: she would have to give up politics. And Shaughnessy had no intention of doing that.

By 1989, every Liberal in the country knew that a leadership contest was on the horizon. John Turner had steered the party to two election losses and the knives were out. Twice in 1988, once in April and again in the middle of the election campaign, he had faced mutiny within his own caucus and not so subtle prompting to step down.

Jean Chrétien, nursing his 1984 loss, had been waiting for his chance to assume the helm from Turner. His team was in place, his organization pulling itself together again in every region of the country. Caucus malcontents, specifically Nova Scotia's David Dingwall and Toronto's Sergio Marchi, made no secret of their allegiance. All they awaited to declare support for Chrétien was a signal from John Turner that he was leaving, and with the announcement of his resignation in May 1989, he obliged. The party set the date for the leadership convention a full year ahead, to June 1990, and braced itself for a year-long marathon that was expected to end with Jean Chrétien's coronation. He was one of the most popular politicians in Canada, regarded as a straight-shooter who spoke, as the title of his bestselling 1986 autobiography declared, "straight from the heart."

But Shaughnessy would not go over to Chrétien's side this time. Paul Martin Jr., thought of as "Windsor's own" although he represented a Montreal riding in Parliament, intended to run as the leading challenger to Chrétien, and his was the best show in town, she decided. This was about Windsor, and Shaughnessy had been around long enough to recognize the importance of local connections.

Her next political objective was to rally the hometown behind the Martins' leadership aspirations. Though the elder Martin had long ago been supplanted as the Liberal dean of Windsor, he was still the city's leading citizen and still influential. If Shaughnessy could win his approval, through her efforts on his son's behalf, she would solidify her claim to his former riding.

The task was pure joy for Shaughnessy, even if her candidate's chances were slim, and even if, contrary to her left-wing leanings, Martin Jr. was positioned as the choice of the party's right wing. Shaughnessy's politics were pragmatic – she was far less ideologically leftist than Jerry, for instance – and she threw herself wholeheartedly into Martin's campaign. There were advantages in supporting the underdog. The hierarchies of front-running campaigns are packed with long-time supporters and party veterans; neophytes and outsiders have little chance to get in the game. But there was room for Shaughnessy in Martin's camp, as much room as she wanted to take. And she wanted a big role. "It's the most fun you can have standing up," she told the *Windsor Star* as the delegate selection process got under way in Ontario.

Her first job was to dispel Martin Sr.'s reservations about her style or her loyalty. Fortunately, she had an ally in the same household: Nell Martin, his wife, was enormously fond of Shaughnessy. The two women shared a down-to-earth irreverence that bound them together. In the early days of the leadership race, Nell and Shaughnessy would huddle in the kitchen, plotting and laughing, while Martin made himself scarce. They would talk about who was in and who was out in Windsor's incestuous political pond, and whom they needed to cultivate. The sum total of their plotting, Martin Jr. said, was to introduce endless complications into the elder Martin's life. He would inevitably find himself with a fresh to-do list: talk to this person about the candidate's policy, remind that person of a favour owed, phone up the newspaper with a story suggestion.

Shaughnessy's style could be intimidating to the more traditionally minded men in her life. Even Martin Jr. could sometimes be shocked by Shaughnessy's language.

"There is not a sailor on Her Majesty's ships or a pirate ship anywhere in the world that could handle the Queen's English quite the way she could," was the way he phrased it. Still, the younger Martin was already aware, probably more so than his father, of Shaughnessy's intellectual strengths. When the Hiram Walker's distillery was faced with the prospect of shutdown in the late 1980s, just as the campaign was starting to simmer, Shaughnessy and Martin had a long discussion in which she expounded passionately on the connections between local industries and their communities, a conversation that remained in Martin's mind years later when he had to confront the tensions between local and global economies as the country's minister of finance.

Shaughnessy was becoming adept at the power-by-association game, making connections and networks work for her. Don Brown was a powerful lawyer; Paul Martin Jr. was a potentially powerful politician. She could act as matchmaker.

Early in 1990, Shaughnessy decided that Brown should be doing fundraising for Martin. Though Martin was a serious contender and the only plausible challenger to Jean Chrétien, he wasn't pulling in the necessary resources in Ontario. Shaughn was wise to the magic of fundraisers by this time: campaigns could not function without them, and those who raised the money earned a lot of political leverage in the process. She spoke to Don Brown regularly, as a colleague and a friend, and she prevailed on him to help out. Then she contacted Richard Mahoney, Martin's executive assistant and right-hand man throughout the leadership race, and suggested that she had a prime fundraiser lined up to assist the candidate in Ontario.

It was in January 1990, around the time of the first Liberal leadership debate in Toronto, that Brown and Martin met for breakfast in one of the city's hotel restaurants. The two weren't strangers: they had been in the same bar admission course and had kept in casual touch through the years. After the usual pleasantries, Martin got to the point: "Can you help me out, Don? Can you raise some money for me?" he asked.

Brown believed he could, and in a matter of a few weeks, he raised $75,000 in Toronto's well-heeled legal community. One event was held at his own home in Rosedale; the other, at a private club, with 200 guests paying $200 a head to meet the candidate. In later years, Brown would perform this service for other leading Liberals; in 1997, for example, he helped Allan Rock in his campaign for re-election. Shortly after the 1993 election, he earned the distinction of being the top private fundraiser for the Liberal Party.

It would take at least $1 million to run a proper leadership campaign, according to Richard Mahoney, but $2 million was the usual target. The money paid for staff — Martin had 40 to 50 people working for him across the country — as well as travel, posters, buttons, campaign paraphernalia, office equipment, and rental costs. Brown's speedy and fruitful fundraising efforts were warmly received. "We were unbelievably grateful," Mahoney said. "Don and Shaughnessy were my new best friends."

Martin's leadership bid was to be formally announced on a cold January day in three cities. The initial announcement would be made in Montreal, to reinforce Martin's status as a Quebecker. The next stop would be Toronto, to consolidate his ties to the business community. The end of the journey was the sentimental favourite: home in Windsor, united with his father to celebrate the campaign launch, just in time for the nightly news broadcasts.

But on the day that Martin was to descend on these three cities, a huge wall of fog beat him to it. By the time he'd made the first announcement in Montreal, most flights in and out of Quebec and Ontario were cancelled or postponed. When Martin finally did get himself on a flight, he ended up on a propeller plane, run by the soon-to-be-defunct City Express airline, which was prevented from landing at Toronto's island airport by poor visibility. As the tiny aircraft circled the skies, Martin's Toronto appearances had to be cancelled. No launch at Glendon College; no footage on the CBC's newsmagazine, *The Journal*. The flight landed late in the day at Pearson Airport and sat idling for an hour on a strip near Terminal 3. Martin and his entourage had to pass through Customs on arrival, before they embarked on an almost comic scramble to salvage something of the day's program.

In Windsor, Shaughnessy and Mahoney were trying desperately to keep the crowd in the room, so that no matter when Martin arrived, his appearance would be triumphal. The candidate was supposed to be there at 6 p.m. By 9 o'clock, the 750 people assembled for the event were bored; Paul Martin Sr., 86 years old, was cranky. Mahoney walked over to the cash bar and slapped down his American Express card. If nothing else would persuade people to stay, free drinks might. At the same time, Shaughnessy started pushing people up on the stage to speak. Ever the political pro, Martin Sr. performed as required, and even Shaughnessy took her turn at the microphone, trying to keep the room entertained, telling jokes and extolling the virtues of Windsor's two Paul Martins.

When the candidate eventually arrived, surrounded by his bedraggled team and a police escort laid on by loyal locals, Shaughnessy fluttered about, introducing herself to his aides and to the national reporters there to cover the event. "If I can be of any help to you, if you need to know anything about what's happening down here in Windsor, just call me," she said, pressing her phone number into everyone's hands. Within a few weeks, many of these individuals would indeed be calling on her.

Shaughn intended to deliver Martin Sr.'s old riding – now called, after another redesignation, Windsor–St. Clair – in its entirety to the Martin leadership effort. Like all other ridings across Canada, it had 15 delegates to send to the convention. She would be happy with nothing less than a full slate of Martin supporters. The meeting to select delegates in Windsor–St. Clair was scheduled for February 17, making it one of the first to be held in the country and in the province. A strong showing out of the gate by Martin would demonstrate that Chrétien had a serious fight on his hands leading up to the June vote. The pressure was on Shaughnessy and Richard Mahoney to deliver in Windsor – and deliver big – not just for sentimental reasons, but for strategic purposes too. The media and the party would be watching closely.

The lead-up to the Windsor vote was high-stakes political gamesmanship at its most intense – Shaughnessy's favourite hobby. Though Eugene Whelan was officially retired from elected politics, he was active behind the scenes and working for Jean Chrétien. The Martin camp had inherited many of the former Turner supporters, largely because of simmering resentments left over from the last leadership race. Whelan and his daughter Susan, who was considering a future candidacy herself at her father's urging, were Shaughnessy's chief rivals in the campaign for Windsor's delegates.

At the first meeting, in Essex-Windsor on Friday night, tempers flared. Though everyone expected that Whelan's old riding would go to the Chrétien forces, the depth of the animosity between the Martin and Chrétien forces came to the fore. Shaughnessy and one of her 17-year-old charges in the Martin campaign, Charlie Angelakos, got into a shouting match with an aggressive Chrétien organizer, Toronto MP Jim Karygiannis.

As Dena and Jerry looked on, Karygiannis taunted Shaughnessy.

"At least after the last election, I got two letters after my name – MP." Shaughnessy just laughed. "You're a thug, Karygiannis, picking on a 17-year-old. Go find someone your own size." As they exchanged insults, Essex-Windsor's Liberals voted to send 12 Chrétien supporters to the Calgary convention in June.

The next morning, though, belonged to Shaughnessy's side. At a little hall filled with friends of the Martins, and as Martin Sr. looked on, Windsor–St. Clair's Liberals gave their entire slate of delegates to the local boy. Martin Sr. was duly grateful. "I'm very proud of him but I'm very proud of my own riding," the candidate's father was quoted as saying when the meeting was over. "It's a great victory for my son."

The bond between father and son was strong. Martin Sr. had been through this three times before, always as a losing candidate, and it was agonizing to watch his son endure the same uphill struggle. The calls would come at 5 a.m., Martin Sr. demanding to know from Shaughnessy or Richard Mahoney the organizational details of the campaign nationally and locally. During those months, from late 1989 to June 1990, he referred to Mahoney as simply "the organizer" and left frequent, urgent messages for him at headquarters in Ottawa. "Do you know a good newspaperman in Ottawa?" he would ask repeatedly. "We've got to get some good press here." The distance between Windsor and Ottawa was immense, and Shaughnessy, on the ground in the same city as the elder Martin, was invaluable to the campaign in this respect too, keeping him busy and in the local loop. Once she located uncommitted delegates or weak backers of Chrétien, she would ask Martin Sr. to phone them and seal the deal for his son. She was also shuttling back and forth between Windsor and the campaign's Ontario headquarters in Toronto, relaying information and confirming strategy up and down the line.

Martin was still the underdog when the Liberals convened in Calgary in late June. But this would hardly stop his supporters from having a good time. Shaughnessy bustled around the Saddledome, giddy in the heavy political atmosphere, sporting a Paul Martin

T-shirt with the big "PM" on the front (she'd added shoulder pads to make her hips look smaller).

The day before the leadership vote was one of the most bizarre in Canadian political history. It was June 22, 1990, and the Meech Lake constitutional accord was drifting to an ignominious death, sitting unpassed in the legislatures of Manitoba and Newfoundland. It had to be approved by June 23, or it would die because it failed to meet the three-year deadline laid out in the Constitution for all provinces to pass constitutional amendments. It remains a bit of a mystery why the Liberals chose June 23 as the date for their convention, though a year earlier it had been reasonable to expect that this day would pass without incident and with the Meech Lake provisions ensconced in the Constitution. However, thanks to Jean Chrétien, among others, an anti-Meech spirit had been whipped up in the country, especially among Liberals.

Television monitors throughout the Saddledome began to broadcast a series of emotional statements from both architects and detractors of the accord. The Conservative government in Ottawa announced that the deadline would be extended for Manitoba, but not for Newfoundland; Newfoundland Premier Clyde Wells denounced this arbitrariness, saying he would not be manipulated into holding a vote; Quebec Premier Robert Bourassa rose in the National Assembly to pronounce Meech Lake dead, and then the recriminations began.

Back in Calgary, while the chief enemy of the accord, Pierre Trudeau, breezed through the corridors like a rock star, the leadership candidates and their teams huddled in private, preoccupied with their speeches. As thousands of Liberals massed for the evening's presentations, arriving early to stake out their camps' territories in the hall, it seemed as if there was nothing of more import happening anywhere in the country.

The one exception to this sentiment was found in the Martin camp, where supporters, including Shaughnessy, wore black armbands to signify their grief over the failure of the Meech Lake accord. Was Shaughnessy in mourning? Not likely. She didn't feel strongly about Meech one way or the other. But the team demanded she mourn and so she did, sitting in the stands among a sea of Martin delegates wearing the T-shirt, the armband, and the mandated glum expression.

The next day's vote was anti-climactic. Chrétien's victory had been assumed, and it was delivered on the first ballot. He became leader with 2,652 votes, more than double Paul Martin's 1,176 votes. Sheila Copps was a distant third at 499 votes.

The best party after the event was not in the winner's tent, however, but at the bar where the Martin organization had chosen to lament its loss, Winston's on Calgary's Electric Avenue. Windsor had staked out its own block of turf on the deck, and Shaughn sat at the head of a table that was graced by the presence of Northwest Territories MP Ethel Blondin, co-chair of the leadership convention. It was a feather in Shaughn's cap to be seen with Blondin, a woman who had presided over the week's proceedings, on centre stage almost all the time, and whose aboriginal heritage lent her a high profile. (The Liberals saw themselves as the only real voice for women, youth, and aboriginal people in Canada. Special commissions within the party were set up to manage their concerns.) As the night wore on and the liquor flowed, some of Martin's younger supporters grew less gracious in defeat. But Shaughnessy revealed no bitterness. As she told the *Windsor Star* the next day: "You are not going to hear any whining from me. [Chrétien] is my new leader and I will be proud to follow him."

The next day Liberal delegates in Calgary were relishing their victories, nursing their losses, or medicating their hangovers while the country's attention was still absorbed by the demise of the Meech Lake accord. Some of the Martin team had gone for a picnic in the mountains, others were roaming around the Palliser Hotel.

Shaughnessy was wandering the halls, cheery as usual and teasing those who had consumed too much at the wake the night before. Along with a reporter friend, she ran into the Martins, father and son, who invited the women for a brief drink. Somehow the hotel's lobby bar miraculously opened for the small party, and they sat down to a casual conversation that eventually veered to the nature of political loss.

Paul Martin Jr. explained that his defeat the day before had been relatively easy to handle, compared with the devastation he had felt in 1968 when his father lost the Liberal leadership to Pierre Trudeau. He was inconsolable and angry after that vote, he said. He was much more at peace with this loss because it was his own; he had control and he could examine his mistakes dispassionately. "It is far more difficult to lose when you're on the sidelines as a spectator," he said. His major worry that day was for all the people who had supported him. Paul Martin Sr. was one of those, and he echoed his son's sentiments. The loss in 1968 hit his son harder than it did him, for the same reason. But in 1990, watching his son lose, the disappointment was hard to disguise.

The three politicians, veteran, rising star, and rookie, discussed how to learn from defeat and how to comfort those who work so hard in unsuccessful campaigns. Wise politicians see loss through the prism of companionship, community, and camaraderie; they have to help their supporters do the same.

Shaughn understood instinctively that the concern of the Martins would be for the people around them – their families and campaign workers. In her usual generous fashion, she spent that encounter reassuring them with amusing stories about events at the convention and back home in Windsor. It was clear by this time that she had won the affection of Paul Martin Sr. Difficult though it was on the day after his son's first significant political defeat, she made the old man forget his misery and laugh.

6

Eyes on the Prize

The early nineties were a trying time for Canadian politicians. Voters seemed determined to defeat, isolate, and reject everything their legislators offered. Keith Spicer, once a newspaper editor and then chairman of the Canadian Radio-television and Telecommunications Commission, headed a citizens' forum on the state of the political culture in Canada; he hoped to plumb the depths of the anti-politician frenzy that had seemed to erupt during the Meech Lake debate. Spicer reported in 1991 that there was "a fury in the land" – much of it directed against the prime minister, Brian Mulroney. In 1992, the citizenry delivered another rebuff in the form of a defiant no to the Charlottetown constitutional accord. Put to the voters in a referendum, it was decisively rejected in almost every province of Canada.

It was hard to imagine why anyone would want to be a politician at that moment in the nation's history. As a class they were loathed and despised. But a shrewd politician – and there were many in the Liberal Party of Canada – saw that this mood of antipathy nourished the momentum for change. Jean Chrétien knew this, repeatedly urging his troops to stay calm and focused on the larger goal of chasing the Tories from office. Shaughnessy Cohen understood it too. The best strategy was to align herself with the anti-Mulroney sentiment and use it to her advantage. Fortunately, Windsor had never embraced Mulroney's Tories. When the rest of the country had handed the Conservatives majority governments in 1988 and 1994, the two Windsor ridings that had rejected Liberals sent New Democrats to Ottawa instead.

In August 1990, two months after the Calgary leadership convention, Shaughnessy penned a provocative letter to the *Windsor Star*. Her ostensible purpose was to criticize the federal government's foreign policy. More calculatingly, she was working to keep her name in front of the voters as an opponent of Brian Mulroney.

Sir: The broadcast news of Aug. 28 brought videotape of our prime minister and American President George Bush speeding about with their spouses and entourage in the Atlantic Ocean off Kennebunkport, Me., while discussing the crisis in the Gulf of Oman. This image is, I am certain, disturbing to many Canadians.

Mulroney has sent three rustbuckets [a term stolen from a navy spouse as she stood on the Halifax docks waving goodbye] to the Gulf of Oman. These are, by all accounts, outdated and hastily equipped vessels which are assigned to an area which is ripe for actual, armed conflict and which are staffed with personnel who are untrained in the very type of anti-missile warfare which they are likely to encounter. Surely the gall of Brian Mulroney is unprecedented in Canadian politics. The man has once again bowed to bravado and expediency; but, this is not the first time he has done so to remedy his poor showing in the polls at the expense of the well-being of Canadians.

We should be reminded of his famous declaration of war on drug pushers at a time when there was no data to suggest that there was any major problem in Canada. We should also be reminded of his rush to negotiate the U.S.-Canadian free trade deal which has resulted in so many job losses and plant closings in Windsor and elsewhere in Canada.

With little consultation and virtually no rational explanation to the Canadian people, Mulroney has in furtherance of his great love affair with his self image, set aside years of Canadian foreign policy, made life very uncomfortable for countless military families and potentially made our navy the laughing stock of the world.

Meanwhile, back at home, he is noticeably absent in the Oka crisis, a situation which public opinion polls show most Canadians are concerned about and he has precious little to offer to us in terms of a game plan to remedy the Meech Lake debacle which he so cavalierly engineered this past spring.

The man confuses bravado with self worth and showmanship with leadership.

Shaughnessy Cohen

The letter bears all of Shaughnessy's rhetorical trademarks. The one-time psychology student loved to analyze the motives and personalities of her political foes: Brian Mulroney had a "self-worth" problem, she opined. She also had a fondness for linking her concerns to the greater good of ordinary people, in this case the beleaguered military sent to war with inadequate equipment and their families left behind. And despite her own tendencies to name-drop and be impressed by the famous, she had a knee-jerk reaction to elitism in others. Shaughnessy embraced all things American in a spirit of friendly equality. What she perceived as Mulroney's fawning deference to the United States she found demeaning to the nation.

Shaughnessy's political fortunes were rising, in fact. She was overtaking Brian Ducharme as the slickest Liberal player in town. Ducharme's reputation had suffered another bruising when the

David Peterson government collapsed on his watch as provincial party president in 1990. The *Windsor Star*'s political columnist, Gord Henderson, tracked the decline shortly after the Liberals' electoral disaster in September.

"Poor Brian," he wrote. "Less than five months ago this city lawyer and Peterson confidante [*sic*] was on top of the world . . . Those interested in judicial appointments and other coveted posts, I was told, would want to be on good terms with the new party president. Hint. Hint.

"No longer. This 'big cheese' job turned rancid on election night and now Ducharme's enemies in the Windsor area are pushing for his immediate resignation."

Henderson wouldn't be expected to reveal his sources for that story, but there's no doubt that in happier days Shaughnessy would have been one of the Liberals talking up her very important friend, especially his influence on her perennially favourite perk of power, judicial appointments. She wasn't likely to be the source of the whispers of Ducharme's demise, but she would have known who his "enemies" were. Some had harboured resentments since the nasty battle against Mike Ray in 1985; they were her detractors as well as Ducharme's. Still, for all those foes, Shaughn knew where she could find friends, and many of those were in the media. She was learning how to play the pundit's game in Windsor, cultivating media sources and presenting herself as a person in the know.

That reputation earned her a spot on the local CBC-TV supper-hour news. As the Liberals' spokesperson on a new weekly political affairs panel, moderated by Percy Hatfield, Shaughnessy joined New Democrat Joe Comartin and Conservative Bill Krause for a 10- to 15-minute broad-ranging discussion of national developments. She approached her performance with gusto, working the phones in the days prior, shaking the Windsor grapevine, all in preparation for the role of well-informed Liberal insider. And because she was in regular touch with people like Mary Clancy and Richard Mahoney, she could deliver the federal and provincial party lines with authority. Mary, already an important presence in the 80-member Liberal opposition, supplied Shaughnessy with gossip from the Hill. Mahoney was working as an Ottawa lobbyist, laying the groundwork for a deeper involvement in Ontario Liberal politics.

On camera, Shaughnessy perfected a posture of amused tolerance while Comartin and Krause made their points, her eyes crinkling or rolling behind oversized red-framed glasses. (Though she had previously worn blue frames, she decided that the big-Liberal-in-town persona required her to wear red at every opportunity.) When her turn came, she was ready with a swift verbal jab at her opponents, always delivered with a sweet smile. Then she would introduce her spiel with a segue such as "Well, I happen to know" or "Don't be ridiculous."

"You couldn't get a better political panellist," said Hatfield. "She had great insights, she was partisan, and she always knew a good gossipy story along the way."

The ratings for the show soared; viewers liked Shaughnessy especially and applauded the tone of the weekly debate. Once entranced by the media savvy of her old friend Carrie Flaherty, Shaughnessy now had her own place in the media spotlight. Several months into the season, Hatfield apologized for the pathetic honorarium the panellists were paid in exchange for their weekly appearances.

"Are you kidding?" Shaughn said to him. "I'd pay you to do this show!"

Her love of the CBC, in principle and in self-interest, soon vaulted her into another public crusade: the campaign to save the local CBC station from a scheduled closing. A Windsor group called Friends of the CBC sprang up and Shaughn became legal counsel and one of the chief spokespersons for the organization.

The Liberals started preparing for the next federal election in 1992, expecting Mulroney to go to the people after the usual four years. Shaughnessy believed, somewhat naively, that the coming campaign would be easier than the last. She had, after all, been the candidate in 1988, and political protocol usually dictates that the previous hopeful is given a chance to run again, uncontested within the party.

Moreover, she'd worked to polish her political image and acumen. Though it would be a life-long process of re-education, Shaughnessy was developing a bit of savvy about clothes, deportment, and communication skills. With some reluctance, she abandoned the rumpled, casual look that had distinguished even her professional appearances and put aside the golf shirts, jeans, and baseball caps that constituted her leisure wear. She was guided in this effort by her friend Norma Coleman, a former political communications expert at Queen's Park. Coleman had served as a volunteer in Shaughn's 1988 campaign; now she moved into a key role as confidante to the would-be candidate.

One of Coleman's accomplishments while working at Queen's Park was the makeover of David Peterson. Along with the image guru Gabor Apor, she transformed Peterson from a bespectacled, chubby nerd into the dashing and handsome premier. She vividly remembered the day Peterson emerged from his office wearing contact lenses, a perfectly tailored dark suit, dazzling red tie, and sleek haircut. He stood, awaiting her inspection. "Are you happy now?" he asked in exasperation.

Norma and John Coleman had moved to Windsor in the late eighties when Norma was seven months pregnant. When her daughter, Katharine, was born, tragedy struck. The tiny infant was infected with viral encephalitis and given faint hope for survival, let alone a normal life. Katharine's first days at home were marked by long sessions of screaming and intermittent seizures. Coleman couldn't leave the house. She was heavily dependent on a committed circle of friends who would come by to lend a hand or just keep her in touch with the world at large. Shaughnessy was one of those friends. She would visit regularly, marching straight through the door and up the stairs to see little Katharine in her crib. "God, she's beautiful," Shaughnessy would tell Coleman. Over the years, as Katharine's condition degenerated (she died in November 1990, at the age of five), Shaughnessy remained at the family's side, always ready to help. "I think she learned a lot from us and from Katharine, about support for people and families who have these things in their lives," said Norma.

She returned Shaughnessy's kindness in tangible ways, offering the benefit of the political communications expertise she'd gained at Queen's Park. She talked to Shaughnessy about the importance of profile. Get in those parades, she'd say, get up on that stage. Even if it upsets the local pooh-bahs, specifically the New Democrats who held the majority of Windsor's federal seats, make it clear that you are a woman who demands to be seen. Sure enough, Shaughnessy did insist upon her right to take the platform at local events and the reigning MP, Howard McCurdy, would grit his teeth while she waved at the crowd.

She was becoming a media darling too. Unlike other politicians who often see the media as a blunt instrument – "Can you give me some publicity?" they ask reporters – Shaughnessy honed her skills to a deft sharpness, learning the importance of the well-placed leak, the rumour, the whisper to an important ear. With Coleman's tutoring, she realized that she didn't have to take out advertisements or push her name up front to have her purposes served.

But the goal of becoming an elected politician was still to be achieved. A number of hurdles lay ahead, among them the animosity of her foes within Windsor's Liberal ranks. She had played for the losing side in the leadership race; with Chrétien's people now controlling the election organization network, Shaughnessy could not expect much help from national headquarters or from local Chrétien loyalists. Furthermore, this election was starting to look like it might be a romp for the Liberals and, as Ducharme observed, that meant the nomination battle would be more intense than the campaign. She could not take the nomination in Windsor–St. Clair for granted. "I didn't have control of the riding association and I didn't try to take it over," she recalled several years later, when interviewed for a television documentary about women in politics. "I wasn't aggressive enough to try and shore up my support."

Two rivals for the nomination emerged in the summer of 1992, both busily signing up new members. George Dietrich, a well-liked lawyer, was off to a fast start and showed every sign of becoming a serious threat to Shaughnessy. So too did Harold Downs, the former mayor of the Windsor-area community of Tecumseh. Downs had run as a New Democrat in 1988, but he switched to the Liberals for his next election bid. He was popular, and Ducharme said he had recruited the anti-abortion movement in Windsor to help support his nomination. Whenever a morality issue invades politics, the fight becomes particularly nasty.

Ducharme, in charge of Liberal candidate recruitment in the region, was naturally interested in seeing Shaughnessy win. He had some influence in declaring the cut-off date for memberships, and he decided it was best to stop the process before it got out of control; he didn't want Windsor–St. Clair hijacked by a single-issue interest group. The Liberals had already witnessed the phenomenon in a number of ridings in the 1988 election and the 1990 leadership contest. To some it was an alarming trend. But the man overseeing the Liberal election effort was David Smith, a former Toronto MP and minister of small business in the Trudeau years. He had supported Chrétien in 1984 and 1990 and had no incentive to help Shaughnessy win the nomination. What if the nomination battle got heated? He thought that a lively nomination process would lure more Liberals into the fold. As the party's national campaign chairman, he had his eye on the larger picture. Too many Liberals in Windsor–St. Clair? That was not a problem for David Smith.

Shaughnessy needed some high-level intervention. If the race for members carried on much longer, she'd lose the candidacy she believed was hers. Ducharme telephoned Sheila Copps, who had been assigned special responsibility to ensure that the Liberals attracted women candidates. Gender imbalance is a problem for all political parties – fewer women ran federally in 1997 than in 1993 – and the Liberals had a long-standing commitment that at least 25 per cent of their candidates be women.

A conference call was scheduled between Ducharme, David

Smith, and Sheila Copps. It was a blunt exchange. Copps insisted that the party had an obligation to Shaughnessy, a woman and a former candidate. She didn't mince words, Ducharme recalled.

"I've worked my ass off to get women involved in this party," Copps told Smith. "I'm not going to see us lose this woman candidate. She's already run once for us. She's owed this. Shut down the nominations and call the goddamn date."

Copps earned the loyalty of a number of Liberal women that year, fighting hard on their behalf and making it possible for them to enter the political fray. And many, notably Jane Stewart, who was also recruited that year, said that Copps was correct to focus her attention on the nomination process.

Even though she was no naïf in politics – her father, Robert Nixon, was a former treasurer of Ontario, a veteran of the provincial legislature, and a buddy of Jean Chrétien – Stewart was still daunted by that first step. For women, Stewart said, it was the most difficult stage. To begin with, women are not generally part of the old boys' network that is so crucial to rising within the party. They are outsiders at the start and often remain so. Then the outsider has to ask for something more than a simple vote. "You've got to ask people to give you – to *give* you – ten dollars. It's awful," she said. Add to this the toll of taking on friends or colleagues who were allies in the past and should have remained comrades in the party trenches. "It's in the family, the Liberal family," Stewart said. "That makes it tough. Your competitor can be your neighbour or the person you canvassed with in the last election."

Thanks to Copps's intervention, the cut-off date for new members in Windsor–St. Clair was declared as September 24. Any memberships registered after that date were not valid. Under party rules, candidates are not told the cut-off date until a week later, in this case, October 1. Almost immediately, George Dietrich protested. Dietrich's father had died on September 21, and few memberships had been sold or processed as a result. While Dietrich was planning his father's funeral, he had 180 signed and paid-up memberships in his hands. But with the candidate otherwise engaged, the memberships had not been sent on to Toronto to be registered. Dietrich appealed for an extension on compassionate grounds. Shaughnessy, unsentimental, had a simple answer to that request: No.

"If I had given them an extension, I would have lost," she candidly admitted to reporters. "Guess what? I wanted the nomination."

When Dietrich's supporters grumbled publicly about Shaughn receiving special favours from the party brass because she was a woman, she fired back in her own defence. The appeal to her compassion, she said, was designed to prey on her feminine sensibilities. "They wouldn't have asked a man that. Females are supposed to cave in when a man asks them something and if we don't, then we're bitches," she said. Dietrich subsequently bowed out of the race.

On November 23, 1992, Shaughnessy took the nomination by about 100 votes. Sources close to the counting told the *Windsor Star* that Shaughnessy had won 280 votes while Harold Downs won 176. Victory came with a price – more grumbling and more enemies within the Windsor Liberal Party rank and file.

Three months later and just after Shaughnessy's 45th birthday in February 1993, Mulroney announced his resignation and the kickoff of the Conservatives' leadership campaign. Jean Chrétien, who would have preferred to fight the supremely unpopular Mulroney, was still reasonably confident that his Liberals would end up forming the government by the end of the year.

Indeed, Liberal headquarters in Ottawa was boasting about its high level of election readiness. Paul Martin, along with the party's policy director, Chaviva Hošek, spent months working on a detailed account of the party's platform and promises that came to be called the Red Book. In May, a campaign college was held over several days on Parliament Hill. There newcomers such as Shaughnessy, Jane Stewart, Paddy Torsney, and Allan Rock were schooled in Liberal policies and tactics. Liberal women were given specialized sessions. Sheila Copps talked to them about what to wear while campaigning. "Avoid big prints and big earrings," Copps warned. Shaughnessy and Anne McLellan, a candidate from Alberta, immediately snapped their focus on veteran Mary Clancy, sitting resplendent in a loud print jacket and dangly earrings.

The summer of 1993 was a tense time of waiting for Liberals. The Conservatives' new leader, Kim Campbell, was doing well in popularity polls, and "nervous Nellies," as Chrétien dubbed them, were fretting that the Liberals could be facing a third consecutive election loss. Shaughnessy was not one of the nervous crowd. She was sure of Chrétien's chances, perhaps less sure of her own because of Howard McCurdy's strong hold on Windsor–St. Clair. But she was eager to give it another try.

The election call finally came in early September. The vote would take place on October 25. Had Campbell left it any later, she would have been in danger of stretching the Tories' term beyond the five-year limit. As well, she had to set a date no more than one year from the October 26, 1992, vote on the Charlottetown accord. Any longer and the whole country would have had to go through another expensive enumeration.

Shaughnessy entered the election campaign with barely two hundred dollars in the bank. She had spent most of her limited resources on the nomination fight and she had relegated her law practice – her only significant source of income – to the back burner. There was no campaign manager in sight: Brad Robitaille and Brian Ducharme were tired of the political game and had retreated to rebuild their legal careers. There was no campaign organization in place: her law office quickly turned into a confused mess of election materials and legal files.

She turned to an old friend, Ron Doherty. "Please, please say you'll do it!" she pleaded. "I need you." Doherty knew he wasn't her first choice, but he jumped at the chance to run a political campaign.

As soon as he agreed, Shaughnessy piled half of the debris from her law office into a cab and sent it over. Ron arranged a vacation from his job at CN, found an office, and prepared to mount a shoestring campaign in Windsor–St. Clair.

His first decision was to allocate most of their resources to a rented truck and lawn signs. The old-fashioned tools of stump speeches and colourful signs are still the nuts and bolts of any campaign. The work of planting signs all over town mobilizes volunteers and puts the candidate in touch with voters at the door-to-door level. And after a tough, frustrating day of slogging through the neighbourhoods, hammering in a few signs can be a therapeutic release. Some fierce hammering took place in Windsor–St. Clair the day that sand was poured in the gas tank of the Cohen campaign truck.

Shaughnessy's two opponents were Howard McCurdy, running for his third term, and Conservative Tom Porter, a local lawyer. All kinds of nastiness soon erupted. Porter accused Shaughnessy's people of leaking a story to the media about alleged improprieties in his real estate dealings. Shaughnessy and her team weren't above such tactics (their fingerprints were all over a story in the *Windsor Star* about a neighbourhood squabble involving Howard McCurdy's barking dog), but this was a matter that Shaughnessy had personally assured Porter she would not exploit – and she didn't. Still, Porter was so upset by the leak to the newspaper that he retained Harvey Strosberg for legal advice on a possible libel or slander suit. Below the surface, though, local Tories fought one whisper campaign with another.

At about the midpoint in the campaign, details of Shaughnessy's untidy financial affairs were revealed to the *Windsor Star*. Reporter Chris Vander Doelen, who wrote later that the information came from a variety of sources, including the Conservative camp, set about investigating the allegations. He looked through court files in Sarnia, where he discovered that the Murrays' old family priest, Father Charles McManus, was suing Shaughnessy for non-payment of a $14,000 loan. In his suit, Father McManus claimed that Shaughnessy had made only three payments of $198 in 1991 before her cheques started to bounce. Added to this was Shaughnessy and Jerry's non-payment of a $120,452.43 mortgage on the Windsor–St. Clair house and another $57,705 loan. Court documents showed that a writ of seizure and sale was being issued to the sheriff of Essex County to recover the mortgage and the Toronto-Dominion Bank was suing the Cohens for the loan. What Vander Doelen didn't know was that Shaughnessy had already taken this situation in hand. When it was clear that she had a real chance of becoming a member of Parliament, she was forced to confront the skeletons in her closet. She confessed to Brad Robitaille that she was in serious difficulties with creditors. Once again, it was the sheepish, embarrassed Shaughnessy who appealed for help. She was in trouble, it was her own fault, and she was scared.

Robitaille knew that politics was as much to blame as her procrastination. Shaughnessy just wasn't interested in anything but politics, he said. "At the end of the day, when criminal lawyers headed back to their offices to prepare and send out bills, Shaughn was mucking it up politically and was not taking care of the business side of her practice," he said. "Though she was an excellent advocate, she made very little money." Shaughn's annual income from her practice in the early 1990s ranged from $30,000 to $50,000. "Shaughn's political pursuits cost her dearly," Robitaille said. "The debt load became intolerable, not because of dishonesty or inability to pay, but because her financial affairs were simply not in proper order."

Robitaille moved quickly to remedy the situation. A bookkeeper was hired to manage Shaughnessy and Jerry's money. Rosalina Pinpin (affectionately dubbed "the dragon lady" by Shaughn) took direct control over all their finances, paying their bills, setting up a savings plan for mutual funds, and doling out a limited amount for Shaughnessy to spend at her discretion. Chastened, Shaughnessy didn't utter a word of complaint against this strict regimen, knowing that she had no choice. A refinancing plan consolidated more than $200,000 in debts and was managed with the help of a businessman who chose to remain anonymous. Rather than risk impropriety by funnelling funds directly to Shaughnessy, this benefactor approached the chartered banks and "went to the wall," Robitaille said, to guarantee a loan.

Robitaille was furious when parts of the story were leaked to

Vander Doelen. "She was just getting on her feet financially when she was kicked in the stomach." Even though Vander Doelen's bosses decided not to publish the story until after the election, his inquiries sent a shudder of fear through Shaughnessy's team.

Money seemed to be a problem on every front. The campaign in Windsor–St. Clair had few resources and relied heavily on the goodwill of volunteers. Young people would be lured into canvass duty by the promise of pizza at the end of a long day. But as the weeks passed and the Liberals' hopes soared nationally, more and more people started coming by to do telephone work or stuff envelopes. Doherty was reduced to inventing jobs or having them done twice, just to give willing workers something to do.

Shaughnessy's undiminished sense of fun infused the campaign headquarters. She would keep the volunteers giggling with silly stunts. "Let's all walk like Joe Clark," she'd say as she strutted stiffly around the room. One day she visited Herb Gray's campaign office and marvelled at the difference between her own chaotic head-quarters and the calm, highly organized atmosphere surrounding Windsor's senior politico. Though the *Star* had described Shaugh-nessy's campaign as part of the "big red machine," those close to the action knew that a better metaphor for the Liberal operation in Windsor–St. Clair was "big red circus."

Shaughnessy gazed in awe at a map of Gray's riding, all colour-coded by zone with push-pins and tiny flags denoting the names and assignments of organizers in Windsor West. While Gray's vol-unteers weren't looking, she shuffled all the flags and push-pins, scrambling the names and duties of volunteer captains. Some weeks later, she popped by Gray's office again and was stunned to discover that no one had corrected her little act of campaign vandalism: the flags and pins were right where she had left them. The truth was that nobody noticed; the map and the so-called organization were merely for show. Herb Gray had held his riding for so long and was so well liked in Windsor that no one seriously believed he had to mobilize a machine to be re-elected. He simply had to put his name on the ballot.

Not so for Shaughnessy, who had to be prodded and cajoled into the important business of campaigning door to door. She much preferred to chatter on the phone, her feet up, checking in with her pals in the heat of the campaign elsewhere in the country. If she was quiet for too long in the back office, Ron Doherty knew that she was playing computer solitaire and would have to be pulled out to do more canvassing.

Once she was on the street, calling on voters, she enjoyed herself, using the occasion, as she had in 1988, to visit with con- · stituents. Her workers often had to send out search parties; Shaughnessy invariably accepted invitations for tea or a beer. At one home, she allowed a woman to wash her hair with nettles from the garden, after this prospective voter told her that they could thicken her thin, wispy hair. "I'm getting my hair washed, do you mind?" she replied when one of her frantic volunteers finally tracked her down.

Her legal career occasionally haunted her at the door, though the reception was mixed, depending on whether she'd met the person as defence counsel or as prosecutor. Gary McNamara, a local Liberal active in municipal politics, recalled walking door to door with her, checking the names at the next homes to be canvassed. "Shit," she'd say. "I prosecuted this guy. I'm not going to his door." She would linger on the sidewalk while McNamara braved the encounter alone. But as often as not, she would see the name of someone she'd successfully defended. "I got this guy off," she'd say. "Watch this."

At the doors, the voters were talking about the need to get rid of the "Mulroney government," even though Mulroney himself was long gone. Shaughnessy's workers were starting to believe that their candidate had a real chance of being part of a national Liberal sweep, prompted in large part by the widespread disgust with the Tories.

Garry Fortune, Herb Gray's aide, phoned Ron Doherty every day to check on Shaughnessy's progress. Doherty had hints that headquarters in Ottawa was watching this riding closely, because it was a tight race but winnable. Various volunteers were dispatched from the Ontario headquarters to offer assistance as the campaign wore on.

One of the key measures of performance was the number of lawn signs on display. Doherty knew that 50 new sign postings daily was the minimum. One day he was able to boast that 300 households had agreed to show Shaughnessy signs on their lawns.

On October 16, the Chrétien plane was scheduled to touch down in Windsor. Shaughnessy was excited about the visit; she wanted something new to wear. Burrowing through her papers at the campaign office, she plucked her cheque from the Judy LaMarsh Fund out of the pile. The fund had issued about $2,000 to each woman candidate in 1993, to be spent on whatever she chose. "I'm going to go cash this cheque," she told her campaign workers, "and find something fabulous to wear." After a trip to the bank, she stopped by the office to pick up Doherty. He noticed a strange parcel on the top of the car; inside it was a wad of bills. Shaughnessy had absent-mindedly left hundreds of dollars lying on the top of her car. Her clothes-buying mission was similarly scattered. Shaughnessy returned with a pantsuit. Norma Coleman drew the line: "You are not wearing pants. Take that back to the store and buy a dress, for heaven's sake."

When the Liberal entourage and accompanying media stepped off the plane, Shaughnessy was standing at the foot of the stairs, resplendent in a red dress, waiting to greet every passenger. As she embraced the national reporters she knew personally, she whispered: "I think I'm going to win! Can you fucking believe it?" With the leader, she was slightly more reserved. "I think I'm going to win," she told Chrétien. He replied: "You're not going to just win. You're going to blow them away!"

Doherty said this reality sank in with Shaughnessy some days later while she was looking over faxes coming into the office. Shaughnessy Cohen headquarters was suddenly inundated with unsolicited resumés from political staffers in Ottawa, some of whom were currently working for Tory backbenchers.

Shaughnessy's prospective victory was widely assumed in Windsor by then, but each time it was discussed, it delighted her anew. On the local Windsor CBC Radio station, her friend Karen Hall was part of a regular media panel. As the campaign was winding down, Hall was asked for her thoughts about Windsor–St. Clair. Before she could catch herself, she said, "Shaughnessy Cohen is probably going to win." Hall took some heat for that utterance: people who knew of her friendship with Shaughn thought she was offering an endorsement, instead of a prediction. Shaughnessy clearly thought so too.

One rainy night, as Hall was getting ready for bed, she saw headlights outside her house and heard scuffling at her front door. She came out just in time to see Shaughnessy and Jerry scrambling back into their car, like children caught knocking on neighbours' doors. Left on her front step were ten jumbo-size boxes of her favourite addiction: Twinkies. As a thank-you for her "prediction," Shaughn and Jerry had sent her a wee reward. Karen could only smile. If the gift had come from someone else, she might have been piqued by the suggestion that her journalistic views could be bought or rewarded. Shaughnessy was just expressing her thanks for making her happy.

Brad Robitaille, who had begged off full-time duty but still wanted some kind of involvement in Shaughn's campaign, was in charge of organization for E-Day – election day. Shaughnessy, reasonably confident, was nonetheless restless all day and filled her time with visits to friends and supporters. She paid a call on Nell Martin, who was too tired to come down the stairs to see her. Since her husband's death in September 1992, Nell had become frail. Shaughnessy had visited her often. She was touched to learn that Nell had used up all her reserves of energy that day to go out and vote for Shaughnessy.

For campaign workers, the election day drill is to identify Liberal voters and get them to the polls. Ron Doherty and Jerry knew that if between 10,000 and 15,000 Liberals went out to vote, Shaughnessy would win. Of course, no campaign organization can mobilize that many voters on its own. They had to hope that the larger issues in this campaign, especially the anti-Tory factor, would provide the necessary motivation. Those hopes were well founded in 1993. As the results started to pour in, the extent of the rout was stunning. Every Conservative but two was defeated. Jean Chrétien and his Liberals had won 177 seats, and Windsor–St. Clair was one of them. Shaughnessy trounced McCurdy with 22,960 votes to his 9,021.

Cathy Roberts, who watched her big sister come into her own that night along with their parents and a clutch of other Murrays, recalled how natural the victory seemed. "We were never surprised by it – that was just Shaughn." But they knew that at least some part of her would be leaving their world. "We were proud, a little bewildered – and a little awestruck," Cathy said.

When the result was official, Shaughnessy was ready with a symbolic gesture of farewell to her old life as a lawyer. She turned to a friend, Doreen Ouellette, the wife of Judge Ken Ouellette, and said: "Can you give this note to Ken for me?"

Written on a scrap of paper was this taunt: "I don't have to watch my language for you anymore."

ー   ー

Within a week of her election victory, Shaughnessy flew to the capital to survey her new stomping grounds as a member of Parliament. She walked the long path from Wellington Street past the eternal flame to the centre door of the Parliament Buildings, under the Peace Tower. As she came into the main foyer, tears welled in her eyes. She slid into the corridor by the Railway Committee Room and tried to compose herself, surprised at her own emotions. "I know, I know," she said to a reporter friend, accompanying her on this first walk through the building as an MP. "I just feel so privileged, so honoured, so lucky to be here." That feeling would last for years.

Her swearing-in was turned into an event for her closest

colleagues. Jerry came with her to Ottawa, as did Brad Robitaille, Brian Ducharme, and Ron Doherty. Richard Mahoney was there too. Sporting her favourite red-and-black-checked jacket, Shaughnessy took her oath of office with uncharacteristic solemnity.

The group didn't have a chance to celebrate the occasion. As soon as the swearing-in was over, they all caught a flight back to Windsor, to attend the funeral of Nell Martin. The feisty matriarch of the Martin clan had lived long enough to see her son sworn into cabinet and to watch Shaughnessy reclaim her husband's old seat for the Liberals.

Shaughnessy remained devoted to Nell's legacy and that of her husband. As she left her swearing-in, she vowed that her first letter as an MP would be a request for the federal building in Windsor to be named after Paul Martin Sr. When Windsor unveiled a rose named in Nell Martin's honour – a gorgeous, deep-red hybrid – Shaughnessy became a one-woman floral promoter. In the summer of 1996, she carried two of the rosebushes from Windsor to Paul Martin Jr.'s farm in the Eastern Townships of Quebec and lovingly planted them at a treasured site in the garden.

Those early days after her election set the tone for her entire political career. They were marked by an overwhelming sense of privilege to be in Ottawa, a strong attachment to the Windsor family and friends who got her there, and a sense of duty and loyalty to her Liberal mentors, none so much as Paul Martin.

These impulses made Shaughnessy an intriguing, sometimes contrary politician, but not one who could be ignored. As he came to appreciate Shaughnessy as a colleague over the next few years, Martin would warn others that his old friend had two basic approaches to her political dealings.

"If you have a problem, she'll solve it for you," he said. "If you don't have a problem, she'll create one for you."

7

Welcome to Ottawa

The honeymoon for newly elected members of Parliament is cruelly brief. When the new Parliament opened with the Speech from the Throne on January 18, 1994, rookies like Shaughnessy were still adjusting to the realities of life in government. One of the first lessons the freshmen absorbed was that very few people on the Hill were at all impressed by their election victories, least of all the MPs who were returning for their second or third terms. Even within their own caucuses, the camaraderie could be superficial and deceptive.

Montreal MP Sheila Finestone described the jolt of the new politician's arrival in Ottawa. "With our constituents, we're used to smiling and glad-handing. But you learn quickly that there's no smiling and glad-handing here. You don't dare," Finestone said. "In your constituency, everyone's a potential supporter. In Ottawa, everyone's a potential competitor."

The reality, said Finestone, is that caucus politics does more to hone politicians' killer instincts than the battles with their counterparts in other parties.

"You keep sizing up your opposition and it's not on the opposition benches . . . It's in your own party." Everyone wants to make a contribution, be a star, be important, but there isn't room, said Finestone. Jobs, titles, and responsibilities are handed out according to gender, language, and regional considerations; political smarts alone are not enough when the "groups" are pitted against one another. For Liberal women, this system can be especially damaging. Although they are supposed to be blazing their way towards equal representation, some of the class of '93 suspected that their aspirations would be hindered by an unspoken limit on the number of women who would be allowed to fill the top positions.

"Fewer women make it up the ladder," said London West MP Susan Barnes, who knew that this system made her – another woman lawyer from southwestern Ontario – a natural competitor to Shaughnessy. "Even though nobody talks of quotas, it's 'If you've got enough, you've got enough.' Nobody ever asks whether we've got enough men doing something."

Whether the fight is for position or policy, it is a fact of parliamentary life that squabbles within party caucuses can be far more vicious than fights with the opposition.

"Everyone has a knife here," said Liberal Derek Lee, MP for Scarborough–Rouge River. "But at least the opposition is two and a half sword lengths away." (Opposition and government benches in the House are indeed carefully distanced to symbolize that the debate takes place beyond the reach of violence or aggression.) By the time Shaughnessy took her seat in Parliament in 1993, the idea of genuine, spontaneous debate in the Commons was almost ludicrous, since virtually every utterance was poll-tested, rehearsed, and massaged for general consumption. Moments of real emotional difference between the parties – the tense exchanges surrounding the Quebec referendum of 1995, for instance – became newsworthy because they were so rare. Most of the serious debate in Parliament would take place behind closed doors, within the caucus. Certainly, for the next few years, that was where individual Liberals would be tested.

The average citizen might believe that politicians are measured by how well they perform in front of the public. But the reality of day-to-day life in Ottawa is that much depends on how well politicians perform in front of each other. This is what the caucus is for: a chance to parade yourself and your causes in front of fellow MPs. Prime Minister Chrétien rarely missed a Wednesday caucus session.

Shaughnessy soon picked up the routine. When Parliament was in session, MPs attended a series of meetings on Tuesday evenings or Wednesday mornings before the national caucus session. These smaller gatherings were organized geographically. Shaughnessy was expected to attend the southwestern Ontario caucus at 8 a.m. and the Ontario caucus at 9 a.m. before she headed to the full caucus on Wednesday at 10 a.m. Once the full caucus convened, the chairs of the four major regions – Ontario, Quebec, the East, and the West (including the North) – delivered five-minute summations of the major concerns from their areas. Then the floor was opened to speeches from individual MPs; these lasted until noon. Immediately after, the Liberal women met for their own caucus session.

Chrétien assessed not just the message but how it was received. "It's difficult to measure. I know those who impress me and those who don't impress me. But that does not mean that somebody who doesn't impress me doesn't impress somebody else. It is a very subjective thing."

He liked Shaughnessy because she could make him laugh. "She was always smiling," he said. "Whenever she got up, she had a great presence and she would always start with something rather funny. She was not what I would call one of those guys who are very serious, and get up and carry the weight of the world. She was not like that. She was not carrying the weight of the world. She would share it with the rest of us, easily."

Shaughnessy had to find her place in the pecking order of the caucus, and she could be irrepressible if she had a point to make. Peter Adams, chair of the Ontario caucus for most of her time in office, remembered that one of his major goals was "getting her to shut up." If her issue hadn't been addressed to her satisfaction, he said, she would keep popping up to ask why the discussion had veered. She loved to mutter and quietly heckle for the benefit of those around her or sometimes to upstage another speaker who was monopolizing the floor.

At one caucus gathering, Kingston MP Peter Milliken was on his feet, dissecting one of the government's proposed moves on the social front. He was discussing what it meant to families and noted, as an aside, that he was single.

Shaughnessy shouted: "Why don't you marry Mary [Clancy], then? She needs a husband!"

Milliken, forgetting that he was at the microphone, announced to the room at large: "I'll marry Mary if I have to," he said, and the room exploded.

After three decades in federal politics, Jean Chrétien had an instinctive understanding of caucus dynamics. He knew that the meeting room would barely contain the 218 egos, both MPs and senators, packed inside it, and he knew that rivalries within the party were often the fiercest.

"Within caucus, like it or not, there is a natural competition for positions – should a person be chair of a committee, become a parliamentary secretary, eventually become a minister... and there's regional competition too," Chrétien said. "Sometimes you have two good MPs next to each other. So they watch each other pretty well."

There was an exception to this rule in Chrétien's brand-new caucus. Two MPs who should have been regional competitors – Shaughnessy Cohen and Roger Gallaway, the MP from Sarnia-Lambton – were friends and allies from the moment they met on Parliament Hill. They'd compete to be the centre of attention, but they didn't begrudge each other promotions or favourable publicity, as neighbouring MPs often do.

Roger is a large bear of a man with a boisterous laugh and a wicked sense of humour. Like Shaughnessy, he grew up in a small, southwestern Ontario town – born, raised, married, and settled in Point Edward, a village on the edge of Sarnia. He always lived within a block of his parents, aunts and uncles, and cousins. His wife, Jane, a kindergarten teacher, also had family close by. Roger and Jane's four children, most of them teenagers by the time their father was elected to Ottawa, were raised in the midst of this huge extended family.

Though deeply irreverent and not at all impressed by political titles, Roger brought to Ottawa strong convictions about the value of community and public service. He was a small-town lawyer who had served on countless local boards and committees, and he was mayor of Point Edward from 1991 to 1993. His riding had been held for two terms by Conservative Ken James; Roger had not really expected to win when he threw his hat in the ring for the Liberals.

Within a week or two of the 1993 election, a reception was held at the West Block to welcome the new Liberal MPs to government. Arriving alone, Roger positioned himself near the bar, a little baffled, a little overwhelmed. He looked around and spotted Shaughnessy, also standing by herself. She was surveying the crowd and suddenly locked her gaze on Roger. They realized, without a word, that they were having the same reaction to this event: What the heck are we doing here?

"We started talking and within 10 minutes we were goofy. Within 20 minutes, it was hysteria. I don't remember what it was about but it wouldn't matter anyway. They were the kind of jokes that don't translate," Roger said. They had so much in common – both from border ridings, both from big families in southwestern Ontario, both large people with self-deprecating humour – that it was inevitable they would become best friends.

More than friends, in fact; Shaughnessy and Roger were a team – sometimes a comedy team, sometimes a trouble-making team, but always plotting, strategizing, and assessing the strange terrain where they found themselves. They paid close attention to the players in the caucus: who was up, who was down, who was a grandstander, who seemed to be struggling. Both were distrustful of inflated egos. "It's not about *you*" was one of Shaughnessy's favourite lines.

Roger wasn't her only ally in those early days. All those hours of telephone conversation with Mary Clancy, all that work for Paul Martin's leadership campaign, all that mentoring by Herb Gray back in Windsor stood her in good stead. It turned out that boarding school experience was another asset. Away from home and family again, she had to make a separate life for herself among the other temporary residents of the capital. Shaughnessy had a theory that there was a high correlation between success for women politicians and their girls'-school education. Carolyn Bennett, elected in 1997 from the Toronto riding of St. Paul's, said girls' schools provided good training in developing the confidence that politicians need. "We grew up chairing meetings," said Bennett, a graduate of Havergal College who became a well-respected doctor. "We knew Robert's Rules of Order."

By 1993 Mary Clancy had been in Ottawa five years and knew her way around: where to shop, where to eat, whom to know and whom to avoid. But Shaughnessy was one of the few people who could tell her things too. If Mary chattered too much at the breakfast table, for instance, Shaughnessy would calmly remove her coffee cup and pour its contents down the drain. "You've had enough. Just listen to yourself," she'd say.

Shaughnessy was coached — and did some coaching herself — on the topic of whom "we like" and whom "we don't like." They adored Finance Minister Paul Martin, respected "the Boss," Jean Chrétien, and had a rotating list of favourite and not so favourite cabinet ministers. People with pets, especially dogs, were judged to be basically good; people who betrayed their friends were swiftly condemned. Embarrassment of the government was a capital offence; Shaughnessy and Mary were merciless towards any caucus member who spoke out publicly against Liberal policy.

It was a routine that could be carried to unflattering extremes. Shaughnessy was capable of using sarcasm, ostracism, even loudly whispered insults against her targets, and once the enemy was identified, she expected her friends to join in the assault. Several of her caucus colleagues were distressed and disappointed by this facet of her personality. It was understood that one had to establish a place in the hierarchy, that rookies especially had to fight for rank in the pack, but there was a cost.

"Shaughnessy had her favourites and her not-favourites," said fellow MP John Godfrey. "The price of cleverness and publication – Radio Shaughnessy – is that it can hurt people. And of course they're not going to be your allies and your friends when you need them."

Susan Barnes was disturbed that Shaughnessy occasionally confused the notions of "like" and "respect." "With Shaughnessy, it wasn't like/don't like. It was respect/don't respect. Quite frankly, in political circles, respecting someone is more important than liking them," she said. Mary Clancy insisted there was never anything personal; nonetheless, there was damage done.

The best advice that Mary gave Shaughn concerned living arrangements. She introduced the new Windsor MP to another new arrival, Anne McLellan, a law professor from the University of Alberta and Mary's old roommate at Dalhousie. McLellan had been appointed minister of natural resources. Short, compact, her dark brown hair controlled by a tidy blunt cut and eyes intense behind gold-rimmed spectacles, Anne struck Shaughnessy as a dead ringer for the "Honey" character in the Doonesbury cartoons. ("I do not look like a cartoon character!" Anne would protest in mock indignation.)

Mary was keen to have her friends join her at Queen Elizabeth Towers on Laurier Street, a 15-minute walk from Parliament Hill. Mary already shared an apartment there with a Montreal-area MP, Shirley Maheu. The apartments were comfortable and well maintained, and the rent was manageable. Mary and Shirley were hoping to find a four-bedroom unit that would accommodate all four women. Instead, they opted to move out of their place (they were sick of the carpet and the state of the air conditioner) and take an apartment a few stories higher.

Anne and Shaughn moved into Mary and Shirley's former apartment almost immediately. They furnished their digs with chairs, couches, tables, and desks from Shaughn's old law office – pieces purchased from the Bombay Company. Her boardroom table became the dining table, her teal waiting room sofa and chairs graced the living area, and the gaps were filled with prints and knick-knacks brought from home every week. Anne favoured artsy pictures for the walls; Shaughnessy slapped up such odd items as a commemorative poster from the Kingston Prison for Women and a poster from a Detroit car show. The apartment was tidy but not immaculate. Neither Shaughn nor Anne was a meticulous house-keeper. Each had her own bathroom, though Shaughn would often stand at the door of Anne's bathroom as the minister applied her morning makeup, gossiping about events from the night before. Anne's oversized black minister's briefcase was always stationed in the front foyer. Shaughn's papers were more likely to be scattered around her bedroom and the dining table. The phone rang con-stantly. If a call came through the prime minister's switchboard, meaning that Chrétien or one of her fellow ministers was on the line, Anne would take the phone with its extra-long cord into her bedroom and close the door.

Their rent was about $500 each, which entirely consumed the $6,000 annual allowance they received to cover their housing in Ottawa. Additional payments for hydro, telephone, cable, or fur-nishings came out of their MPs' salaries. In 1993 Shaughn, as a new MP, received a salary of about $65,000 a year, plus a tax-free allowance of $20,000. Anne, as a cabinet minister, earned roughly $45,000 more in salary than Shaughnessy.

Though apparently very different people from a distance – Anne, seemingly so serious and quiet; Shaughnessy, funny and loud – they actually had much in common. Both were lawyers with aca-demic partners. Anne's partner, John Law, was, appropriately enough, a professor of law at the University of Alberta. Jerry was at the University of Windsor. Both men had daughters from previous marriages who lived with them – John had Jessie, Jerry had Dena. Anne and Shaughnessy were childless themselves; they doted on their dogs and the pets of all their friends. (Shaughnessy and Dena had managed, shortly before the election, to persuade Jerry to allow Brandy, an abandoned, docile Brittany spaniel of undetermined age, to come to live at the Amherstburg home. Brandy's arrival was followed by the purchase of Maggie, a high-strung Irish water spaniel. Shaughnessy couldn't wait to get home every week and fling herself at the dogs.) Shaughn and Anne were definitely "dog people." Whenever they entered the home of a dog owner, they would instinctively drop into a crouch on the floor, as canine experts advise, to show that they were friendly and no threat. They encouraged their Ottawa friends with dogs to bring them to the apartment and happily served as dog-sitters for a miniature dachshund named Nell when her owner was out of town.

The apartment was a warm and friendly refuge, where tea was always brewing and the television always on – tuned to Newsworld, the Cable Public Affairs Channel, or one of the ridiculous comedy shows, such as *The Nanny* or *Cybill*, that the women loved to watch. News broadcasts were interactive exercises: the two would cheer their friends when they appeared in stories from Ottawa ("Quiet, quiet – watch what Paul says now," they'd whisper); hoot and critique if they themselves ended up on camera ("Maybe I was a little bit strident there?" Anne would ask Shaughnessy, who would raise her eyebrows, a laugh behind her eyes, and reply, "Maybe just a bit"); and boo and hiss if someone said something stupid ("Oh shut up!" they'd yell if a Reform MP came up on the screen).

For all the competition within parties, McLellan said, the women who did form friendships in Ottawa did so with an intensity that men generally couldn't match. "Even though one might expect competition, really there isn't. There isn't that kind of competition you find with guys that I think sometimes gets in the way of a close friendship – a real, close friendship," she said. "With women, that is possible. With people like Shaughnessy, Mary, myself, Jane Stewart, Paddy Torsney, and people like that, that was not only possible but very real."

Anne was Shaughnessy's compatible roommate, but Mary was her inseparable soulmate. They shopped together; they went to lunch together; they went to caucus together. They were loud, raucous, hilarious, and irreverent together. It was the Mary-and-Shaughnessy show, and it was not for the faint of heart.

Their banter was not unlike a comedy routine, and they would inflict it on everyone from store clerks to ambassadors. They required only an audience, preferably stuffy people, perfect strangers, or serious journalists. On one occasion, CBC reporter Jason Moscovitz approached Mary and Shaughn in the Commons foyer to solicit their comments on some newsworthy development. Moscovitz, a quietly competent, intense veteran of the Hill media, is also a small man. He stood before them, microphone poised for their remarks. Suddenly Shaughnessy bellowed: "Jason in the land of large women!" Moscovitz could only blush.

The two also took this show on the road, beyond Parliament Hill. Mary's fondness for expensive clothes earned her Roger's nickname, "the member from Halifax–Holt Renfrew." At Holt's, clerks in the hat department came to recognize Shaughn and Mary. After a bad day, they would come in to try on hats, or rather to see how ridiculous Shaughn looked in every one she put on. She had neither the head nor the carriage for a hat, and the sight of anything on her head would send the two into whoops of laughter.

These high spirits were a tonic at boring meetings or stiff affairs. Ottawa is filled with people who take themselves too seriously, and Mary and Shaughn were expert at cutting the pompous down to size. But the two women were also in danger of not being taken seriously at all. Mary had already established a respected position within the party as the women's issues critic for the Liberals from 1988 to 1993 and had comported herself grandly in 1990 as a co-moderator of the leadership debates. But Shaughnessy had yet to make her mark; in fact, she had suffered a stinging attack at the very outset of her parliamentary career.

A little more than two weeks after the new Parliament opened in January 1994, Shaughnessy was pilloried in the satirical magazine *Frank*. In its February 3 edition, under the headline "Just Off the Turnip Truck," *Frank* gleefully described Shaughnessy as "supremely unappealing," "leather-lunged," and a "handsome endomorph." Its two-column profile was a rehash of previously reported innuendo from the mainstream press, including the stories about her debts. Shaughnessy wasn't sure whether this material was supplied by Tories or New Democrats back in Windsor or by people within her own party – the Liberals who came to despise her during the nasty nomination battles of the mid-1980s. Clearly someone was carrying a grudge and working hard to undermine the credibility of the new MP for Windsor–St. Clair.

Despite its claim of being an "alternative" voice in national political coverage, *Frank* is in fact highly effective at reinforcing old prejudices and propping up the conservative boys' club of Parliament Hill. The only difference between *Frank* and more establishment defenders of this culture is that *Frank* uses ridicule, exaggeration, and sometimes falsehoods to enforce the very traditional standards that rule Ottawa.

On the issue of Shaughnessy's financial woes, for instance, *Frank* reflected the mood of judgment that prevailed in the early 1990s, when debt became a moral issue. To be in debt was to be corrupt; to be bankrupt financially was to be bankrupt in character too. Reform Party leader Preston Manning, with his preacherly lectures on the country's finances, encouraged this tendency to fuse financial deficits with personal deficiencies.

Canadians were being told that their souls were already lost, that the only hope was the elimination of the debt for the sake of their innocent children. Canada was over $600 billion in debt and the annual deficit hovered around $40 billion. The Canadian Taxpayers' Federation set up a doomsday "debt clock," ticking away the billions until bankruptcy – or the Revelation, whichever came first. In this atmosphere, it wasn't surprising that Shaughnessy's indebtedness became a morality play and a measure of her character.

Lost in the reporting of Shaughnessy's financial affairs, though, was the fact that many newly elected MPs are deeply in debt – not because they've squandered money recklessly, but because of the severe financial demands of the political life. Industry Minister

John Manley, immediately after his nomination for the 1988 election, had to borrow money just to get along until the vote.

"We wanted to start preparation for the election campaign and there was absolutely no money. I went to the Toronto-Dominion Bank and signed a promissory note for $10,000. It wasn't until well after the election that it was paid off. If we had lost, I probably would have ended up paying it myself... It's not uncommon for people to go into debt, especially when the party hasn't been in power."

Lawyers who had to wind down their law practices when elected – people such as Shaughnessy, Manley, or Allan Rock – could find themselves saddled with the lingering financial obligations of their previous lives but none of the revenues. Manley and Rock, for instance, were faced with paying two years of taxes when they gave up law to go into politics, and both had to borrow thousands of dollars just to quit their jobs.

It has been estimated that the low-end cost of getting elected is about $120,000, from nomination to election, taking into account lost income, the expense of campaign material and equipment, and the myriad expenditures involved in becoming known in the community. Shaughnessy had faced all these costs twice in five years, but her annual income was never more than $50,000 in the years preceding her election. Jerry's salary was adequate, but not enough to assume the expenses associated with the campaigns. Their resources had been squeezed even more by their purchase of the house in Windsor–St. Clair. The rental income from this two-storey home barely covered the mortgage payments and maintenance. Nor had Shaughn managed to do any significant fundraising for herself, even though she had recognized its importance in the leadership campaign.

Privately, Shaughn was chagrined by the way she was being portrayed in the press. Embarrassed by her own financial sloppiness, fighting a losing battle with weight gain, she was stung by personal attacks, satirical or otherwise. Norma Coleman, who had helped Shaughnessy understand and cultivate the media, said her friend could be hurt by bad coverage. Often she walked into dangerous situations all by herself; she had an ill-defined sense of the boundaries, and sometimes didn't realize that the journalists she thought were her friends could be scathing when it suited their purposes. Her beloved *Windsor Star*, home to her friends Karen Hall and Norma's husband, John, the editorial-page editor, made sure that Shaughn's constituents knew about the *Frank* story. In this report, though, Shaughn had a chance to defend herself.

"You get it over with," she told the paper gamely. "I got Franked and it's done."

It probably helped that she was from a small town, where gossip and innuendo keep conversation going. Her family loved to tell the story of Shaughnessy, then married, a lawyer, and living in Windsor, walking into the Thamesville Red & White grocery store with her sister Cathy. She noticed two women whispering and glancing furtively in the direction of the oldest Murray girls.

Shaughn sauntered over to the gossiping matrons. "Okay, let's get it straight," she said, pointing to her sister. "She's the one who's divorced. I'm the one who married a Jew."

Say it first. Declare it openly. Take away the nefarious power of a whisper campaign. These were Shaughnessy's survival tactics in the small-minded towns of Thamesville, Windsor, and Ottawa. One night Mary was sitting with Shaughnessy, reviewing yet another barbed offering from *Frank* magazine, an article whose entire purpose was to draw attention to the physical proportions of the Clancy-Cohen team. Normally, Mary recalled, she would have been devastated by such a report. She was extremely sensitive to remarks about her size. Shaughnessy, though, ridiculed *Frank*'s investigative skills. "We're fat! Who knew?" she said. "I wonder who told them!"

This was one of Shaughn's great gifts to Mary. Shaughnessy hated shame in all forms. Why should Mary be ashamed of herself? Why should anyone be ashamed of what they are? Gradually, she got Mary to laugh at herself and her vulnerabilities.

In a CBC *Rough Cuts* documentary on women in politics,

broadcast in May 1997, Shaughnessy talked about how female politicians have to accept that they will be judged by their physical appearance.

"Yes, I have had comments about my size," Shaughnessy told interviewer Jane Taber. "I am a big woman. It is not a secret that I can keep very well from the world . . . And certainly people have no compunction about what they say to you about that once you are in public life. You know, I get people who will call me and talk to me about my foundation garments . . . They have a sense of propriety about you, so they think it is okay to tell you your slip is showing, or to hike up your bra, or [that] your roots are showing."

She also explained that women have to modulate their voices to be taken seriously – a fact that she was constantly impressing on Anne McLellan, whose high-pitched tones also earned her rebukes in the media. Shaughnessy had acquired her own communication skills by working in the courtroom. For a woman who was often seen as loud and troublesome, in fact, Shaughnessy had a keen eye for the subtleties of communication, especially between men and women. She spoke too of how her legal training had prepared her for the world of Parliament Hill.

"I was a criminal lawyer. I think for almost 10 years I was the only woman practising in the criminal courts in Windsor, so I had a tough baptism with the boys," she said. "There was a technique the men would use to intimidate, and that is they would step into your space. So rather than standing at a normal distance from you, some of them, the old-timers especially, would move into my space so that basically my chest is up against your chest. [With] my chest you don't have to be very close for that to happen to me! . . . And I learned a long time ago how to deal with it – and I learned also, subconsciously, that was a bullying tactic."

Shaughnessy was always watching for subtle body language, said Sheila Finestone, not just to protect herself but to understand others. Even while she spoke, her blue eyes would roam the room, taking everything in, looking for the unsaid and the unarticulated. "She'd have her eyes open for the person who was sitting alone, who was off to the side, who seemed troubled."

That trouble, among her fellow caucus members in that first term in Ottawa, was often family trouble. Personal problems are part of the package for an elected politician. Individuals who become MPs have essentially two choices on how to maintain their family lives: at long distance, as commuters to Ottawa, or by moving their families to the capital.

For cabinet ministers, the choice is usually the latter. So much more time is required of ministers, even on weekends, that it makes little sense to try to maintain a life away from Ottawa. Of the three dozen ministers and secretaries of state in Jean Chrétien's cabinet through the first term, almost two-thirds established their principal residences in Ottawa. Of course, the ability to do this rests on the willingness of ministers' families to pick up their lives, break away from careers and community, and relocate to the capital for an indeterminate period.

Despite the fact that this is a world in which working women are a commonplace, it appears to be easier for women spouses to make that move than it is for male spouses. Lloyd Axworthy, Allan Rock, and Herb Gray were married to strong, independent women who nonetheless decided to make their homes in Ottawa and adapt their work to the demands of their husbands' careers. But Anne McLellan and Jane Stewart had husbands who opted to keep their careers in their home cities.

When women do leave their families behind in the ridings, the desire to maintain the family connection is intense. Female cabinet members may have some choice about whether to move their families to the capital, but backbenchers have no choice at all. MPs who aren't in the cabinet are expected to be back in their ridings every weekend, every summer, and during breaks. So for most women in Ottawa, whether they're in the cabinet or on the backbench, political life means an endless round of travel and rushed phone calls to family members to somehow stay connected. Shaughnessy often ducked into the lobby of the Commons to call Jerry at his office, just to ask how his day was going. "And how are my dogs?" she'd ask. Jerry would politely point out that "her" dogs were under his care about 80 percent of the time.

The glue of Shaughnessy's life was loyalty. The bonds were strongest with Jerry and her family, but she had long-lasting ties to the friends she'd developed throughout her career. Taken too far, loyalty can be a sentimental burden or, worse, a blindfold. But as a tool in politics, loyalty can be powerfully effective. And loyalty came naturally to Shaughnessy.

Christopher Matthews, a former aide to Tip O'Neill when he was the U.S. Speaker of the House, wrote in his 1989 book, *Hardball: How Politics is Played by One Who Knows the Game,* that "loyalty is not simply a virtue but a building block of political strength." Politics is about cultivating and maintaining networks, he said, and "loyalty is the linchpin of this network of support."

In an interview with Ian Timberlake of the *Windsor Star,* published November 20, 1993, Shaughnessy and her friends discussed her preoccupation with loyalty. "Ask Cohen about her value system and she talks at length about her belief in loyalty to friends, a loyalty she says extends to her constituents and to her party," Timberlake wrote. He quoted one of Shaughnessy's challengers for the 1993 Liberal nomination, George Dietrich, who suggested that Shaughn's money troubles could be seen as loyalty taken to a fault. "Dietrich said she has helped financially with the campaigns of friends elsewhere in Ontario. 'Now that's a very expensive hobby.'"

Brian Ducharme echoed that observation. "I think maybe one of her weak points is she tries sometimes to do too much for people. She's got a soft spot for new Canadians who are trying to get into the country... I know she has a heart of gold when it comes to her friends... I feel sometimes she overcommits herself, wants to help everyone and loses focus... She's an extremely well-meaning person and a very loyal person."

After her election in 1993, Shaughnessy had to consider where her loyalties lay in the political realm. Unlike other Liberals elected in Windsor in decades past – Herb Gray, Mark MacGuigan, Eugene Whelan, Paul Martin Sr. – Shaughn chose not to establish her own faction in the region. She would not be another Windsor warlord, competing for turf with other Liberals in this crowded partisan community. She would lash her political future to the steady mast of Herb Gray and commit her loyalty and energy to him. They had known each other for years, though he was the one who had sought an introduction at the start.

"It was at a dinner meeting of the Essex Law Association in Windsor," Gray recalled. "Frankly, I came ... because I'd received an invitation to it signed by someone I hadn't met before, the new secretary of the association, one 'Shaughnessy Cohen.' I said to myself: 'I have to attend this dinner. I have to meet this new arrival. How interesting ... a lawyer who's a Jewish man from Ireland!'"

Gray valued Shaughnessy's friendship. The relationship he enjoyed with his neighbouring Liberal in Windsor was far different, far closer than the one he had experienced with Paul Martin Sr. "He was a more remote figure to me," Gray said. "Shaughnessy and I were more relaxed with each other, more likely to cooperate." The two even held joint meetings of their riding associations and joint holiday events in Windsor. Gray was very much Shaughnessy's mentor, even her disciplinarian when the situation called for it. He warned her about appearing too often in the various "notebook" or gossip columns on Parliament Hill, which frequently reported some of her riskier or funnier antics. "There are risks in using humour too much," Gray said. "There's a risk you won't be taken seriously."

Shaughnessy believed that what was good for Herb Gray would be good for Shaughnessy Cohen. She became a trusted confidante of all his assistants, especially Jerry Yanover, his long-time adviser, and Garry Fortune, his special assistant. Fortune's brother, Brian, had been Shaughnessy's campaign chairman in 1988, and Brad Robitaille, Ron Doherty, and Brian Ducharme were his close friends too. On any given day, the Windsor MP and the tall, bespectacled Fortune could be seen plotting or laughing together in the Commons foyer or at the National Press Club. When they were in Windsor, Fortune would often accompany Shaughnessy on her rounds through town, winding their way from meeting to meeting. On one over-scheduled day, the two ate no fewer than six meals as they attended two breakfast gatherings, two lunch engagements, and two dinner meetings. This, unfortunately, was all too typical of an MP's life in the constituency. Such itineraries help explain the weight gain that accompanies elected office. Food is served at every event; to refuse is impolite and sometimes unwise – schedules are so hectic that it's difficult to predict when the next opportunity to eat will arise. Opportunities for exercise, meanwhile, are remote.

Shaughnessy's relationship with Fortune was affectionate and strategic. She knew that if she allowed one of Gray's chief advisers to keep a close eye on her, she could in turn keep a close eye on the boss. She needed to be wise to the ways of Windsor's most powerful minister.

Shaughnessy was a woman in politics, and such women are accustomed to stepping out of the limelight. Whether it was the influence of her large family, the boarding school years, or the sheer force of socialization, Shaughnessy knew how to be a team player. For women, though, being part of a team is a very different experience than it is for men. It's more about being a good sport, accepting the second-string position with grace, and understanding that physical appearance and deportment will be judged as harshly as performance.

Shaughnessy boasted that she was a good team player and insisted that she was content to be a good sport. Wherever Shaughnessy's political career was about to take her, she decided that the mantra of team loyalty would serve her best. And if her profile had to be downplayed, at least in the short term, she could only hope that politics had long-term rewards. Those wouldn't come soon, as her first, unsettling year in Parliament would prove.

8

Social Insecurity

In 1994, the Liberals confronted an uncomfortable conundrum: how to remain Liberals while reducing the deficit. The prime minister opted for a characteristic balancing act. The Liberals would lean a little to the right in economic policy, a little to the left in social policy, and if all went well, the government would end up in the careful middle. He put Paul Martin in charge of the fiscal house in Finance and made Lloyd Axworthy responsible for social programs in Human Resources Development. But instead of a balancing act, the country got a tug-of-war. Shaughnessy would find herself in the middle of this drama, drawn to one side by her loyalty to Martin and then to the other by her growing fondness for Axworthy.

The connection to Axworthy began with Shaughnessy's first committee assignment. When the MPs arrived in Ottawa, they were asked to fill out a form listing their top three preferences for committee duty. Shaughnessy's first choice was the Justice Committee, a natural place to use her talents. She also liked the idea of a spot on the Finance Committee, where she could remain close to Martin's agenda.

The task of appointing MPs to committees and as parliamentary secretaries is complicated, a juggling of personalities and political imperatives. The job officially falls to the party whip – in the Chrétien government's first term, the former Rat Pack member Don Boudria – but the decisions rest heavily on input from ministers.

When the committee assignments were released at the beginning of February 1994, Shaughnessy found herself among the six Liberals named to the Human Resources Development Committee. She wasn't particularly keen, but it wasn't an inconsequential position. The committee would soon become the repository of the lofty hopes and fond ambitions of the Liberal left.

On the last day of January, Lloyd Axworthy had outlined to the House his intention to undertake a sweeping overhaul of Canada's social security system. The prelude to this overhaul had several steps: first, the Human Resources Committee would be directed to "consult broadly, to analyze, and to make recommendations regarding the modernization and restructuring" of the system. Its process of consultation would be as comprehensive as possible and would demand weeks of hearings in every part of the country. Second, the government would then put forward an "action plan" of proposals – "options and choices" – for reform; and third, the committee would conduct another round of hearings to solicit reactions to the action plan, all of which would lead eventually to legislation. Axworthy spoke of the urgency of the task, its complexity, and its ambition, declaring that the responsibility to put forward a new blueprint for the social safety net was "the reason we are all here." He ended by declaring such reform an opportunity to define "who we are and where we want to go" and he invited the members that day to reach for the stars.

The Liberal backbenchers on the Human Resources Committee were allowed to think of their mission as a consolation prize for being left out of the cabinet. While ministers were cutting and compromising in the name of deficit reduction, the MPs of the committee would uphold and help maintain Canada's social safety net. Lofty notions indeed.

Toronto was well represented in the group, as expected. It was the only major city in Canada to have elected a full slate of Liberals, and its more than two dozen MPs from the greater Toronto area formed the backbone of the party's majority in Parliament. Two prominent social activists from the city, Maria Minna and Jean Augustine, joined Shaughnessy on the committee. So did Maurizio Bevilacqua, an up-and-coming young Liberal who had supported Paul Martin in the 1990 leadership race. Bevilacqua earned his spot by virtue of his position as parliamentary secretary to Axworthy. (All parliamentary secretaries sit on the Commons committees associated with their portfolios.) Like Shaughnessy, Bevilacqua would find himself right in the middle of the tension between Martin and Axworthy that came to be seen as the central conflict of the Liberals' first mandate.

Whatever her initial disappointment, Shaughnessy was eager to portray her position on the Human Resources Committee as a feather in Windsor's cap. In the *Windsor Star*, she was quoted as saying: "This committee will have a key role in the restructuring of Canada's social programs and in putting Canadians back to work... It is important and significant that our region has a voice on this committee."

On the day of the committee's first meeting, she walked into the room and plopped herself down beside Winnipeg South MP Reg Alcock. "What the fuck am I doing here?" she said, joking with Alcock that she had no idea why anyone thought she could make a worthwhile contribution to such a critical project as this. Her self-deprecating manner instantly appealed to Alcock. He silently breathed thanks that he had a good-natured colleague with whom to share the weeks of committee hearings.

Alcock was similarly perplexed to find himself in that room. Asked to name his choices for committee assignments, he had listed Industry, Finance, and International Trade. In block letters along the bottom of his form, he had printed, "I DO NOT WANT TO BE ON THE HUMAN RESOURCES COMMITTEE." Years of working in family services in Manitoba, as well as more recent experience as a

Liberal member of the Manitoba legislature, had left him eager to expand his horizons. His last position had been as opposition critic for finance in Manitoba, and he had hoped for a chance to build on that knowledge in Ottawa.

But Alcock, a long-time associate and supporter of Lloyd Axworthy, understood that he was expected to serve as an ally for the minister. Alcock allowed himself to be persuaded that the Human Resources Committee would be at the centre of a new Liberalism that was about to emerge. If these MPs could find a way, after listening to Canadians, to rethink and reshape the role of social programs, they would do the nation a great service.

Almost immediately, the committee sprang into action, squeezing its big mandate into a tiny twin-prop plane that ferried the MPs to a series of hearings across the country. At the same time, Axworthy appointed a special task force, made up of key thinkers on social policy such as the former anti-poverty activist Patrick Johnston, to guide and advise him.

The Commons committee, charged more directly with gathering the views of the citizenry, instantly became a lightning rod for discontent. The unemployed, the poverty activists, the union folks – all saw the "doing more with less" discussion as a barely disguised threat to social programs.

"It became a focus for people's fears about what was happening in that basket of services," Alcock said. "We who saw ourselves as advocates for the system all of a sudden became the objects of scorn and derision from the very people that we'd been working with." At stops in Montreal and Vancouver, where union-led protests were most fierce, Alcock and Shaughnessy laughed nervously about how in another time, they would have been out there picketing too. Axworthy, an old hand who had served in Trudeau's cabinet as well as Chrétien's, was dismayed by labour's portrayal of him as Mr. Mean on the social front.

Apart from the ideological discomfort these Liberals felt, there was also the matter of creature comforts. This committee, sent aloft on a gruelling round of hearings, introduced rookies such as

Shaughnessy to the rigours of an MP's life on the road. The small aircraft chosen for the odyssey frightened her, and she would do almost anything to avoid having to fly in it. On several occasions she joined the committee a day late, pleading schedule conflicts, just so she could take a commercial flight to the hearings. In Whitehorse, agitated at the prospect of getting into that plane once again, she contacted Transport Canada and organized an aircraft inspection, vainly hoping that she could have the plane permanently grounded.

If Shaughn had put as much effort into the committee as she had into complaining about travel and working conditions, her fellow MPs might have been more sympathetic. But even the Commons clerks noticed that Shaughnessy seemed bored at the hearings. She carried on conversations with others during presentations, and her attendance record wasn't perfect. Her interest seemed to perk up only when she saw the opportunity to score points with cabinet ministers, especially Lloyd Axworthy.

However, her political radar was telling her that neither Lloyd nor the left was in fashion at that moment. If she wasn't picking up that message through the media or the experience of the committee, she would have been hearing it from her old friends in the Paul Martin leadership camp.

Even Patrick Johnston had reservations. Johnston was one of the better-regarded Liberals on the left of the party. Once the head of the National Anti-Poverty Organization, he had been an unsuccessful candidate for a Liberal nomination in 1988 (he was defeated by an anti-abortion campaign in Scarborough West by Tom Wappel) before moving to the helm of the Canadian Council on Social Development. Johnston's ideology was all about community and social responsibility. But he approached his job on Axworthy's task force with few illusions.

"There was an inherent contradiction from the get-go in the government trying to overhaul the whole social security system while at the same time trying to reduce the deficit by massive reduction in public spending. You can't get there from here," Johnston said. "I came to see my own role during the exercise as essentially trying to limit and minimize the damage. Not a particularly noble calling, but about the only contribution I thought I could realistically make at the time in the face of the Finance juggernaut."

David Walker, the Manitoba MP who was parliamentary secretary to Paul Martin at the time, also came to the conclusion that Axworthy's mission was very likely impossible. Walker was a former political science professor from the University of Manitoba who had worked as research director for the Angus Reid polling firm. He had a keen interest in the future of social programs, informed by the knowledge he'd gained through polling and the study of demographics.

The social policy exercise was squeezed on two sides, Walker said: on one side by the demands to address the deficit, and on the other by the forces pushing for decentralization of the federal government. Those two sentiments found clamorous expression on the other side of the House, in the voices of the Reform Party and the Bloc Québécois opposition. And there were plenty of new Liberals, elected in rural or suburban areas, who felt similar unease about additional federal spending exercises.

But what had happened to the so-called social Liberals? A lot of them ended up in cabinet – Sheila Copps, David Dingwall, Brian Tobin, Sergio Marchi, Allan Rock, not to mention Axworthy himself. While technically they had more power than other MPs, they were obliged to plead their convictions in private. Canadians didn't hear their impassioned arguments against program cuts. If, in the end, controversial, budget-slashing decisions were announced, these left-wing Liberals would be expected to slap broad smiles on their faces and go out and help sell a policy of belt-tightening.

Shaughnessy understood this reality and perhaps saw it coming. She relied on her instinctive loyalty to the larger team and to Liberal policy, whatever shape that policy might ultimately take, to guide her through the shoals of cabinet rivalries. Martin claimed her allegiance for reasons of regional and historic connection; Axworthy did so by virtue of this committee assignment and because she had always regarded herself, like him, as a left-of-centre Liberal. She would not choose between them, but instead worked to keep her ties to both strong and personal. These were the associations that mattered to her above all. It was a pragmatism that was not without its critics.

Bob Nault, a five-year veteran of the Commons by this point, said Shaughnessy's strategy was typical of MPs who come from previously non-Liberal ridings. These are people who treat their stint in Parliament as "borrowed time," said Nault, and derive their authority from who they know, not the positions they take. "They tend to play the game differently," he said. Though they may be confrontational with colleagues, they are not so eager to fall on the wrong side of cabinet ministers. "They don't want to take people on, because they want to be liked." Shaughnessy was that kind of MP, he said.

But the force of her personality could not be ignored either. It was one thing to cozy up to cabinet ministers; it was another to have the sentiment returned. Certainly, that was how it worked with Axworthy. People who saw him as cold or distant could not believe their eyes when they saw the warmth that Shaughnessy could elicit. An episode in point was a trip to Copenhagen in February 1994, when Axworthy took Shaughnessy and a few other loyalists with him to attend an international summit on social policy reform. Ethel Blondin and Patrick Johnston were in the party and returned with indelible memories of Shaughn's ability to loosen up Axworthy.

"As the head of the delegation, he was under a fair bit of pressure and came in for heavy criticism from some of the non-governmental organizations," Johnston said. Moreover, the airline had lost his luggage and Axworthy, under siege from people he once believed were his allies in social policy discussions, was forced to weather this criticism in a borrowed, and ill-fitting, suit. After a few days, Axworthy proposed that members of his group go out for a quiet dinner. It was anything but quiet, largely because of Shaughnessy.

"It was the first time I had seen him so relaxed and at ease since we had arrived in Copenhagen," Johnston said. "In fact, it was the first time I had seen him that relaxed in a long time. I attributed it to Shaughnessy's effect on him. Lloyd obviously loved her sense of humour and, perhaps more important, he seemed to trust her. At the end of the day, I don't think Lloyd trusted too many people."

Though Shaughnessy's personality was one ingredient in this chemistry, everyone knew she had sealed her relationship with Axworthy with a tactical decision closer to home. Some might have called it nepotism; Shaughnessy considered it a smart political career move.

Shaughnessy's budget allowed for two staff members in her Parliament Hill office. She wanted two young people, good at their jobs, possessed of a sense of humour, with Liberal connections. Almost immediately after her election, she found one in Sandra Leffler, member of a family that had strong roots in Windsor and in the party. Her mother, Myra, was a prominent volunteer for the party; her sister Johanna had been the campaign manager for Richard Mahoney in his successful effort to become the Liberal Party of Ontario president in 1993. Mahoney and Brad Robitaille gently nudged Sandra in Shaughnessy's direction, believing – correctly – that her organizational skills would prove crucial to Shaughnessy. With one staff member installed, Shaughnessy embarked on a headhunt, asking around the Hill for names of people who might be interested in working for her. Sharon Sholzberg Gray, Herb's wife, told her about a young man in need of a job. His name was John Ommaney and his mother, Denise, was married to none other than Lloyd Axworthy.

Shortly after, Shaughnessy bustled into her office and reported to Leffler about the high-level prospect who would be in for an interview. "We've got Lloyd Axworthy's stepson coming in today," she said with a twinkle. When Ommaney showed up, his dark good looks and disarming smile worked instant magic on Shaughnessy.

"Oh, I'm going to hire him. He's cute as a bug's ear," Shaughnessy told Leffler as soon as he left the office. By the end of the day, she had already told all her female friends that they must come by to see the "boy toy" she had hired.

"Yes, I was sexually harassed," Ommaney deadpanned later, when recalling his early days with the MP. Shaughnessy would later become his unflagging champion for bigger and better jobs within the Liberal establishment. In the meantime she could count four cabinet ministers in her immediate orbit: she lived with the natural resources minister; she had hired the son of the human resources minister; she and the finance minister, thanks to the 1990 leadership race, were on the best of terms; and she enjoyed a strategic alliance with Herb Gray, the solicitor general. So what if she wasn't in the cabinet? She had the ministers' attention.

"That was the thing with Shaughnessy," said Roger Gallaway. "She regarded herself as an equal to cabinet ministers – without the car and the staff, of course."

That didn't mean that Shaughnessy was without ambition, uninterested in a title or a position. Resigning herself to a relatively low profile in parliamentary business, she decided to go after a leadership role within the caucus. At the last minute, at the end of February 1994, Shaughnessy put her name forward for head of the Liberal women's caucus.

Paddy Torsney, the only other candidate who had announced a desire for the job, was a little puzzled by Shaughn's entry into the race. "Hey, wait a minute," she thought. "Isn't this the same woman who urged me to run a while ago?" Indeed it was, but Shaughn had changed her mind. She had to have some title to brag about to the folks back home.

The vote was held in the women's caucus, which met right after the main caucus session of Liberal MPs and senators. Most of the 40 members (four senators and 36 MPs) were in attendance and the contest was friendly. These women, after all, were expected to work in one-for-all, all-for-one fashion around the men's club of Parliament Hill. Most came to Ottawa with an interest in social policy and a fundamental commitment to the notion of women's equality. Women such as Georgette Sheridan, Susan Barnes, and

Mary Clancy had been among the few women law graduates in their classes in the 1970s. Others such as Maria Minna, Bonnie Brown, and Sheila Finestone had come to politics from their roles as community activists or social workers. Petty rivalries may have divided them but their symbolic significance united them. They were proud to look around the room and count their numbers. Laughter and good-natured teasing punctuated the voting in their large West Block meeting room.

When the secret ballots were counted, Torsney and Shaughn had received exactly the same number of votes. So they settled it the old-fashioned way – with a coin toss. Torsney called heads, Shaughn called tails, and the coin was flipped. It spiralled up into the air then down onto the floor, where it rolled behind a desk. "Oh . . . ," Torsney said. "Is anything about this going to be straight-forward?"

The coin had landed heads up. In this oh-so-formal way, Paddy Torsney became the leader of the Liberal women's caucus. Shaughnessy was philosophical; more important than the job was the demonstration of her ambition.

In Ottawa, ambition runs as freely as tap water. To be tagged as lacking in ambition is the same as being called lazy or stupid. Every MP has it in one form or another. Some dwell on grand policy ambitions, dreaming of making the world a better place with daring ideas or far-reaching vision. Others are focused purely on power for its own sake. Every caucus has a healthy quotient of both types. Most MPs, though, including Shaughnessy, come to Ottawa with some modest expectation of effecting change in a few specific areas and, at the back of their minds, of possibly being famous and powerful too.

If Shaughnessy was to have any influence, she concluded, she would exercise it from the intersection of the personal and political. She had long ago learned that her connections to people could help her make a difference. Principle and policy had their place, but her instincts were trained to react to injustices viscerally and emotionally.

On the very first day of the Commons sitting, for instance, Shaughnessy was aroused by a practice that offended her sense of religious tolerance. The traditional prayer that initiated the day's business shocked her. Straight from the pages of the old Church of England prayer book, its wording referred to the royal family and "our Father."

Shaughnessy looked around her and saw Herb Gray and Barry Campbell, both Jews, Gurbax Malhi, a Sikh, and Elijah Harper, the Manitoba aboriginal MP. The Commons prayer spoke not at all to the spirituality of these politicians. So she began pestering Peter Milliken, then chairman of the Procedure and House Affairs Committee, to have the prayer changed. She wasn't alone. With 200 new members in the Commons in this 35th Parliament, there was far less patience with the usual excuse: "That's how it's always been done."

It took less than a month to remove this anachronistic relic from the chamber. Milliken deliberately waited until a Friday to put a new prayer before the Commons, calculating that fewer people would be around to protest. He was correct. With little fanfare, the reworded devotion was unveiled on February 18, 1994. The blunt Christianity of the old prayer was replaced by a more neutral "blessing" and an opportunity for private prayer.

In another way Shaughnessy managed to land a victory for women's rights in the House, albeit in comical fashion. Early in the new session, Shaughnessy was in the Commons with her colleagues, getting ready to cast a vote. Though only a skeleton crew of MPs are present in the House for most of the debates and routine proceedings, there are three times when MPs are expected to be in their seats: during the daily Question Period, during addresses by foreign dignitaries, and, most important, during votes. The public may regard Commons votes as mostly ceremonial, largely pointless exercises, but they are deadly serious business on Parliament Hill. Votes are the great equalizers between ministers and backbenchers and between government and opposition – it doesn't matter who they are or what they're doing, if MPs are in Ottawa, they are expected to be in place when the bells ring. Dinners, meetings, or flights home will all be abandoned if a vote is suddenly called in the Commons.

On this day, Shaughnessy was dutifully in the House, but her notoriously weak bladder prompted her to slip out of the chamber minutes before the vote. She hurried through the majestic stone foyer just off the Commons and towards the washrooms: men only. She walked a little more quickly, looking for the women's washrooms, which she expected to find nearby. No luck. She walked farther still. No sign of a women's washroom anywhere within 150 feet of the entry to the chamber on the second floor. She discovered, in a panic by this point, that women's rooms were to be found behind the House, near the Speaker's chambers, or up or down two flights of stairs and down corridors.

When she finally returned to the House, she found she'd missed the vote. In the face of a reprimand, Shaughnessy countered with the charge that the state of the facilities in Parliament was decidedly sexist. "There's no women's washroom out there! What the hell is that?" she demanded.

Within a few weeks, workers moved into the large men's washroom off the lobby and divided it into two smaller facilities. For some time, it was referred to as the Shaughnessy Cohen Memorial Washroom, in honour of her missed vote in the House.

There were as well many unpublicized, mainly private acts of kindness that marked Shaughn's early months in Parliament, a side of her that some parliamentary colleagues didn't see for the entire time they knew her. It was a matter of how much she was willing to reveal and to whom. Those who were closest knew there was extraordinary sensitivity beneath a sometimes abrasive surface. She was conscious of the aspirations of others, especially young staff members or recent university graduates, to whom she offered generous advice and for whom she would lobby her cabinet contacts to help secure promotions or new positions. She knew the names of the Commons pages and was interested in their lives. If necessary, and perhaps because of her experience at Hiatus House, she did not hesitate to use her position to help relatively powerless young women. It was well known that Shaughnessy would react swiftly if she heard a report of sexual harassment. A call to the offending male staffer, at whatever level, and a call to his boss were enough to fix the problem.

A more public crusade concerned an issue that had been simmering since late 1993 and was in the news sporadically through 1994. It prompted one of her characteristic, deeply felt expressions of personal outrage and determination to right a wrong in the name of tolerance and diversity.

On Remembrance Day 1993, four Sikh veterans were refused entry to a Legion hall in Surrey, British Columbia, because they wouldn't remove their turbans. The national umbrella organization of the Royal Canadian Legion refused to take a stand on the matter, saying that the decision was within the purview of individual Legion branches. That position, or non-position, angered Shaughnessy. She wanted any Legion that refused Sikhs to be chastised, and she proposed a boycott of Legion poppies at Remembrance Day to her friends. But as an MP, she could make a more effective gesture in the House of Commons.

In early February 1995, she rose to table a motion: "That this House, recognizing the fundamental Canadian right of religious freedom and the courageous contributions of our veterans of all faiths, urge the Royal Canadian Legion and its constituent branches to reconsider their recent decision so that all of their members will have access to their facilities without having to remove religious head coverings, including the Sikh turban and the Jewish kipa."

She went on to speak about her views of tolerance and how they had been instilled in her. "Although I proudly represent the riding of Windsor–St. Clair, I was not raised there. I grew up in a small town, a village actually, Thamesville, Ontario, in the riding of Chatham-Kent. I grew up in a warm, wonderful home with caring parents, four caring sisters, in a caring village of only 1,000 people. I grew up thinking that our way of life, my family's way of life, the way we related to one another, the expressions we used, our relationships to our extended family, the food we ate, and all the things we did were just plain Canadian.

"However, as I grew older and my personal world expanded, my perception of what was Canadian changed radically. My parents adopted three sons, my brothers, who are proud to be aboriginal Canadians. I went to a university. I made friends with men and women of colour, of varying religions and heritages. I married a Jew and I raised with him our daughter in a new multicultural world.

"This motion is not just about the Canadian Legion," she said. "This motion is about Canada, our multiculturalism, and our tolerance of our fellow citizens... The Newton Royal Canadian Legion hall in Surrey, B.C., refused to permit four Sikh veterans into the hall because of their religious headgear. The four individuals were a retired Indian air force technician and three Sikh World War II veterans. Thirteen other veterans trooped from the hall to show their support for the Sikh members.

"On entering the Legion hall, removing hats out of respect for fallen comrades is a dearly and deeply held tradition. On May 31, 1994, delegates to the Royal Canadian Legion's national convention voted against a bylaw... that would have required all of its 1,700 branches to admit those wearing religious headgear into public areas of Legion halls... They claim that it is their right to make this decision because they have a private club. They say that because they took a democratic vote, the majority must rule...

"My father, who is a veteran, and my constituents who are veterans are proud to march next to the many great Sikh veterans, the many great Jewish veterans who wear kipas or yarmulkas. They are proud to march with them and we all should be. Instead of forbidding them from entering our institutions, instead of giving them a hard time, we should be thanking them for the freedoms they have preserved, so that Shaughnessy Cohen can go to mass, so that she can serve in the House of Commons, the freedom that others have in this society that we would not have if it were not for them.

"I call on this House to support this motion. I call on all members to urge the Royal Canadian Legion and its constituent branches to reconsider their recent decision."

Shaughnessy was extremely proud of this speech, getting on the phone (naturally) to all her friends and urging them to read the official record. Jerry was delighted too, recognizing it as one of the more important contributions Shaughn had made to public debate since she arrived in Parliament.

This act came in the aftermath of Shaughnessy's unhappy experience on the Human Resources Committee. The previous October, Lloyd Axworthy had released his promised action plan on social reform, titled *Improving Social Security in Canada*. Among the many ideas on which this Green Paper invited debate were several that rankled the considerable segment of the Canadian population that regarded the country's social safety net as a sacred trust. Passages such as "Given the constraints on government spending, we cannot do everything" and "Action on some of these suggestions would require tough choices about our priorities as a nation" drew immediate suspicion and condemnation.

Critics denounced the earlier consultation work of the Human Resources Committee as a sham, its hearings a mere camouflage for the not so secret plan to gut Canada's social programs. Oddly, one of the most effective spokespersons for these critics was none other than Bloc Québécois leader Lucien Bouchard. After Axworthy introduced his paper to the Commons, Bouchard poked a sharp stick into the heart of the Liberals' dilemma.

"I think that when it comes to being sensitive to the situation of the disadvantaged, the minister has retained his progressive, left-wing tradition. The problem is that the cure is a right-wing one. While the diagnosis is left-wing, the cure is right-wing. I am not saying that the minister's heart is not in the right place, on the contrary. The problem is that his wallet is not in the same place, as a Liberal minister. Now that he has become minister, he finds himself in a peculiar situation, stuck between a finance minister and a prime minister whose primary objective is to reduce the deficit and the debt on the backs of the disadvantaged," Bouchard said.

Shaughnessy was not enjoying her role in this process, which was testing her resolve to be a team player. No one was going to thank this committee for doing its part for fiscal prudence. Social security reform was headed to a sorry end which could doom not just the ideas but the careers of the people involved. Shaughnessy began to dread the prospect of travelling again, locked into those contentious hearings.

By November 1994, Shaughnessy was unable to hide her distaste for the committee, even from the media. She told Paul McKeague of the *Windsor Star* that the committee was struggling with "gulfs" between its members. She was candid about her differences with MPs from other parties, but she was vague about disagreements with her Liberal colleagues.

"This is not especially fun," she told McKeague, reciting for him the discomforts of life with this committee – the endless travel, the angry protests, the cold she had caught while on the road.

On December 20, 1994, this headline appeared on the front page of the *Windsor Star*. "Food for Thought... But Not the Public." The very unflattering story, by Canadian Press reporter Linda Drouin, was accompanied by a photo of Shaughnessy. "Members of a committee studying reforms to social programs gobbled sandwiches as they worked through lunch Monday listening to pleas for fairness in the social system. But the witnesses – many representing welfare groups – were told to keep their hands off the free food supplied to the MPs and staff."

The story described MPs such as Reg Alcock scarfing food while hungry witnesses had been refused anything but scraps from the table. Windsor's MP was mentioned nine paragraphs down: "MP Shaughnessy Cohen (L. Windsor-St. Clair) asked no questions of the witnesses who appeared during several hours of testimony but spent a half-hour at the food table on the side of the room, chatting and nibbling on the free lunch."

Shaughnessy was outraged by the story, getting on the phone immediately with her friends to launch a "we don't like" campaign against Drouin. It was not true, she said, that she had spent a half-hour at the table or that she had asked no questions.

She was even more incensed when the *Star* followed this story with an editorial cartoon by Mike Graston, depicting an overweight Shaughnessy eating her way to ignominy. That depiction hurt. Shaughnessy saw it as an assault on her physical appearance, her work ethic, and her reputation in Windsor.

When it came time for the committee to write its report at the end of 1994, during the Christmas and January break, the members were run as ragged as they had been while travelling the country. Most of the Liberals on the committee were polarized: Reg Alcock, Maria Minna, and New Brunswick MP Andy Scott on one side; Shaughnessy and Maurizio Bevilacqua on the other. Alcock, Minna, and Scott were determined to push pro-active social policy reform as far as it would go, despite the overwhelming view, held even by their minister, that the left's hands were tied. They wanted to insert strong, uncompromising statements about the government's role in preserving social programs. They were furious at the counter-efforts of Bevilacqua and Shaughnessy to include paragraphs that they believed were dictated by bureaucrats more interested in the fiscal agenda. Eventually, the three tried to pull together their own report, working late into the night in their offices, firing dispatches to one another by computer and reworking the master document. Shaughnessy was barely involved in the substance of the report, stepping in only to act in what she saw as the loyalist/enforcer role for her cabinet friends. This enraged fellow committee members such as Alcock.

"Most of us had come out of the service system and understood the need for changes but thought changes could be shaped that didn't do violence to people," he said. "We were not prepared to write something that was innocuous." Shaughnessy saw the battle as a duel between naive idealism and pragmatic Liberalism. "Let's just do what we can for now," she would say. The left-leaning group suspected that their report was just a sideshow in a larger war between Axworthy and Martin, and that Shaughnessy was trying to position the committee in the safe, non-controversial middle. Certainly Shaughnessy didn't want to lose either ally in cabinet. She was hedging her bets.

One year and $6 million after the work began, the committee's report was described as a waste of time and money, even on the eve of its release. The final document reluctantly acknowledged that big social program reform required big money. The committee had not succeeded in finding a way to do more with less.

"$6-Million Study May Gather Dust," the front-page headline of the *Windsor Star* proclaimed on February 2, 1995. Shaughnessy tried to put the best face on the committee's work, but the most positive declaration she could muster was that the Liberals might implement reforms later – once the deficit and debt were under control. "There's life beyond the debt wall," Shaughnessy was quoted as saying.

This became the mantra of the Chrétien government in the next few years: "We'll be Liberals later." Shaughnessy was one of the hundreds of Liberals in Ottawa who had to accept that Liberalism – at least the kind that cost money – would have to be postponed.

9

Law and Order

Paul Martin's draconian budget in February 1995 brought a final end to the dreams of the activists on the Human Resources Committee, but the futility of their attempt at social policy reform had been obvious for months before. Lloyd Axworthy's social policy task force had fared no better. In May 1994 its members had gathered at the Government Conference Centre in downtown Ottawa — a site haunted by several doomed attempts at constitutional reform in the eighties and early nineties — and found they could not even agree on which chapter of their report to draft first.

Fortunately for the Liberal left, there was consolation to be found right across the road at the Congress Centre where, that same May weekend, thousands of Liberals had assembled for the party's first post-election convention. They basked in their first opportunity in a decade to hold a policy convention as the governing federal party. Though the mood of the gathering was triumphal, there were plenty of questions hanging in the air. What was the party supposed to do with its regained hold on the nation? Liberals, elected and otherwise, appeared to have resigned themselves to cost-cutting government. The trick was to find ways to be Liberal without spending money.

One possible answer landed on the floor of the convention, thanks to some high-level manoeuvring by backroom strategists and by the women's contingent within the party. Labelled Resolution Number 14, it was a six-point plan to severely limit gun ownership in Canada, and it was put before the delegates by the National Liberal Women's Commission, an arm of the party designed to ensure female representation in the ranks and in policy decisions. The gun control resolution called for increased penalties on the criminal use of firearms and their illegal importation, a ban on private ownership of military assault weapons, strict controls over ammunition sales and handgun ownership, and, most significant, a national system of gun registration.

No one missed the symbolic importance of the resolution or its sponsor: gun control was being flagged as a bona fide women's issue for the Chrétien government. Women voters were crucial to the Liberal Party; in sheer numbers and motivation to vote, they were a powerful group. Moreover, women were not, by and large, Reform voters. A strong gun control policy would seal the gender advantage that the Liberals enjoyed. At the same time they could steal some of Reform's thunder as the party of law and order. Canadians appeared to be in the mood to get tough on crime. Prime Minister Jean Chrétien took Resolution Number 14 and ran with it at the convention's close.

"Tough talk is easy," Chrétien said, to loud applause from more than two thousand Liberals in the room. "What Canadians want and what we must provide is tough action. There shouldn't be any more weapons in our streets or in our playgrounds." He said that he wanted gun control legislation introduced in the Commons by the fall.

Chrétien knew it would be a hard sell, though. This government needed a white knight or two to carry gun control to the Canadian people. The duty fell to Justice Minister Allan Rock, the idealistic novice who was quickly emerging as one of the stars of the Chrétien cabinet. A former corporate litigator, he was earnest, young, and attractive — especially to women voters; central casting couldn't have produced a finer champion for gun control. And he appreciated the political dividends of good timing. "It was a very difficult time for all of us because we were faced with a ruinous financial situation," Rock said. "We had to make some tough choices. But in the justice field there were things we'd undertaken in the Red Book that we could follow through on because they didn't depend on economic circumstances. They were issues of principle, or they were social policies that weren't costly in the economic sense but were important from the point of view of Liberal philosophy."

Chrétien said that his government believed fundamentally in the links between the old "Just Society" and a fiscally sound society. "Of course those great ideas for money from 1993 to 1998 were not encouraged, let's put it this way, because we had to balance the books. But it's all interrelated ... It is the kind of society you want, and you cannot just settle problems through justice. You have to have an economy to sustain it, and you have to have the ideals of sharing among people."

The other benefit of this justice focus, said pollster Michael Marzolini, was that it allowed the party to put Allan Rock, an "asset" to be exploited, in the window. Rock didn't need to be conscripted to the anti-gun crusade. He was adamantly opposed to gun ownership. If allowed his own way, he would have taken guns out of the hands of all citizens, except police officers and military personnel. At the very least, he liked the idea of removing guns from all urban areas. He had the party's backing for that notion: Marzolini's firm had developed an ad campaign before the election for "gun-free zones in the three major urban centres." But the Liberals' enthusiasm for the scheme was tempered in the end. First, rural MPs had pleaded with Chrétien in early 1993 to downplay gun control in the Red Book. Then Marzolini found in pre-election focus groups that, despite their fondness for gun control, women voters shared with men voters the fixation on employment issues.

"What has this got to do with jobs?" women asked Marzolini's pollsters when they were shown the gun control proposals. After the election, Rock had been pulled aside by MPs such as Derek Lee who, although they represented urban areas, advocated a go-slow, incremental approach to gun control.

But by the spring of 1994, the pressure for anti-gun legislation was mounting, especially after a high-profile shooting death in Toronto in April, the killing of 23-year-old Georgina Leimonis at the Just Desserts café. Shortly after the convention a Toronto police constable, Todd Baylis, was shot dead. The 1989 tragedy at the École Polytechnique in Montreal, where Marc Lépine shot and killed 14 young women before turning a weapon on himself, remained fixed in the public memory.

Bob Nault, a no-nonsense kind of Liberal from the Ontario riding of Kenora–Rainy River, was serving his second term. Not yet 40 years old, he saw himself as just a regular guy from a part of the country where, as he said, "guns are part of the furniture." He fervently hoped that the Liberals would leave gun control alone, but he knew he was up against formidable opposition. Eddie Goldenberg, the prime minister's right-hand man since the 1970s, had proved impervious to Nault's pleas. In the midst of the 1993 campaign, when Nault was unpleasantly surprised to see a press release issued on the Liberals' anti-gun position – even after he and others had managed to keep the stricter measures out of the Red Book – he placed an angry telephone call to Goldenberg. By way of reply, Nault simply received a fax, a poll showing that most Canadians were in favour of strong controls on guns.

"I knew then that it was going to happen, that it was part of the agenda," said Nault. "We all know who makes decisions around here."

Most of the initial angst about gun control legislation surfaced at the newly established "rural caucus" of Liberal MPs. This group of about 30 members had come together soon after the 1993 election to form a united front in the face of international pressure on Canada's trading arrangements. Nations belonging to the General

Agreement on Tariffs and Trade were rethinking the whole system of supply management, a re-evaluation that could have serious implications for Canada's agricultural industry. But these mainly economic concerns soon gave way to more immediate alarm over gun control.

David Iftody, an MP from the rural riding of Provencher, Manitoba, was chair of the rural caucus. Just 37 years old when he was elected in 1993, Iftody was a rookie to politics and to the issue of guns. He wasn't a sportsman or a hunter; he'd never handled a gun. He was somewhat mystified when the more experienced MPs at the Monday-evening meetings – such as Bob Speller and Leonard Hopkins, both from rural Ontario – began to voice ominous warnings about the looming gun control debate. The rural MPs would be sacrificed for this urban obsession, they predicted. "If we don't get up on this early, and do something about it, we're going to be in trouble."

In 1991, when Kim Campbell, then justice minister, had introduced far more modest gun control proposals, these MPs had been inundated with protests from their constituents. Combative voters had poked their chests in the heat of discussion, angry phone calls flooded their offices. Only their opposition status had saved them back then. Although the federal Liberal caucus had taken an official position in favour of Campbell's gun control bill, these rural MPs could argue that their own government would never instigate such a thing. Now they were in government; now they couldn't blame anyone else for stricter gun control. They could only plead with their pro-gun-control colleagues to back down.

The rural MPs were sure that the enthusiasm for this measure came directly from the Prime Minister's Office and that Rock had been picked to carry the brief for what they saw as a blinkered, politically suicidal policy. Women within the party were claiming this issue as their terrain too, especially the female MPs on the Justice Committee, such as Sue Barnes and Paddy Torsney.

"To me, working on gun control was really important," said Barnes, who, in her role as vice-chair of the Justice Committee, put in long hours for over a year on the issue. "I thought it was specifically important to the women of this country."

"It was a no-brainer," said Torsney, 33 at the time and one of the Liberals' strongest advocates for the interests of young women. "We'd talk about this in the women's caucus and I'd be the one saying, 'Let's go, come on, let's get it done.'"

Barnes and Torsney made it their mission to assemble everything they could about gun control – to seek out the experts, wade into the controversy, and separate the facts from the emotion. They talked to gun clubs and they met with key gun control advocates in victims' rights groups. They argued with their rural colleagues and they armed themselves with statistics about violent crime.

Jean Chrétien recognized the early signs of caucus dissension. He ordered that a special caucus committee be established to develop, away from the glare of media scrutiny, a collective stand on gun control. (The fact that this committee had to be established was another indication that the really interesting divisions in this Parliament were not between the government and other parties but within the Liberal caucus. It was the first of several such committees.) The choice of chairpersons was critical. Here especially the personal became the political. Who you are and where you come from telegraphs volumes about your views on a subject as divisive as gun control.

Shaughnessy was an ideal representative for those in favour of gun control: she was from an urban riding, close to the gun-toting United States, she was a woman, and she was a lawyer. Herb Gray respected her hard-earned smarts. "She knew justice issues from the street," Gray said. Furthermore, since being elected, she had demonstrated unswerving loyalty to cabinet instructions, even if it meant rubbing the raw nerves of fellow caucus members. She liked Allan Rock and had gone out of her way to back him when he spoke in the caucus. At social events she fluttered around him whenever she had the chance. Pointedly, she had told Reg Alcock, head of the social policy caucus, that she wanted to work more directly with the justice minister. These efforts paid off: Shaughnessy was named co-chair, representing the pro-gun-control forces.

Bob Nault, on the other hand, was the perfect personification of the anti-gun-control forces. Though he was also an Ontarian, his riding, on the border with Manitoba, shared more in common with the West than it did with southern Ontario. Nault was chosen as the other co-chair. Their committee was directed to listen to the MPs and cobble together a compromise position. The hope was that the basic elements of the gun control legislation would be developed by the caucus.

"We needed a male and a female, we needed an urban and a rural," Nault said. "Shaughn was a lawyer – that's a good thing – [but] she seemed very committed to the minister." That link to Rock was seen by some, especially Nault, as a liability. In their eyes, Rock was not much more than "some slick Bay Street lawyer who had never set foot on gravel." Nault himself was a former trainman for CP Rail and a union man. Bay Street people set his teeth on edge.

"The perception from a lot of us was that Allan Rock was not a politician; he was very naive and thought that just because the party said this is the way it's going to be, there wouldn't be a battle. He thought we would just go quietly, like lambs to the slaughter," Nault said.

Shaughnessy seemed more willing than Rock to listen to the views of the gun control foes. Indeed, she was getting lots of practice in her off-hours away from Ottawa. Everyone around her, from her father to her brother Richard to her next-door neighbour, gave her a hard time about the Liberals' gun control stand. The biggest event on Bruce Murray's calendar was his annual fall hunting trip. "We never could convince her, though," Bruce said. "She would just walk away."

Shaughnessy had her own reasons for arguing against guns. In 1990, she had served as the Crown lawyer in a gun-detention hearing against a man named George Skrzydlewski. The part-time Chrysler worker had been amassing weapons in his Tecumseh Road apartment; a neighbour, Bill Clark, had complained to police.

When the police went in to seize the guns at Skrzydlewski's home, they found a rifle, three handguns, and seven thousand rounds of ammunition.

At the hearing into whether his guns should be seized and detained, however, no one could produce any firm evidence that Skrzydlewski was mentally unstable or unfit to own guns. He was a member of a gun club, and his handguns had been certified with the proper documentation from the Rondeau Rod and Gun Club. Fellow members there had found him "high strung" but not overly threatening. Police were ordered to return the weapons to him.

A year later, on November 21, 1991, Skrzydlewski confronted Bill Clark outside the apartment building and fired nine bullets into him in retaliation for Clark's complaint to the police. Clark died, leaving a wife and young daughter. Later it was learned that Skrzydlewski had declared to at least one member of the gun club that he wanted to kill Clark. As well, he had a history of paranoid schizophrenia. But the law had no means to keep guns out of his hands.

Shaughnessy was sickened by Clark's death. She believed that if she and the courts had had enough information and legal authority at the time, Skrzydlewski would never have been allowed to retain the gun that killed his neighbour. What this sad story taught her was that so-called "responsible gun owners" could turn out to be threats to society too. "The overwhelming sense I get is that people want to feel more secure in their communities and part of that is feeling that guns aren't omnipresent," she told the *Windsor Star*.

The Nault-Cohen caucus committee began meeting twice weekly in a large room in the Wellington Building, across from Parliament Hill. At each gathering, a group of about 15 to 20 MPs sat around the table, hearing presentations from individual caucus members. David Iftody walked in the first day and saw Shaughnessy sitting in the chair at the head of the table, her arms folded, a menacing scowl on her face.

"She didn't smile. She didn't acknowledge me," Iftody said. "She was Allan's agent on that committee. We all knew that going into the meeting."

Then again, Paddy Torsney would sometimes watch in amazement as Shaughnessy seemed to be agreeing with the foes of gun control. "Hey, whose side is she on, anyway?" Torsney would ask herself, as Shaughnessy solemnly nodded and told gun control opponents that they were raising valuable concerns.

"She really did start to sympathize and see that this wasn't easy," Nault said. "Politically, she became very sensitive to the fact that we were going to get beat up badly. And we did, politically, get beat up badly."

The committee members realized that they would get bogged down if they tried to sort out the complicated questions of how, when, and where to limit firearms. The important thing, they decided, was to focus on values and the big picture: what kind of society did Canadians want? They had to think in the long term; gun control legislation was not so much a chance to "clean up the streets" as an opportunity to shape a safer nation.

Organized opposition to gun control was building, however. On September 22, 1994, just as the Commons resumed after the summer break, more than 10,000 demonstrators converged on Parliament Hill for a massive rally. Allan Rock was worried that the public debate was dragging on too long. He told reporters on the eve of the protest that it was possible he was playing into the hands of the gun control foes by prolonging consultation. "But on the other hand, if I don't complete the process I'm engaged in now, I could be fairly accused of being arbitrary and not taking the views of others into account."

Perhaps as much to their own surprise as to that of their colleagues, Bob Nault and Shaughnessy were able to cobble together a consensus report. It was 10 pages long and began with three premises. First, any legislation would have to be directed at crime control while respecting the needs of legitimate gun owners. Second, public education should focus on a long-term goal of changing the view of firearms use in society. Finally, gun control had to go hand in hand with social programs devoted to crime prevention.

Through more than three dozen recommendations, the caucus committee struck a careful compromise between two opposing positions. Much was said about changing values and getting tough on gun crime, to please Shaughnessy's side. But important caveats were attached, including a recommendation not to ban handguns and to make registration of firearms an issue of crime prevention, not an element of the Criminal Code.

The committee's report was unveiled in caucus in the first week of November, to huge applause. Co-chairs Cohen and Nault were given a standing ovation. But that warm fuzzy feeling lasted less than a month.

On November 31, 1994, Rock came to the Commons with his proposed gun control package, called *The Government's Action Plan on Firearms Control*. It wasn't the final legislation that Chrétien had promised to present by the end of the year, but the announcement of the package served as a loose fulfillment of the commitment. Before he outlined the details in the chamber, Rock explained it in the lobby to the nervous rural Liberal MPs, who were watching every step in this process to gauge their chances of political survival. The package included a ban on short-barrelled handguns and military-style rifles (though anyone who owned such weapons legally as of January 1, 1995, would be permitted to keep them); restrictions on ammunition sales; and, most controversially, a national gun registry system to begin in 1996. Failure to register would be considered a criminal offence.

David Iftody was first shocked and then angry. The caucus committee report had urged the minister not to make failure to register a matter of criminal penalties; a summary offence was sufficient. But Rock was insisting on the hard line: failure to register firearms would be an indictable offence.

"He stood there with that goofy smile," Iftody said. "There was this odd, incredible silence. One by one the guys started walking away."

Rock made no apologies to his fellow Liberals. As the gathering broke up, he moved to the foyer, where he told reporters he was immoveable on the subject. "This is not an invitation for further discussion. This is final."

The mood in caucus turned ugly; the rural MPs felt betrayed.

"There was a big debate about the fact that we had done this for nothing," Nault said. "It didn't reflect the report as well as we thought it should have, and that became a very difficult issue in the ensuing months in the caucus."

Shaughnessy faced a tough decision. Should she side with the MPs who were defending the report she had co-signed? Or should she accept what Allan Rock and the Prime Minister's Office clearly wanted?

One of Nault's allies in the cabinet was Deputy Prime Minister Sheila Copps. He had served as her campaign co-chair during the 1990 leadership contest. When it appeared that the rural MPs had been done in by the cabinet, he went to Copps to plead for high-level intervention. Copps was no friend of Rock's. The rivalry between them had intensified as Rock, with Chrétien's blessing, vaulted into a leading role at the cabinet table. Though technically lower in rank than Copps, he was deemed higher in stature because he was a favourite of Eddie Goldenberg's and was unencumbered by affiliation with any leadership challenger before 1993.

Copps began to investigate what had happened between the delivery of the caucus committee report on November 3 and the unveiling of Rock's proposal four weeks later. Rock had vetted the package with the cabinet while the prime minister was away on his first Team Canada trip to China, so Chrétien had not had the opportunity to state his position. With no prime-ministerial imprimatur on the package, Copps stepped into the vacuum and spread the word that Rock had both misrepresented its substance and misled ministers by saying it was consistent with the caucus committee report. Copps approached Shaughnessy and sought her help in establishing that there was a significant disconnect between the caucus consensus and the proposed legislation. Shaughnessy made a strategic calculation and concluded it was better to be with Rock than against him. If Rock was a rising star, Shaughnessy was ready to rise with him, and she could not overlook his influence on those coveted judicial appointments.

She told Copps she didn't see any major discrepancy. Then she warned Rock that Copps was agitating against him, backed by the rural MPs. She also, indiscreetly, flagged the simmering fight to at least one reporter in Ottawa. When word reached PMO ears that a story could appear, officials there cautioned Shaughnessy, in no uncertain terms, that she had breached a cardinal rule of team discretion. She shrugged off the reprimand. "I'm not going to shut up just because they tell me to," she told her reporter friend.

In deciding that she would be Rock's accomplice, Shaughnessy earned some valuable points with the justice minister. But the episode did nothing to build her friendships within the cliquey — and leaky — Liberal caucus.

"At the end of it all, a lot of people didn't have a positive feeling about Shaughnessy," Iftody said. Nault and Iftody began to steer clear of her. They and the other rural MPs decided that the only way to fight Rock and the prevailing forces on gun control was to just keep talking about it.

"We kept this alive for six months," Nault said. "We kept at least six to ten MPs on their feet at each caucus." At every available opportunity, these MPs would stand up and accuse Rock of turning his back on the caucus consensus.

Shaughnessy was moonlighting on another justice issue that year, in the service of the minister to whom she remained most closely attached, Herb Gray. During the summer of 1994, news of a made-in-Canada "spy scandal" involving the Canadian Security Intelligence Service and right-wing groups in Canada made the headlines. Various media outlets, including the CBC's *fifth estate*, reported that a CSIS informant named Grant Bristow had infiltrated a white-supremacist organization known as the Heritage Front, and that he had gone on to spy on the Reform Party before the 1993 election. Other stories soon followed — that CSIS had infiltrated everything from Canada Post to the CBC. The opposition called for a royal commission to investigate the allegations. The

Reform Party in particular wanted to know if it had been branded an "enemy of the state" by Canada's security service, acting on direction from its political masters. Gray was the "political master" in Reform's sights; as solicitor general, he was in charge of CSIS.

But once again, it wasn't the attack from the opposition benches that troubled the government as much as the hints of sabotage behind the lines. This time it was Scarborough MP Derek Lee who presented the greater challenge to the government's handling of the affair. Lee was chairman of the National Security Subcommittee, an offshoot of the Justice Committee, and he was ready to conduct a probing investigation of the so-called "Heritage Front affair." Lee had long been a champion of Parliament's rights of investigation; in later years he would write a textbook on the broad-ranging rights of committees to subpoena witnesses and evidence. Security issues were his particular passion.

Herb Gray and his department believed there was another completely adequate and proper way to investigate this matter. The Security Intelligence Review Committee is a government-appointed panel whose members include lay people and security specialists, designed to "spy on the spies" and monitor possible espionage excess. It reports directly to the solicitor general. Gray did not want the National Security Subcommittee to hijack the work of SIRC, no matter how fervently the Scarborough MP believed in Parliament's right of investigation. He couldn't prevent Lee's inquiry, but he could attempt to contain it.

The obvious candidate to do Gray's bidding on Lee's subcommittee would have been Gray's parliamentary secretary, Patrick Gagnon. But the Quebec MP was consumed with the coming Quebec election and the referendum that would inevitably follow if the Parti Québécois won, as it seemed destined to do. So the hobbling of Lee's work was handed to Shaughnessy. She would again serve as the minister's loyal deputy, putting down dissent within her own caucus and preventing renegade MPs from veering too far from the government's agenda.

Her willingness to serve cabinet ministers' bidding was now

emerging as her main strength. She had done it on the Human Resources Committee, she was doing it on gun control, and now she would do it for the "spy scandal." Happily for Gray and Rock, Shaughnessy was undisturbed by the enmity this earned her from some other Liberal colleagues. Her conditioning in the Murray family, where bold individuality was rewarded, made her almost impervious to antipathy from people "we don't like."

Shaughnessy thrived on this job. It appealed to her love of mystery and mischief and allowed her endless opportunities to annoy Derek Lee, whom she regarded as a humourless stuffed shirt. Lee was not amused to see Shaughnessy join his committee, as a full-fledged member, an appointment clearly made by the whip on Gray's instructions. He knew immediately that she came with a mission. Her role, he said, amounted to issuing full reports to Gray's office on the goings-on at committee and characterizing any threat to the government's agenda as the work of traitors or enemies. Lee didn't know whether to be more bitter about Shaughnessy's presence or about the fact that Herb Gray had dispatched her. "I think there were probably other ways of communicating with me than sending in snipers from my own caucus," he said.

Shaughnessy wanted backup – and a bit of fun. Roger Gallaway joined the subcommittee after Shaughnessy made her wishes known to Gray's people. Roger was happy to help. Like Shaughnessy, he was clear on the task: slow down Lee's work, obfuscate when opposition members such as Reform's Val Meredith became too conspiratorial, provoke delays by any method. They were told by Doug Kirkpatrick, Gray's executive assistant, among others in Gray's office, that they should bury or delay the subcommittee's hearings until SIRC had a chance to report and the issue had cooled in the media.

Roger and Shaughnessy revelled in this devilry. It did not, obviously, represent their finest hours as principled parliamentarians, but they were observing a fundamental rule of politics: do a favour today for a cabinet minister, and tomorrow you may find it easier to get your own principled ideas through Parliament. They also trusted Gray's judgment. If the éminence grise of the Liberal government thought the subcommittee's work was harmful, who were they to challenge his view? They threw themselves, gleefully, into obstructionism. When Roger joined the committee, for instance, they asked for a delay in the hearings of a couple of weeks so the MP from Sarnia-Lambton could get up to speed.

"We got into absolutely crazy discussions," Roger said. "Sometimes we'd move for adjournment... We would demand sandwiches – free dinner! We'd get in there, eat the supper, and move for adjournment. When we didn't win, we'd get into arguments over certain words. We could go on for an hour about punctuation."

One of Shaughnessy's favourite delaying tactics was to promise to work on some clause of the report, in conjunction with the able lawyer and Library of Parliament researcher assigned to the committee, Phil Rosen. Shaughnessy would commit herself to producing material for a forthcoming committee meeting and then simply fail to deliver.

Lee was furious. "She didn't have any scruples about it. It was so obvious," he said. Almost all the meetings were held in secret and that made things worse. "If we weren't in camera, the public might well ask: 'What the hell is this? Ms. Cohen said she'd be prepared to deal with that issue on Tuesday and two weeks later, she's still not ready.'" Lee felt powerless to deal with her, not just because she was acting on Herb Gray's behalf but because of the loyalty culture among Liberals.

"She was a colleague, so on the record, I wasn't going to impugn her integrity," he said. Off the record, though, Lee denounced Shaughnessy as a minister's stooge.

The gun control debate moved from proposal to legislation in early 1995. On February 14, Rock introduced Bill C-68 in the Commons. The next few months would test the Liberals as nothing else had. This single issue moved them from soaring, 80-percent approval ratings to the low 50s.

David Iftody, disgusted and exhausted, had stepped down as head of the rural caucus just as the bill was about to come to the House. He was not angry at the prime minister as much as he was annoyed with the people around his leader.

"I firmly believe that he got really bad advice," Iftody said, "and it was too late for him to turn back. There were 25 or 30 of us who were stuck in the burning house. Nobody wanted to come in and get us, and worse yet, some of our colleagues were saying, 'Shut the doors and bolt them because we don't want them here anyway.'"

That was probably the worst of the controversy, Iftody said: facing the allegations — some of them whispered, some uttered directly — that the MPs who opposed gun control weren't real Liberals anyway and the caucus would be better off without them. Neither Rock nor Shaughnessy said this aloud to the dissenters, but Iftody described the justice minister as "remarkably insensitive" to the political damage he was causing with gun control. He said Rock would regularly report to his caucus the accolades he was receiving in Toronto for his stand. The rural MPs would mutter in their seats, "How brave of you, when you're not paying the price."

The months of hearings on Bill C-68 were excruciating and difficult, said Sue Barnes, the Justice Committee vice-chair. Shaughnessy wasn't officially on the committee; she attended the hearings as an associate member, a status reserved for MPs who sit on subcommittees but not the larger committee itself. She started to "sub in," as it's called, to keep watch on developments for Rock. But in this role she was more than a pair of eyes and served a function far beyond that of minister's lackey. She would warn him about possible conflicts and advise him on where he had to back down, for the sake of caucus unity. While arguing in favour of the gun control measures as a strong statement of Liberal values and of her own abhorrence of violence and victimization, Shaughnessy never lost sight of strategy. "She was very blunt with me and gave good but sometimes pointed advice," Rock said.

Throughout that spring, the Justice Committee heard hours of testimony on the legislation. It toured the country, visiting gun clubs in rural areas. It heard from police officers and women's groups and from Suzanne Laplante-Edward, the mother of one of the women killed at the École Polytechnique, who had taken up the cause of gun control to help deal with the tragedy that befell her family.

"We took the claims of the interested parties very seriously," Sue Barnes remembered. "It was at the beginning of our careers in politics ... We were given room to grow ... We worked as a team to make sure that was a great piece of legislation. I'm very proud of it – I felt like I did my job."

Other MPs, less enthusiastic about the bill, felt they had to do their jobs too. As the committee moved into clause-by-clause consideration in the early days of June – an excruciating process that stretched into the wee hours night after night – the tension became palpable. Once again, it wasn't the Reform Party or the Bloc Québécois whipping up the worst storms. The Liberal MPs were series of amendments that threatened to draw the process out even longer.

In particular, Lee wanted to introduce an amendment to make sure that firearms manufacturers didn't become tangled in the red tape of certificates when they were merely transporting goods to and from the factories. His Scarborough riding was home to a gun manufacturer, and he was looking out for the legitimate interests of his voters. But Sue Barnes and others believed that the raft of Liberal-sponsored amendments would gut the bill. However reasonable Lee's proposal may have seemed, the pro-gun-control MPs were resisting any attempt to alter the legislation. One amendment, they figured, would open the door to a host of others.

As the House neared the summer break, the pressure was on to get the gun control bill into the Commons and passed – if only to avoid a long, hot summer of sustained anger in the country. Rock had had his fill of caucus dissent as well.

One June day, the Liberals on the Justice Committee were abruptly summoned out of their work on Bill C-68 and told to report to the office of the whip, Don Boudria, on the first floor of the Centre Block. They shuffled in and sat down, Shaughnessy among them. Boudria asked where they were headed with the bill. They all began to speak at once. Lee tried to explain his amendment.

Suddenly Allan Rock was in the room. Gone was the friendly and earnest minister – in his place stood the steely corporate litigator, facing down the MPs who were causing him such problems.

"I've just come from the Prime Minister's Office," he said. Lee was unimpressed. He didn't think Rock had spoken to Chrétien himself. If it was the prime minister ordering the MPs into line, Lee thought, then he would listen. But if Rock was acting on behalf of the prime minister's advisers, Lee wasn't interested. He was not the first to bridle at the prospect of taking orders from unelected individuals around the prime minister.

"Enough is enough," Rock said coldly. "No more fucking amendments. Do you hear me? No more fucking amendments." He turned on his heel and left the room. Off to the side, Shaughnessy smirked. "Now that's the way to treat these guys," she murmured. Later, she told Rock she liked this tough side of him. It was the kind of take-no-prisoners political behaviour she savoured.

The incident left a lasting if less favourable impression with her colleagues. Her friend and co-conspirator Roger Gallaway took a dim view of the episode. "To tell you the truth, that really jaundiced my view of the committee process," he said. "I've never forgotten that."

Lee was also livid, but he could see a victory in it, too. "It made me stronger. It showed me what a committee could do. It showed what could happen."

Reflecting later on this striking departure from his usually conciliatory methods, Rock said he saw no other choice but to get tough with the committee. "That process had gone on too long, and there were issues being raised by the committee that were beyond its mandate," he said. "And they were repeating various exercises, and just prolonging the whole examination of the bill at a point when the prime minister wanted the thing done. He wanted the bill through committee, back to the House, take your vote, and move on."

Move on they did. On June 13, 1995, the gun control bill came to the Commons for the third and final reading. The days and hours before the vote were anguish for the rural MPs. Iftody had already gone to the prime minister's office a few weeks earlier and notified him that he wouldn't be voting in favour. For 45 minutes, Iftody sat in front of Chrétien and explained that it was the only way to preserve a valuable seat for the Liberals west of the Ontario border. The prime minister, alternately stern and exasperated, tried to persuade him to vote with the caucus. Iftody said he was ready to take his punishment.

"It's the most difficult thing you can imagine," Iftody said. Bucking the party line is a dangerous business: committee assignments can be withheld, promotions can be denied, reputations can be discreetly undermined. "I was elected at the age of 37. I'm a year and a half into my job and I find myself in the prime minister's office, sitting face to face with him and knowing there's a spear that's going to come late in the night and kill me."

The day of the vote, Bob Nault paced for hours up and down the Sparks Street Mall, debating what to do. If he voted against the bill, the immediate payoff would be great in his riding. He'd be praised as a rebel and a hero in the community. But in the long term, he thought, he'd be marginalized within his own party. And how would that serve the riding?

Shaughnessy was one of the final speakers on Bill C-68. She declared how proud she was of her caucus and the Liberal cabinet. She spoke of Windsor's support for stricter gun control, because Windsorites could see from their border vantage point the ills of a society that didn't restrict firearms.

When the time to vote came, Shaughnessy stood proudly with 192 other MPs in the House and said yes to gun control. So did Bob Nault. So did Bob Speller, David Iftody's roommate.

Iftody did not. He and eight other Liberal MPs, including Len Hopkins, voted no. While Shaughnessy, Mary, and Roger went out to celebrate, while Rock greeted reporters with relief, while Sue Barnes went back to her office to receive the congratulatory bouquets sent by friends and family, the dissenters made their way off the Hill in despair.

The party would have the summer to recover and to put it all behind them. Shaughnessy, like the rest of her colleagues, happily left Ottawa and returned home. For her it was back to Windsor, Jerry, Pelee Island, and the ever-present dogs.

The Place to Be

The summer break meant a respite from the gruelling weekly commute between Windsor and Ottawa and a brief return to some vestige of domestic normality for Shaughnessy and Jerry. She had phoned him almost nightly during the gun control battle and he was proud of her efforts. American-born, he had a deeply rooted opposition to guns. While Shaughnessy fought the good fight in Ottawa, Jerry took every opportunity to promote her work on behalf of a safer Canada back home in Windsor. For a few weeks, though, they could quietly retreat.

"Home was her refuge," Jerry said. "This is where she came to get away from things."

The Amherstburg house was also the focus of the greatest of Shaughn's intentions in the realm of interior decoration. She bought dozens of decorating magazines, assembling a scrapbook of dream rooms for the house, which had expanded, thanks to Jerry's handiwork, from a small cabin to a sprawling bungalow.

Shaughnessy's vision was a sunny, open space, painted yellow to show off the warm, glowing pine of the furniture she collected.

The reality was a huge, 30-by-30-foot living-room area cluttered with the pine dining tables she had bought dirt cheap on antiquing treks over the years. Her cupboards were filled with the multi-coloured Fiestaware and kitschy knick-knacks she could not resist. Cathy, Judi, and Patty often accompanied Shaughn to the flea markets. Jerry sometimes tagged along too. Shaughn would point to her husband ambling well behind the women and say to the merchant, "Here comes my husband, Jerry. But you can just call him 'the wallet.'"

In the summer of 1995, as they did every summer, they stole away as often as possible to Pelee Island. Here, Shaughnessy practised a unique form of busy leisure. A typical day on the island would go something like this: Shaughnessy would wake early, as usual – around 6 a.m. – and tune in to American radio, usually some outrageous talk show that made her laugh. Tea in one hand, a paperback in the other, she'd lounge on the porch, absorbed in reading before the day began.

Just an hour or two into these summer mornings, the phone would start to ring. More often than not, it was Mary or Roger, or another political friend, ready to dissect some new issue in their world or plot strategy to win the day on another. It might be Garry Fortune, asking Shaughn to accompany him on a mission for Herb Gray in Windsor. Or it might be a cabinet minister's assistant, responding to a matter that Shaughnessy had been pushing.

In the afternoons, Jerry would take out his sailboat. Shaughnessy adamantly refused to accompany him. "It's boring," she'd say. "I get claustrophobic in that small space with nothing to do, nothing to see, except water all around." So while Jerry sailed, Shaughnessy would either head down to the store, to visit with the locals on the island, or tool around the dusty roads, paying calls on Margaret Atwood and Graeme Gibson, Carolyn and John Kirkendall, or Barry Wayman and Tom Brown.

John Kirkendall was a Michigan judge, and Shaughnessy was delighted to count him among her friends. The two could sit for hours down on the beach, in the Kirkendalls' cabana, gossiping about the legal worlds they both knew so well, and drinking beer. The pine-walled confines of the tiny cabana, incidentally, didn't seem to make Shaughnessy claustrophobic.

Sometimes Shaughnessy would leave Jerry behind on the island and head back into Windsor to handle her constituency business. The summer break was no escape from such details. Much as Shaughnessy loved the life in Ottawa and the adrenalin rush of being at the centre of big national issues, she knew all too well that much of an MP's life is absorbed by local concerns. She could never afford to forget that crucial refrain, borrowed from Tip O'Neill: all politics is local.

This emphasis on local concerns became more pronounced in the years when Shaughnessy was in government. In fact, a curious thing happened to the Canadian civic psyche in the 1990s. As the political parties adopted a global outlook, the voters went local. In the face of sometimes incomprehensible globalization, citizens were paying closer attention to the idea of community and to what was needed to preserve the integrity of the world immediately around them.

Windsor, says Paul Martin, was a perfect training ground for learning how to balance local strength with larger global forces. "Growing up in a small Canadian city, opposite a very large American megacity, I think that we were given, long before global- ization occurred in people's minds, a very clear insight into how that happened," he said.

Windsor could not ignore the overwhelming presence just across the Detroit River. Each morning, when Shaughnessy and Jerry looked out the window of their riverside Amherstburg home, they could see huge American tankers plying the waters. Their view spanned Ohio smokestacks at one end of the horizon and Detroit's outskirts on the other. Their television and radio stations broadcast non-stop news from Washington, Michigan, and other points south. The United States was literally on their doorstep, and the response of Shaughnessy and her fellow citizens was to culti- vate Windsor's sense of community. The strength of local political activism and the vibrant community service tradition in the city illustrated how village imperatives are able to transcend the global – or at least keep them in perspective. The people of Windsor, as Herb Gray likes to boast, are consistently among the most generous contributors to the United Way in Canada.

Shaughnessy never let anyone forget she was from Windsor. Her maiden speech in Parliament was a testament to her love of the city, part elegy to Windsor's rich history of vice – liquor and casinos – and part careful note of all of Windsor's famous sons and daughters. She would constantly nag her Ottawa staff or national reporters to come down to Windsor and spend some time at "the centre of the universe." She insisted to friends that Windsor had the best restaurants, the best clothing stores, the best hairdressers, the best boutiques.

"I was often treated to an expensive cigar from 'the greatest tobacconist in Canada' – who just happened to be in Windsor," Don Brown said. "Many great things and people are located in Windsor – something I did not know until Shaughnessy told me." Windsor figured large in every intervention she made in the Commons and in any debate she had over national issues.

One day in the first term, she arrived in Allan Rock's office for a broad-ranging chat on national issues. Waiting to be shown in, she glanced over an assistant's shoulder at a piece of paper on his desk. It was a list of all the MPs, followed by a few words summarizing the local concerns or favourite projects of each one. Shaughnessy was tickled to see three items beside her name: liquor, gambling, and cars. Though these same three words might have been equally at home under "hobbies" on a ne'er-do-well's resumé, they were Shaughn's proud local obsessions.

Every cabinet minister in Ottawa knew that Windsor's major industries were Shaughn's bread and butter too. She demanded a voice whenever issues involving booze, gambling, or cars were part of the government's business – and even when they weren't.

She was chair of the "auto caucus," another of the issue-based groups within the larger Liberal fold. This collection of more than

40 MPs, most with car manufacturing interests in their communities, kept a close eye on any policy that affected the auto industry. Ford, Chrysler, and General Motors, accounting for thousands of jobs in Windsor, all had plants in Windsor–St. Clair. "If it's good for Chrysler, it's good for Windsor" was her motto. Chrysler alone employed 15,000 people in Shaughnessy's riding.

Industry Minister John Manley was constantly buttonholed at caucus meetings by Shaughnessy, who would invariably have an auto industry issue to raise with him. She could rhyme off reams of statistics dealing with the car companies, Manley said, but she regarded the industry as a continuing-education project. In late 1998 she told him she wanted a full briefing from his department on the details of the Canada–U.S. Auto Pact.

"Look, I really need to understand this case," she said. "Will you arrange for me to be taken through the whole Auto Pact issue in detail so I understand it?"

Manley thought this would be a classic case of carrying coals to Newcastle. "I thought she knew it better than anyone else," he said.

Throughout countless Liberal caucus debates about the power of the big banks, Shaughnessy was quick to see the local implications. The banks were lobbying to gain entry to the lucrative car-leasing business, a business then held directly by the auto manufacturers. The issue was simple for her: the banks couldn't have what they wanted.

"Banks bad, car companies good," she reiterated to her fellow MPs. During one of the caucus debates over the car-leasing issue she wrote the mantra on a Post-It note and – unbeknownst to Martin – stuck it on the finance minister's back, where it remained throughout the meeting.

She was also determined to understand the labour side of the auto industry. Though the auto workers had a nasty habit of voting New Democrat, she decided to take advantage of an MP-business exchange program in 1997 and do a week's internship at the offices of the Canadian Auto Workers union in Toronto. She braced herself to march into the headquarters of the labour behemoth that so dominated politics in her hometown, unsure of how she would be greeted; in fact, she loved the experience. Reporting to friends after her week with the CAW, Shaughnessy declared that she had moved many of the CAW folks from her "we don't like" category into the "we like" category.

Buzz Hargrove, head of the CAW, came to count on her as a supportive, strong advocate of auto workers' interests. "She understood the auto industry," Hargrove was quoted as saying in one of the union's newsletters. "She understood how important it was for communities like Windsor. Because of that she worked with us very hard to ensure the government wouldn't do something that would harm the industry."

Though not a gambler herself, Shaughnessy became an ardent supporter of another of Windsor's economic engines, gambling. The casinos' arrival in Windsor coincided with Shaughn's arrival in Ottawa. In early 1994, a building that had once housed a brewery and later the Art Gallery of Windsor was converted to a casino. Almost immediately, about 15,000 gamblers, 80 per cent of them American, flooded through the doors each day, leaving their cash behind in hundreds of shiny slot machines. A riverboat casino soon followed. Though these establishments were owned by the provincial government, they were operated by the slick folks from Las Vegas's Hilton, Caesars, and Circus Circus conglomerates. Shaughnessy knew the value of the income these gaudy institutions were generating for her city, even if they were a magnet for a few less-than-savoury characters. She looked for ways to increase the gambling revenues, to make the casinos even more successful than they were.

Early in the Chrétien mandate, rumours circulated that Finance would soon announce a tax on gambling winnings. Such a measure would do nothing to encourage casino attendance. Shaughn turned into a tiger; Paul Martin enjoyed some sport.

"That's when she backed me into the corner," Martin later recalled. "There was never any intention of doing it, but basically I tried to scare the living hell out of her. What I didn't tell her was that we had an agreement with the provinces that we wouldn't tax gambling winnings. But I let her stew for a while.

"It was sort of fun," Martin said. "She didn't stew in silence. She would come at you very hard. But always, always with that smile."

"Liquor, gambling, and cars" summarized a good number of the local issues that preoccupied Shaughnessy during her work-weeks in Ottawa. On weekends and in those periods when the House was not sitting, she was back in Windsor dealing with countless others. The life of a government backbencher is more complicated than it might appear to constituents watching at home when their local representative rises to say aye or nay according to the orders of the party whip. Those who take the time to tele-phone or write to the local MP will probably find that politicians obey not just the prime minister, but the voters too.

Shaughn returned religiously to Windsor every Friday, some-times Thursday night, and dutifully made her way back to Ottawa by Monday morning, even though she could spend as much as six hours in transit each way. She had a 45-minute drive from Amherstburg to the airport in Windsor, an hour-long flight to Toronto, a one- or two-hour stopover, and then another hour-long flight to Ottawa. She used this time to read, sign correspondence, and of course talk on the telephone during the stopovers.

Her constituency office was a storefront building on busy Wyandotte Street in downtown Windsor. The front of the office was a tidy arrangement of desks, file cabinets, and posters. Shaughnessy had decorated with works by local artists and framed mementoes and certificates. Photographs of sod turnings, featuring Shaughn with local business people or political celebrities, dotted the walls. Shaughnessy's office was at the back, as was a boardroom. The phone was often the only thing one could find on Shaugh-nessy's desk. Like a pack rat, she accumulated newspaper clippings, scraps of interesting reports, pads filled with doodles, half-written letters and lists.

Shaughnessy was saved from this chaos by the women who

were willing and able to manage the things she couldn't, or wouldn't. Three women worked in her office, each with her own strengths, none with a clear title or rank beyond "assistant." Shaughnessy couldn't imagine forcing staff members to observe rigid hierarchies or job descriptions. Her Windsor staff worked closely with her Ottawa staff, and all were deemed equal.

Heather McNamara loved detail and organization. Her husband, Gary, was a Liberal who served on Tecumseh's municipal council. He'd helped in the Cohen campaign in 1993, and Shaughnessy helped Gary when he decided to run provincially for the Liberals in 1995. "She taught me that every individual is important. She would go into a room and her eyes would be wandering around the room — not looking for the important people, like so many politicians do, but for the 'little' people," he said.

"Shaughn will go directly to those people and acknowledge their support. She'd say, 'The big people, they'll get their due. The ordinary Joes, there's a lot more of them than there are of the important guys.'"

Heather McNamara came to work for Shaughnessy immediately after she was elected in 1993. Her role was essentially that of paid disciplinarian. It was a weekly struggle to get Shaughnessy to pay attention to the myriad small matters that McNamara had attended to that week. Shaughn knew all the ways to annoy McNamara, a neat freak. If the big plate glass window near McNamara's desk was shiny and clear, Shaughnessy would plant sloppy lipstick kisses all over the pristine glass, covering it with unsightly smudges.

"She would often come in to work in play mode," McNamara said. Shaughnessy would arrive at her constituency office almost every Friday, all set to put her feet on the desk and indulge in hours of chat and laughter with friends. After a week in Ottawa, she most wanted to download her information and gossip to her pals. Sometimes McNamara or other staff members just walked over and politely closed the door so visitors to the office couldn't hear the off-colour jokes or howls emitting from the esteemed member's office.

The signal that business was about to be done was the inevitable appearance of the dreaded "green book" – the large House of Commons binder that all MPs use as their organizational bible. In this tome, bits of correspondence, invitations, and important memos are paper-clipped to each leaf, annotated with comments from the constituency worker. "Needs an answer by tomorrow," the notes would read, or "Has already called five times." McNamara also recorded every phone call on individual slips of paper, neatly summarizing the name, address, phone number, and concerns of the constituent, complete with quotes; the issue was flagged in the top right-hand corner of the note. These too would be filed in the green book. The hopeful expectation of every constituency worker is that the MP will attend to these matters, ASAP.

"She'd see the green book and grimace," McNamara said. "That was our control system, the green book – and Shaughnessy didn't like to be controlled."

Marion Fantetti, wife of a policeman from nearby LaSalle, was another constituency worker. Her priority was to handle the network – Shaughnessy's connections in Windsor and Ottawa – and a lot of the diplomacy attached to maintaining those connections. She learned at the feet of the master. For Shaughnessy, the network was everything, Fantetti said.

When a complaint arrived, Shaughnessy had two major questions: "Who do we call? What do we do?" Fantetti said. It was second nature to Shaughn to immediately reach for help from those more powerful when trouble arose. Fantetti didn't find it odd at all that Shaughnessy spent so much time cultivating relationships with powerful cabinet ministers in Ottawa, because she saw how quickly her bosses' phone calls would be returned when a constituent's complaint was registered.

The third assistant was Norma Coleman, who had been with Shaughnessy since the campaign in 1988. She handled the more tangible forms of communication: the press releases, the media relations, and the "householders," regular, mass mail-out bulletins that all MPs send to their constituents. Coleman designed these householders to imitate a broadsheet newspaper, in style and substance. Shaughnessy and Coleman, with their well-tuned antennae, believed that the residents of Windsor–St. Clair were in no mood to see rah-rah Liberal propaganda from their MP. Coleman worked hard to make sure the householders stuck to the informative rather than the persuasive.

There was one constituency task that Shaughnessy, unlike most other MPs, enjoyed immensely. She loved dealing with the eccentric or interesting folks who came to the office. Routine meetings with local businessmen or community activists could be tiresome for her, but she would make time for someone who was entertaining, diverting, or unusual. She was enormously fond of a mentally challenged senior citizen named Don Loucks, who busied himself making complicated, three-dimensional collages, constructed from newspaper clippings, coloured paper, foil – anything he could lay his hands on. Loucks, a tiny, cheery, earnest man, had a style of dress that sharply resembled his collages, a colourful mixture of patterns, pins, and memorabilia. Shaughnessy happily displayed Loucks's work in her constituency office and took every opportunity to introduce him to visitors to Windsor, including the prime minister.

Every MP also has to deal with individuals whose eccentricity propels them towards the paranoid. Their stories are remarkably similar, and they usually fall into one of two categories: people who believe they're being punished or persecuted individually by some shadowy government plot, and people who believe that aliens or an unknown force are infringing on their normal functioning as citizens.

Shaughnessy would listen attentively to these victims, nodding and encouraging them to spare no detail. When the spiel was over, Shaughnessy had a mischievous strategy all ready. Rather than shoo them away, she'd refer the paranoid voter to one of her Liberal colleagues in cabinet.

"You say you're being monitored by aliens?" she'd ask. "Well,

I think you should take this right to Herb Gray – he's the solicitor general, after all, and he'll get the RCMP moving on this." Then she'd write a sweetly worded note to Gray's office, explaining that she had personally referred this constituent directly to the minister's attention. Those with military-related worries – the army poisoning the water, perhaps – were sent to David Collenette when he was defence minister. What was the sense of knowing all these powerful people if you couldn't have a little fun with their position?

The constituency office was only one theatre of local operation for the member of Parliament. Shaughnessy was well aware that she had to be seen around Windsor, everywhere from a parade float to a local bar.

Though she was entitled to use the free hairdressing salon in the Parliament Buildings, Shaughnessy preferred to give her business to Windsor hairdresser Sue Ann Culver. There, comfortably ensconced on a Monday morning or Friday afternoon, Shaughnessy would settle into her chair and invite Culver's dog, Barney, a miniature dachshund, to snuggle under the smock with her.

On Saturday mornings, if she wasn't committed to a formal political event, Shaughnessy would decide whether she was going to do "regular groceries" or "working groceries." If she needed to stock up on supplies, she would pop down to the A&P store at the mall in Amherstburg and fill the grocery cart. If she opted for a working session, though, she would get dressed up, drive into Windsor, and float through the market and into the dozens of shops in her riding. This might turn into an all-day event, as she greeted acquaintances and allowed herself to be buttonholed by everyone who had a complaint to register with the local MP. Jerry would often come with Shaughnessy on these shopping trips and be a quiet support in her dealings with the voters.

Jerry came to share her political passions. He enjoyed spending a quiet Saturday morning with Shaughnessy, listening to *The House* on CBC Radio and hearing his wife's blow-by-blow commentary. Of course, this attachment to politics on the weekends didn't always make him happy. Sometimes Jerry would learn that Saturday mornings were spoken for, that Shaughn had agreed to stand in for Gray at some ribbon-cutting or speaking event in Windsor. Or he would plan for them to spend a night on the town and Shaughnessy, after a day of running around Windsor with Garry Fortune, would say that she was simply too tired of making small talk with people all day.

Jerry was, in many ways, a model political spouse. He supported Shaughn's aspirations entirely, and he would do anything – hammer signs in lawns, be an attentive audience for her stories – to support her work. He also accompanied her to many of the events that politicians must attend each weekend in their home ridings. He would stand off to the side and smile appreciatively as various groups performed dances or gave speeches. Jerry would be at Shaughn's side, sampling new ethnic cuisine or forcing down yet another barbecued hot dog at community events in Windsor.

When it came to meeting her constituents, Shaughnessy's favourite haunt was the Victoria Tavern. This was her real constituency office. The "Vic" is a drinking establishment that has been in operation since the 1890s. The Walkerville Exchange, as the original tavern was called, was intended to serve travellers using the Walkerville depot, a transfer point for passengers switching between local rail and stagecoach lines.

In the decade that followed the tavern's founding, the wooden structure was moved one lot south and a brick hotel was built on the original site, taking over its name and its custom. Here Henry Ford signed the papers that established his carmaking business in Windsor; here too Hiram Walker's employees would relax after work before making their way home to the community he'd built for his employees, called Walkerville.

One hundred years later, the bar's decor reflects all the decades it has seen. If Shaughnessy was furnishing her dream house, in fact, it might look a lot like the Vic. A gilt-framed portrait of Queen Victoria scowls over the patrons; the establishment took her name around 1930. A sturdy but elegant pine cabinet from the early years rests against one wall. Tall round tables covered in brown vinyl fill one corner; the rest of the room is crammed with the standard, bar-issue wooden chairs and tables. Hanging over Shaughnessy's favourite table, at the far end of the bar, a Victoria Tavern sign, in gothic script, is lit up in red neon. The clientele is a typical Windsor mix of businessmen with cellphones and blue-collar guys in jeans and baseball hats, all chatting at the bar and joking with the wait-resses, who banter with the customers like the best politicians in Ottawa.

On a typical Friday afternoon, Shaughnessy would wander into the bar, accompanied by Garry Fortune and a loose collection of friends who happened to be free and in the mood for a get-together. Shaughnessy would, as usual, be the centre of attention, bringing back all the news and gossip from the week in Ottawa. She didn't do all the talking, though – she was just as curious to know the news from Windsor, and she'd sit in rapt attention when anyone, at the table had a story to tell. She also gave her full concentration to anyone who wandered over with a problem to solve. These help-seekers were often dispatched to the table by the Vic's proprietor, Larry Burchell, who stood off to the side, an amused expression on his face, as he watched Shaughnessy practise her brand of personal politics in the warmth of the tavern.

One of the clients that Burchell referred to Shaughnessy was a man named Keith Kersey, an intense, ponytailed automobile designer who was a regular at the bar. Back in his wilder days as a teenager, Kersey had got on the wrong side of the law. He'd been in a fight and had hit a man with a baseball bat. The misdemean-our, combined with an incident at the border, had cost Kersey his mobility rights between Canada and the United States. Because of his criminal record, Kersey wasn't allowed to cross the border. For an automotive designer living in Windsor, this was an immense handicap. Though the big three auto companies all have a strong presence in Canada, the lion's share of research and development on new models is done in the United States, mainly in Detroit. Kersey could barely call himself an automotive designer if he was unable to cross the border. He had been trying for years to obtain a Queen's Pardon, but his case was hopelessly tangled in red tape.

One day, urged on by Burchell, Kersey approached Shaughnessy in the Victoria Tavern and laid out his problem. She was incredulous: "You mean you haven't been able to get it for all this time? And this is over something you did as a teenager?" Shaughnessy said. "Leave it with me."

Within three weeks, Kersey received his Queen's Pardon. Shaughnessy didn't call him to bray about her success or to demand thanks. His pardon arrived without fanfare, and it changed his life. The next time he saw her in the Vic, he tried to express his gratitude. Shaughnessy wouldn't allow it. "You don't have to thank me. That's my job."

Shaughnessy enjoyed the challenge of cutting through red tape and liked nothing better than dreaming up creative dodges around the normal obstacles of the bureaucracy. Early in her tenure, the town of Tecumseh was looking for infrastructure money to finance its new sportsplex. In its planning for the elaborate multimillion-dollar building, the municipality had come up $1 million short. The municipality was stuck, because it had promised the sportsplex would be built without a cent added to local taxes. The only solution was an infrastructure grant, under the much-ballyhooed Liberal program to upgrade roads, sewers, and transportation systems.

But strictly speaking, a sportsplex was not a "local improvement," according to the narrow criteria governing infrastructure money. Shaughnessy came up with an idea: separate out the expense of sewers, maintenance, and other servicing costs to the new arena, and these could be legitimately billed as "local improvements." The money came through, remarkably quickly.

Shaughnessy didn't forget her Windsor causes once she went to Ottawa. Father Paul Charbonneau, at Brentwood, said he didn't need to call his old friend twice: if he phoned her and asked for political help, she'd oblige. Nor did she abandon Hiatus House, using every opportunity to put the shelter on the national map. When women's issues came up in the Commons, the member from Windsor–St. Clair could be counted upon to sing the praises of Hiatus House into Hansard. When Sheila Finestone was the secretary of state for women's affairs, Shaughnessy lured her down to Windsor for a visit. Allan Rock also paid a call.

This boosterism worked both ways. Sometimes, at social events in Windsor, Donna Miller would hear people malign Shaughnessy – for her partisanship, for her achievements (or lack of them), or simply for her style. Donna had a stock answer: "Shaughnessy has been a terrific board member. She provided incredibly wonderful leadership when she was board president. She's been loyal to the organization and loyal to me personally."

Some MPs come to Ottawa with "pet projects," and if they end up on the backbench, these causes can sustain them in the chill outside of the cabinet. They may have no choice but to back the government's major measures, but on smaller issues – the workings of Parliament or matters closer to the everyday lives of their constituents – MPs can make a difference. Liberal MP Derek Lee wrote his manual on Parliament's rights to call for witnesses and evidence; Reg Alcock used his interest in information technology to study the way a new medium could change all kinds of messages in government. Lee argues that every MP should ideally have two pet projects – one that's focused on the constituency and one that's more national in scope – to ensure that their time in public office is well spent.

Early in his time in Ottawa, when he was much younger, Jean Chrétien had his own pet project – to change the name of Trans-Canada Airlines to Air Canada. "You have to have these projects, and you have to be flexible enough to have your projects adjust to the legislative priorities of the government," Chrétien says. "And sometimes to lose your idea to a minister who wants to incorporate it into the legislation."

This is precisely what happened to Roger Gallaway. Chrétien so liked one of his pet projects – a proposed bill that would ensure federal maintenance of prime-ministerial gravesites – that the prime minister made it a government priority and swept it right into law before Roger had a chance to take credit as its champion.

Gallaway is a dogged believer in independent projects for MPs, and at any moment he has several on the go. He put together a private member's crusade against the cable companies in 1996 in the wake of a storm of consumer protest about what was known as "negative-option billing" – charging customers for services unless they explicitly refuse them.

Though the Chrétien government appeared to be behind him in his efforts to halt this practice, the praise grew fainter as his bill came closer to passage in the House. The national unity issue had reared its head. The government came to realize that if non-Quebec customers could say no to French-language cable services, the goals of bilingual telecommunications could be jeopardized.

Much as she wanted to support her good pal Roger, Shaughnessy began to murmur that maybe he was charging a bit too bullishly into a sensitive area. She was swayed by the arguments of her cabinet friends, not the least of whom was Anne McLellan. Shaughnessy also became nervous when Gallaway went on a crusade for fathers' rights in child custody and access. He served as chair of a controversial committee that was often seen as antagonistic to women's concerns in matters of divorce. Donna Miller was on the phone to Shaughnessy frequently, imploring her, in the name of the women she knew at Hiatus House, to get Gallaway to tone down his public rhetoric. And when Gallaway, with his cable bill killed in the Senate, became an abolitionist on the subject of the red chamber, Shaughnessy was similarly uninterested.

"Stir it up" was one of her favourite phrases, but when it came to relations between the cabinet and MPs, she wanted relations stirred very gently, not shaken. She wasn't afraid of confrontation, but she knew confrontation could be counterproductive with cabinet ministers.

Shaughnessy didn't have pet projects of this kind, although she certainly had causes that captured her commitment and she had enthusiasms. At different times she would focus her energy on issues such as turbans at the Legion, Canada's role in the space program, or the fate of lab monkeys at Health Canada. At others, she was determined to see and learn as much as she could of the wider world.

Mindful that the Canadian public had soured on the idea of perks for politicians, Shaughnessy nonetheless was eager to take advantage of the various foreign trips that MPs are offered. All kinds of travel assignments are available to MPs. Sometimes they are intended as educational – parliamentarians examining budgetary reform, for instance, might head to New Zealand to see how that country had privatized its way out of near bankruptcy. Sometimes they are intended as consolation prizes – MPs who don't get their way, who threaten to vote against government policy, or who have their ambitions thwarted in some fashion can find themselves offered a trip to a convention in an exotic locale.

Shaughnessy was on the lookout for ways to go abroad, even though her close friends warned her that she should be careful about accepting them in exchange for real influence in the caucus. Shaughnessy listened, but she argued that she had come to Ottawa to take every opportunity she could as a parliamentarian to expand her world view. She jokingly referred to Lloyd Axworthy as her "travel agent" when he became foreign affairs minister in 1996; she intended to lobby him for assignments abroad when they arose.

In her five years in Ottawa, Shaughnessy did get around, travelling to Copenhagen, Papua New Guinea, the Middle East (on more than one occasion), and Thailand. She especially loved travel in the government's Challenger jets. John Manley won her enduring friendship by being the first to let her ride with him on the Challenger in 1994.

Shaughnessy rarely got into trouble for her foreign forays, even though she was shameless in demanding them as rewards for loyalty or hard work. The bonus was that she returned to Canada with a whole raft of funny stories about this innocent abroad.

In January 1996, for instance, Roger Gallaway and Shaughnessy headed off to the West Bank to serve as election observers in the first Palestinian elections. Their friends back home received regular telephone bulletins about their Middle East adventures: their accidental wanderings into dangerous, restricted areas, the exotic headgear they were wearing. At the same time they were honoured – this was a historic chance to witness democracy in its infancy.

Shaughnessy collected new buddies wherever she went. Roger and Shaughnessy joined separate delegations on the West Bank trip, and when they returned, Shaughnessy kept insisting that she had made some "very, very important" friends on her election observation mission. Lord Allenby, descendant of the First World War hero Edmund Allenby, who captured large swaths of the Middle East for Britain, was one. Shaughn and Allenby, she said, twining her first two fingers, were "just like this." Shortly before they returned to Canada, Shaughnessy and Roger went into one of the fancier restaurants in Jerusalem, where tables were at a premium. "Oh look," she said to Roger. "There's my friend Lord Allenby." When the restaurateur told them the establishment was completely full, Shaughnessy said, "Oh, are you sure? We're friends of Lord Allenby." She waved to her famous friend's table and was rewarded with a beckoning gesture. Within seconds, a table had miraculously appeared for the "very good friends of Lord Allenby."

On a couple of occasions, Shaughnessy took along family members on her foreign trips at her own expense. Her mother accompanied her to Papua New Guinea in 1995, and she took Jerry with her to Asia in the summer of 1998. Jerry also joined her in Jerusalem and in Florida for the space shuttle launches. In August 1995, Jerry and Shaughn were introduced to Dan Golden, the head of the National Aeronautics and Space Administration. She boasted about Jerry's work back in Windsor, especially his cognition work with animals, and Jerry was given a tour of the lab-animal facilities at NASA. (Shaughnessy was intent on setting up a "space cadets caucus" of MPs who shared her passion about space exploration. She wanted to set up a delegation to tour the Canadian space research facilities in St. Hubert, Quebec.)

More seriously, Shaughnessy believed that foreign and domestic issues were strongly linked, and her job as an MP was to understand both. That view was shared by some of her closest colleagues in the

Liberal caucus. Anyone who wants to understand domestic issues in Canada in this day and age must understand the international context, says Toronto MP Bill Graham, who served as chair of the Commons Foreign Affairs Committee.

"There's a blurring," Graham says. "You can't deal with domestic issues any more unless you have a handle on the international situation."

Shaughnessy, like Graham, was one of the MPs who enjoyed good relations with many of the foreign envoys in Ottawa, especially those from the two countries closest to her heart: the United States and Ireland. First with U.S. ambassador James Blanchard and then with his successor, Gordon Giffin, Shaughnessy established herself as a link between the embassy and Liberal parliamentarians.

Giffin's first encounter with Shaughnessy was at a function at the embassy, when she walked right up to him and explained immodestly that she had appointed herself the MP who handled Canada-U.S. relations within the caucus. Though there is no such official position, Shaughnessy seemed well suited for it, unofficially. Giffin was impressed with her flair and her confidence, but it wasn't until a couple of weeks later, at one of those normally stodgy diplomatic dinners, that he fully appreciated the magnitude of Shaughnessy's charm.

Sergio Marchi, by then the international trade minister, was hosting a dinner in honour of Mac MacLarty, then the special counsel to U.S. President Bill Clinton and special envoy for the Americas. Mary and Shaughnessy launched into their routine that evening — the usual round of barbs at each other and standard heckling of cabinet ministers, this time of Marchi.

"It wasn't a typical staid diplomatic evening. It was fun. It was actually like being at an Irish pub all night," Giffin said. "I was sitting in this dining room at Foreign Affairs having a wonderful time. And not engaging in a lot of substantive dialogue."

A lot of people an ambassador meets can be the life of the party, Giffin said, but Shaughnessy combined that social skill with a sharp intellect.

"Often Shaughnessy was a supporter of policies that the United States was interested in, but plenty of times she was quite direct in her ability to let me know when there was a Canadian interest at heart: what the Canadian interest was and how it was either consistent or inconsistent with what we were doing and how we had to get it right," he said. One such issue was the Canada-U.S. dust-up over magazines. Canada was trying to protect its industry with strict limits on content and advertising in U.S. magazines sold in Canada. Shaughnessy bluntly informed Giffin that Canadian magazines needed special protection from the glut of American periodicals filling the shelves in the stores.

A highlight of her experience in Canada-U.S. relations was President Clinton's visit to Ottawa on February 23, 1995. The president was to meet members of Parliament after addressing the House and Senate. Shaughnessy was beside herself with excitement. She and Mary made their way up to Parliament Hill the morning he was scheduled to arrive, only to find the place ringed with humourless security guards. One of these officers made the mistake of trying to keep Mary and Shaughnessy behind the security line.

"We're members of Parliament!" Mary haughtily proclaimed, pushing the man aside before he had a chance to protest. As Shaughnessy followed behind, she sheepishly looked over her shoulder at the security guard and said: "Don't you know who we think we are?"

Inside, Shaughn and Mary took their places in the reception line. As the president made his way to Mary and was introduced, Clinton, ever the charmer, praised Mary on her Halifax hometown and said he was looking forward to the forthcoming G-7 summit to be held there in June 1996. Then he moved to Shaughnessy and warmly shook her hand.

Staring at his retreating back, a lovestruck grin on her face, Shaughnessy turned to Mary and said: "I just had sex with Bill Clinton."

"No," Mary corrected her. "If he had sex with anybody, it was me. It's just been so long that that's what you think sex is."

"Well," huffed Shaughnessy. "At least I once knew what it was. That's the closest you've ever come to sex."

Like successive American ambassadors, Paul Dempsey, the Irish ambassador, also revelled in Shaughnessy's sparkle and intelligence. He forged a bond with Shaughnessy almost immediately upon his arrival in Canada in 1995, when he found himself scrambling to organize a visit of the Irish prime minister. Shaughnessy, in Mary's absence, was acting as the head of the Canada-Irish Relations Committee within the Liberal caucus and was only too happy to help introduce Dempsey to the folks he needed to know in the Liberal ranks, elected and otherwise. He came to rely on Shaughnessy to alert him to political sensitivities on certain issues, and as a lawyer himself, Dempsey could spend hours with her discussing the differences between the legal systems in Canada and Ireland.

The magic of Shaughnessy's enthusiasms, said John Manley, was that they extended so far beyond her official or riding responsibilities. "Being an MP is like being at one of these giant buffet tables. Everything looks interesting and you take a plate; the plate's too small and you just put a little bit of everything on it." As a result, rookie politicians tend to become overwhelmed.

Not Shaughnessy, he said. She somehow managed to take a larger interest in everything. The monkeys at Health Canada's labs were one of Shaughn's most intense concerns, though she kept that project more to herself. "I don't think I should be going around talking about this too much. People will think I'm a flake, don't you think?" she'd ask close friends.

Part of her interest in the well-being of laboratory animals was fuelled by Jerry's work at the University of Windsor. Through Jerry, Shaughnessy had been able to meet some of the leading scientists in the field of animal behaviour and intelligence.

Starting in 1995, Shaughnessy became fixated on the idea of inspecting Health Canada's Ottawa labs, where polio vaccine was being tested on a group of primates. She pestered Diane Marleau, then health minister, until she got approval to do the tour. She had Sandra Leffler make arrangements for her to get the proper vaccinations she'd need to enter the lab. At the last minute, though, she lost her nerve.

"If it's bad, I don't think I can see them," Shaughnessy said. "I just don't think I can take it." Instead, she decided to work more quietly behind the scenes. Her interest didn't flag over the years. In June 1998, she was peppering the health minister's office with questions about the treatment of laboratory animals. She drafted a 15-question letter to Allan Rock that month, probing for answers on everything from the type of species in the labs to how the department defined "ethics" and "care" surrounding their treatment.

Shaughnessy's skills as a lobbyist with cabinet ministers were becoming legendary as the Chrétien government went into its third year of rule. It was more than her unflagging loyalty, in the eyes of her cabinet colleagues. It was her expertise in empathy – at being able to climb into the shoes of a cabinet minister and see an issue through his or her eyes. Shaughnessy was a master at this, said John Manley, describing his idea of a good lobbyist-MP.

"I find the most effective ones are the ones that can understand the issue and understand what they need. They appreciate that there's got to be compromise," said Manley. "It's very rare that you have an issue that is black and white, win/lose, zero sum. Usually there's room to give and take. The most effective ones for me, at least, are the ones who can sit on my side of the desk and understand that I have to please more interests than one."

But Shaughnessy was still toiling in the background halfway through the first term of Prime Minister Jean Chrétien's government, despite all her good work on gun control and in keeping the peace for cabinet ministers. She hoped, as summer turned to fall in 1995, that things would start to change for her.

11

The Powerful and Influential

When Parliament returned in the fall of 1995 the Liberals focused on closing the wounds of earlier months. February's radical budget cuts and June's gun control legislation had left a ragged tear in the fabric of Liberal caucus solidarity, with right against left, urban against rural, and the centre against the regions. Though caucus rifts are hardly unusual, this Liberal caucus had a habit of making its squabbles all too public. In the latter part of 1995, Chrétien intended to keep these differences within the walls of the caucus room as much as possible. He and his deputies would accomplish it with a combination of carrots and sticks.

First came the sticks. Back on the Hill in September, several MPs found themselves shuffled out of their previous jobs. Montreal MP and former cabinet minister Warren Allmand was dumped as chair of the Justice Committee as punishment for voting against the February budget. Derek Lee was off the Justice Committee altogether. Though no one told him directly why, he attributed it to those tense days in the spring when he had seen the darker side of Allan Rock. "There was no doubt that I'd been punished," Lee said.

The MP for Windsor–St. Clair approached the new session with justifiable expectations. Committee jobs were being shuffled and for Shaughnessy – whose loyal service to the cabinet had been widely acknowledged – change very definitely promised opportunity. It was a shock then to discover, just before the first caucus meeting of the session, that she had been dealt an apparent demotion in the Commons.

To those watching parliamentary proceedings at home, one seat in the Commons looks much like any other. But for the denizens of the chamber, where you sit is just as important as where you stand – in the hierarchy, that is. Reform Party leader Preston Manning had tried to resist the traditional seating arrangements and had placed himself in the second row, rather than the first, of his caucus. But soon he abandoned the innovation and put himself back in the usual spot for the third-party leader – in the front row facing the Liberals at the far end of the House.

The Liberals organized their seat allocations according to a complicated formula that recognized seniority, position, and that indisputable standby alphabetical order. The prime minister sat in the middle of the front row, where all prime ministers have sat, and the cabinet was arrayed around him. His parliamentary secretary was placed behind him: Jean Augustine for the first two years and Rey Paghtakan for the second two years. (Though it would be cynical to suggest that these parliamentary secretary assignments were mere tokenism for the sake of the cameras, it was nevertheless a happy circumstance that the television frame of Chrétien in the Commons included either a black woman or a Filipino man in the first term.)

By virtue of the early occurrence in the alphabet of her last name, Shaughnessy had a relatively good seat on the government side of the House during the first two years. She sat across from the Reform Party in a prime heckling position and frequently used it to excellent effect to launch caustic barbs and off-the-cuff speech-lets across the floor.

Reform MP Herb Grubel was a frequent target. In the midst of one of his long-winded economic lectures to the Liberals in March 1995, Shaughnessy interrupted him: "Canadians want the deficit handled," she said. "We are doing that. We are taking a little longer than Reform would because we do not want babies to starve in the street, we do not want children to miss their education, and we do not want old people to not have income support. Hello, Earth to Reform: This is the real world over here."

Shaughnessy looked forward to more of the same. Just before the women's caucus met for the first time in September, she and fellow Ontario MP Brenda Chamberlain stopped by the chamber to look for their new seats. All the seats of the MPs in the class of 1993 had been rearranged. Now it was the MPs with last names in the second half of the alphabet who sat directly behind cabinet members. Mary remained on the government side of the House, thanks to her status as a parliamentary secretary and one of the class of 1988. Unlucky MPs such as Shaughnessy had been moved over to what was called the "rump" – the overflow section on the opposition side of the House. There were so many Liberals elected in 1993 that they couldn't all be accommodated on the government side.

As Brenda watched, Shaughnessy gazed incredulously at her name emblazoned on the side of the desk in the rump. Without warning, she burst into tears.

"Why?" she wailed. "Why did I get put over here?" It was impossible for her to see it as anything other than a slight, despite the logic of seniority and alphabetical order.

Before the Liberals could fully restore unity in the caucus, they found themselves drawn into a much larger unity debate, one involving the whole country. Quebec Premier Jacques Parizeau was preparing for a provincial referendum on sovereignty – an event that would severely test Jean Chrétien's don't-worry-be-happy approach to governance. Chrétien was accused of being too tough on his Liberal colleagues but not tough enough on the separatists. And if there was a federal strategy – many suspected there wasn't – it was not being shared with Liberal MPs, especially those from outside Quebec.

Non-Quebec backbenchers, such as Shaughnessy, were told that this was not their fight; they were to remain spectators. No official trips to Quebec; no statements to the media. At one meeting of political aides that fall, the Liberal whip's office instructed all assistants to phone in and report on their bosses if they heard of any unauthorized activity by MPs on the national unity front. The federal response to this referendum would be strictly controlled by the Prime Minister's Office and the Privy Council Office. Coming on the heels of disciplinary moves in the caucus, this directive prompted several MPs, especially from Ontario, to grumble about being treated like trained seals or decorative props.

They were told that while the referendum campaign was under way, the show must go on in Ottawa, albeit as quietly and as uncontroversially as possible. This meant that days in the chamber were taken up with such weighty matters as Bill C-93, the Cultural Property Export and Import Act. Liberal MPs were instructed to just keep talking, to keep the parliamentary machine running, to maintain the impression that the nation's business was being carried on as usual. A strict schedule of speakers was drawn up. One day, with just half an hour left before Question Period, Ottawa Centre MP Mac Harb unexpectedly cut short his speaking duty by 20 minutes. Peter Milliken, the parliamentary secretary to the government House leader, was eating lunch in the lobby and had to rush back to fill the empty time. He barely knew what was in Bill C-93, except that it had something to do with culture. Still swallowing the last bites of lunch, he began to hold forth, delivering every cultural tidbit that came into his head. Helpful colleagues pushed bits of paper in front of him, possible topics to keep his monologue going. He rambled on about the arts, he took pokes at the Reform Party, and he even reminisced about his summer vacation.

"My honourable friend for Ottawa Centre will appreciate that I had occasion to go to Alberta in July of this year. One place I visited was the Tyrrell Museum in Drumheller. There are a lot of dinosaurs in that museum and I can say that the resemblance between some of the dinosaurs there and members of the Reform Party was absolutely striking. I could tell where their ancestors came from," Milliken said.

MP Marlene Catterall scribbled a note: "You can sit down soon. Shaughnessy will ask you a question." Milliken wrapped up his remarks, collapsed back into his seat, and exhaled. The Speaker recognized the member for Windsor–St. Clair, beaming with the chance to provide relief, of the comic sort.

"Mr. Speaker, if in two years or so some Liberals, perhaps under the leadership of the prime minister, were to travel to [Alberta's] Wild Rose Country, where there have been some sightings of dinosaurs, and sneak up behind a couple of them and knock them off and then try to donate them to a museum, how would this act work to allow us to have a tax credit for knocking off dinosaurs in Wild Rose Country?" Even some Reformers burst out laughing along with the Liberals.

The Quebec referendum was not a matter for levity, however. Shaughn took seriously the prospect of a separatist victory on October 30, which, by mid-month, seemed possible, even probable. Many Liberals were uncomfortable with the government's low-key strategy and believed that voices outside Quebec needed to be heard. When Fisheries Minister Brian Tobin proposed a huge rally in Montreal in support of the No forces, a demonstration to be attended by Canadians from all parts of the country, Shaughn was immediately on the phone to Windsor, urging Jerry to help organize a delegation from her hometown.

Jerry made his way to Ottawa on the eve of the event, set for October 27. Shaughnessy, Jerry, Mary, and their friend Barry Campbell, a Toronto MP, packed themselves into Anne's limousine, along with her driver, Ray Patenaude, and set out for Montreal. They checked into a hotel near Dorval Airport which was, as Mary said, "straight out of a Stephen King novel." Shaughnessy, never completely at ease in the dark, kept phoning Mary to report on how black her room was.

In the morning the group joined a sea of buses from outside

Quebec; thousands had come for the rally. The MPs split up to join the contingents from their respective hometowns and provinces, but Mary fretted that they wouldn't be able to link up again to get home. Shaughnessy, by now in her Windsor bus, yelled to Mary to calm down: "Oh, for God's sake! If you're breathing in the city of Montreal I'll find you!"

Sure enough, even in that mob of 150,000 people waving flags in the streets of Montreal, Shaughn and Mary found each other after the rally. They hopped on a bus carrying the folks from Nova Scotia and pulled Shirley Maheu, Mary's roommate, on board as well.

Maheu, a Montrealer, was hitching a ride as far as the intersection where she was to meet her husband. As they neared the corner, the bus didn't seem to be stopping. Maheu's voice rose, ordering the driver to stop immediately. The brakes screeched and the bus came to an abrupt halt. Maheu jumped out and was nearly run over by an oncoming car, which was emblazoned with a sovereigntist Yes sign.

Whether this last-minute show of emotion worked for the federalist side would be debated in the weeks ahead. What Shaughnessy and her fellow Liberals did know was that the tight referendum result — a narrow federalist victory with just 50.6 per cent of the vote — was far too close for comfort. Nor was the national unity issue laid to rest with the outcome.

The referendum planted a perception of the Chrétien government as out of touch with the reality of Quebec. Chrétien's next move made Canadians wonder whether his Liberals were disconnected from the rest of the country too. Too hastily in the wake of the referendum, the government introduced legislation to "share" Ottawa's constitutional veto with four regions of the country: the West, the Atlantic, Ontario, and Quebec. The failure to recognize that British Columbia had evolved into a separate region over the past 20 years prompted a huge outcry. Chrétien amended the bill, but the lingering image was of a government insulated and insensitive. Word spread quietly that Chrétien would shake up his caucus and shuffle his cabinet, preparing his troops for battle well in advance of the next referendum in Quebec, whenever it might come.

The new roster was announced in January 1996. Some of the changes were inevitable; others were brutal. Chrétien made clear his intention to dispense with several ministers who were not expected to run again for office. Trade Minister Roy MacLaren was ejected from the cabinet but enjoyed a safe landing as Canada's high commissioner to Britain. Foreign Affairs Minister André Ouellet was gone too, given the job as chairman of Canada Post. Heritage Minister Michel Dupuy, who had embarrassed the government with a conflict-of-interest controversy over a letter he wrote to the Canadian Radio-television and Telecommunications Commission, was also sent to the backbench.

But the biggest news of this shuffle was the instant elevation to the cabinet of two newcomers: the veteran Quebec Liberal Pierre Pettigrew and the federalist academic Stéphane Dion. To make room for these Quebec "stars," Chrétien chose to shunt aside two women – both of whom were close to Shaughnessy.

Shirley Maheu was going to the Senate, vacating her safe seat in Montreal, Saint-Laurent, so that Dion could take her place. She was content with the move, grateful that at age 67 she at least had an income. Sheila Finestone was far less contented. The woman who had succeeded Pierre Trudeau in the riding of Mount Royal in 1984 was secretary of state for women's affairs. She was never asked whether she intended to run again. She was simply told that her services were no longer required in the ministry. The demotion of Finestone, at age 69, served two purposes: it helped Chrétien put a younger face on his Quebec cabinet representation, and it cleared the way for Hedy Fry, born in Trinidad and a British Columbia MP, to take her place. Finestone understood, but she was crushed.

Shortly after the cabinet shuffle, the Liberal caucus met in Vancouver – another gesture to soothe British Columbia tempers – in the last week of January to continue plotting post-referendum strategy. Finestone walked into the Hotel Vancouver with her head held high, though she remained hurt and upset by the ejection from cabinet. The first person she saw in the meeting hall was Shaughnessy, who walked up to her and wordlessly swept her up in a bear hug.

"No tears," Finestone said, as much to herself as to Shaughnessy.

"Damn right, no tears," Shaughnessy said. "What's there to cry about?"

From that moment, Shaughnessy and Sheila Finestone became close friends, each acting as a sympathetic check on the personality quirks of the other. Shaughnessy would try to humour Finestone, encouraging her to look at the world less seriously. Finestone would do the reverse for Shaughnessy, drawing out the more gentle, contemplative side that the Windsor MP hid so well behind a thick-skinned demeanour.

A certain amount of armour is essential to the politician's wardrobe, but Shaughnessy never adopted the mien of self-importance worn by so many Ottawa egos. "She took her job seriously, but not herself," Roger Gallaway said. She was contemptuous of colleagues who demanded deference from their staffs or from fellow MPs. The only time she delighted in flaunting her MP's status was when she felt someone was getting pompous with her. She once sat silently stewing while a belligerent Customs agent gave her a hard time after a brief trip across the border to Detroit for lunch. She allowed the agent to search her car and speak condescendingly to her, waiting for the moment when he would ask for identification. The demand came. Shaughnessy flashed her green passport.

"What's this?" the agent asked.

"That's my passport. I'm a member of Parliament and I'll be only too happy to talk to my friends in Ottawa about your manners," she said. Before the agent could reply, Shaughnessy gunned her engine and took off. Did that agent not know who she thought she was?

It was one thing for Shaughnessy to take herself lightly, but quite another matter if she heard anyone describe her colleagues as nobodies. Shaughnessy talked up her friends – they were all very, very important – and she could not bear insults to them.

In December 1995, during the avalanche of post-referendum advice to the prime minister, the *Globe and Mail* columnist Jeffrey Simpson urged Chrétien to reinvigorate the Liberal benches. He offered a few suggestions on who should be put out to pasture, dismissing Shirley Maheu as an "obscure backbencher." As it turned out, the prime minister seemed to agree with him. But when Shaughnessy read the column, she was livid.

That night, back in Windsor, she was at Brigantino's with a group of police officers whom she had known from her days in the courts. After several glasses of wine, Shaughnessy decided to give Jeffrey Simpson a piece of her mind. She called his number at the *Globe*'s Ottawa bureau and got his answering machine. She unloaded all her anger. How could he know Shirley Maheu's value, she said, when he'd never made an attempt to meet anyone in the Liberal caucus? "None of my Liberal colleagues know you either!" she barked into the recorder.

The next day, a Saturday, Shaughnessy cringed at the memory of her rant. She phoned another reporter at the *Globe* and asked: "Hypothetically speaking... say a certain member of Parliament was out drinking last night and in a moment of weakness decided to leave a message on Jeffrey Simpson's answering machine? Hypothetically speaking, could another member of the *Globe* bureau get into his phone and erase the message?"

Told that was impossible and also unethical, Shaughnessy resigned herself to the humiliation. "Oh well," she said. "I guess Jeffrey will be calling me a nobody next."

On Monday, back in Ottawa, a practical joke on Shaughnessy took shape. The *Globe*'s Hugh Winsor, discreetly briefed on Shaughnessy's angry Friday-night phone call, telephoned her office while she was in the House and pretended to be Simpson, "returning her call." Within five minutes, Shaughn was on the phone to the *Globe* reporter she had called on Saturday, asking for advice. "Never mind," she said, "I'll just brazen it out."

She telephoned the number Hugh Winsor had left. "Jeffrey Simpson speaking," Winsor answered. Shaughnessy had assembled a group of her MP pals in the Commons lobby to watch her "give Simpson shit" for his treatment of Shirley Maheu. It wasn't particularly brave, but it was brazen, as promised. She launched into a long explanation of why she'd made the call, how she didn't think the column was fair, and so on. Winsor interrupted her: "Yes, yes, that's fine. But who are you anyway?"

Shaughnessy exploded, shouting that Simpson knew very well who she was; she was the member of Parliament for Windsor–St. Clair and he had visited her campaign office back in 1988! Hearing Winsor laughing, she suddenly realized she'd been had.

"Got me," she confessed.

The coda to this story, which Shaughnessy never knew, was that her phone message to Jeffrey Simpson had not reached its target. After a few words of introduction, the machine cut out, so all Simpson heard on Monday was: "This is Shaughnessy Cohen..." The diatribe went unrecorded. For the rest of her life, though, she was convinced that every time he saw her, Simpson was too polite to mention the intemperate outburst she had left on his answering machine that night.

Shaughnessy's favourite place in Ottawa may well have been the couch in the Commons lobby where she unwittingly gathered her friends to witness her comeuppance at Winsor's hands. A green, floral three-seater, it was positioned against the wall near the entrance to the lobby, just beyond the point where elected members only are allowed. The lobbies are directly behind the green curtains in the Commons, beyond the reach of the media and the public. Political aides may linger around the tables immediately at the door but may not go all the way in.

"It was where Shaughn held court," said Paul Martin. "You would walk into that lobby, and there would be Anne, cramming for Question Period," Martin said. "You'd run smack into Mary, who would insist on being heard. But then, all of a sudden, the court opened up and there was Shaughn. You wouldn't be asked to stop – you'd be summoned. And standing off, watching and enjoying it with a bemused look on his face, was Roger."

Shaughnessy still held out hope for some kind of fresh start for herself in the second session. She was eager to get away from the Human Resources Committee, now that Lloyd Axworthy had gone on to better things at Foreign Affairs. She made it known to her regional boss, Herb Gray, that she was looking for a challenge.

Jerry Yanover, Gray's trusted adviser, had travelled to Windsor a few months earlier at Shaughnessy's invitation to attend a baseball game at Detroit's Tiger Stadium. His favourite team, the Cleveland Indians, was playing against the hometown Tigers, and he joined Shaughnessy, Jerry, Brad Robitaille, and Brian Ducharme.

Shaughnessy had pestered Yanover all day about committee assignments and how she wanted off the Human Resources Committee. Meanwhile, down on the field, the Tigers began to pull ahead of the Indians. Shaughnessy couldn't resist teasing Yanover, gloating over the score and telling him how much better the Tigers really were.

Yanover, deadpan, came back with: "Shaughn, you know Ted McWhinney really wants out of the chair of the Library of Parliament Committee." Edward McWhinney, the member for Vancouver Quadra, was a distinguished former professor of law, who spoke with a professorial mid-Atlantic accent. He had a mastery of historical detail and research, an almost apolitical approach to public life, and, truth to tell, a healthy measure of self-esteem. Shaughnessy was a very different character type, to say the least. Her famous dislike for detail would have made her a disaster at the Library of Parliament Committee, where McWhinney thrived. Shaughnessy said no more about the Cleveland Indians.

In fact, Yanover was one of a number of people in Herb Gray's office who thought Shaughnessy had earned a promotion. Doug Kirkpatrick, Gray's executive assistant, recalling her yeoman service containing the National Security Subcommittee, believed she was ready to move up from follower to leader. He put Shaughnessy's name before the whip's office as a candidate for chair of the Justice Committee, provided all the usual criteria for representation by seniority, gender, region, and talents were met.

It was Justice Minister Allan Rock, though, who mounted the most vigorous campaign to place Shaughnessy at the helm of the Justice Committee. "Shaughnessy was extremely talented politically," Rock said. "She could handle the Reform. She was very capable in the cut and thrust, and she could identify where consensus could be reached."

As the rumour mill started to buzz about the changes in committee assignments, Shaughnessy suspected that something good was coming her way. She and Mary spent hours dissecting every possible move that could be made – who would get what. For her part, Mary did not want to change jobs. She had been parliamentary secretary to Sergio Marchi when he was immigration minister, and unless she could be in the cabinet, Mary wanted to remain a parliamentary secretary. A PS job can be wonderful or dreadful depending on how much the minister is willing to delegate to the backup MP. Marchi had been generous, and she loved the opportunities that had been offered to her in that role. By contrast, the prospect of a committee chair seemed dull and workmanlike, not to mention less attractive financially. Parliamentary secretaries are paid an extra $10,000 a year and are given additional staff. Committee chairs receive no such perks. Mary was lobbying furiously to stay a PS, moving portfolios if necessary. But that prospect seemed unlikely, given Chrétien's desire to give MPs as much and as varied responsibilities as possible. (Indeed, she ended up chairing the Defence Committee, without much pleasure.)

For all the hours of speculation she shared with Mary, Shaughnessy didn't have an inkling of what awaited her. She dared to hope that she might sit on one of the larger committees, such as the Finance Committee. A seat there would put her closer to Martin and expand her knowledge in an area where she was weak.

The call from the whip's office finally came one evening when she was about to leave for the National Press Club. She could hardly believe what she was told: not only was she a member of the coveted Justice Committee, she was its chair-elect! Shaughnessy tore out of her office and almost ran across the street to the press club.

"Oh my God!" she said, twirling down the hallway of the National Press Building. "Can't you just see it in the newspapers? Shaughnessy Cohen, chair of the Justice Committee of the House of Commons! I love it."

Celebrating at the bar with a half-dozen or so journalists, Shaughnessy could not suppress her delight. "Yes, that's me, Shaughnessy Cohen, chair of the Justice Committee – chair of the powerful and influential Justice Committee of the House of Commons!"

The appointment was formalized at the first committee meeting in the second session of the 35th Parliament, in March 1996. More than a step in Shaughnessy's career, the moment represented a bit of history for women in the Canadian Parliament. When Shaughnessy was named to the chair's post, two vice-chairs were also named: Pierrette Venne of the Bloc Québécois, a well-regarded lawyer who had won Shaughn's respect for her hard work, and Burlington MP Paddy Torsney. It was the first time that a Commons committee would be headed entirely by women.

Ironically, the first report that Shaughnessy tabled in the Commons was the National Security Subcommittee report, the same report she had worked so hard to obstruct and frustrate in the first session. An initial report had been issued several months earlier, but it avoided the heart of the controversy, limiting itself to some recommendations about the disorder of documents in the solicitor general's office at the end of the Mulroney mandate and the need for more vigilant attention to the security of those documents. The report that Shaughnessy tabled was the second, more substantial one, dealing with the matter of CSIS infiltration into white-supremacist groups.

Led by Derek Lee, the subcommittee made two recommendations: the first proposed clearer instructions to CSIS about the use of "human sources" and a prohibition on illegal or discreditable activities by those sources; the second proposed that a procedure be developed to allow CSIS to advise third parties that they were the objects of threats or attempts at infiltration.

Just as Herb Gray and his advisers had hoped, the report

garnered almost no attention from the media. The "spy scandal," such as it was, had died long ago. Lee was happy that the committee had been able to question individuals such as former justice minister Doug Lewis, although the inquiry was held in camera. This had been Lee's major preoccupation from the start: the right of parliamentarians to conduct their own investigations and inquiries. He was satisfied. Gray was pleased that the committee had chosen not to challenge the authority of the Security Intelligence Review Committee, which still had ultimate responsibility to report on the dealings of CSIS.

All in all, a harmonious debut for the new chair of the Justice Committee. In fact, this period around the midpoint of the Chrétien government's first term was the happiest for Shaughnessy as an elected MP. Thanks to her new responsibilities, she was beginning to be seen as a serious parliamentarian. Commons clerks who had observed Shaughnessy's diffidence on the Human Resources Committee couldn't believe the change in her style. Using those skills she had honed on the board at Hiatus House and the Health Protection Appeal Board, she comfortably slipped into the seat of authority. Leadership became her.

A strong friendship gradually developed between Shaughnessy and her committee vice-chair, Paddy Torsney. Initially, the two women had regarded each other warily; the competition to chair the women's caucus hadn't helped. Torsney found Shaughnessy's antics excessive; Shaughnessy described Torsney as "a bit young."

Though the two women had similar backgrounds – girls' school, Irish Catholic, southern Ontario – more than 15 years separated them in age and their styles were markedly different. They first met at an Ontario candidates' gathering with Chrétien in the spring of 1993 and were seated beside each other on the bus. Willowdale MP Jim Peterson was also on board, a man known to both of them. Torsney's interest in politics began when she worked as a secretary in Premier David Peterson's office. She knew Jim as the brother of her former boss. Shaughnessy met Jim when the two of them were helping out in the ill-fated 1990 provincial campaign.

She had endeared herself to the premier's brother with her fla-
grantly off-colour humour. Their running joke was that she would
perform sexual favours in return for lawn signs. Torsney's eyes
almost popped out of her head when she heard Shaughnessy loudly
braying to Peterson about that canvassing trip.

But the age gap between the two women turned out to be
their meeting point. Shaughnessy was at her best as a mentor or
sponsor to young people, especially young women. Torsney became
one of the many who appreciated Shaughnessy as a friend and
counsellor. During committee meetings, for instance, Shaughnessy
the lawyer would often spot legal holes in witnesses' arguments and
discreetly alert Torsney so that the younger MP would have a
chance to shine in open debate.

Other people who worked closely with Shaughnessy in her
role as committee chair also learned to see past her reputation for
outrageousness. Phil Rosen, the Library of Parliament researcher
who worked with her first on the National Security Subcommittee, marvelled at the way she could listen to witnesses' testimony and have fun at the same time. She would send furiously
scribbled notes to Rosen and selected others around the table,
apparently consulting with colleagues. The messages would say
something like: "Have you noticed the witness is not wearing any
socks?" Yet when it came time to question that same witness,
Shaughnessy's queries would invariably be pointed and serious.

Veteran observers of the parliamentary scene took a new interest in the member from Windsor–St. Clair. Jerry Yanover, who had
seen politicians come and go for two decades before he met
Shaughnessy, came to count on her unfailing ability to deliver committee business on time. It is the rare committee chair, he said, who
takes the trouble before embarking on an issue to sit down with the
department and the government personnel involved and manage
the work around their schedules. "Shaughn was very astute," he
said. "She looked for open channels."

That assessment was shared by Peter Dobell, of the Parliamentary
Centre, an Ottawa think tank that pays close attention to the effec-

tiveness of MPs. Dobell warned that MPs are often measured by the yardsticks of the public service – in other words, by their ability to put things on paper and to operate within rigid hierarchies. The MP works in a different culture, he remarked – one where the tradition is oral and where hierarchies count for less. By Dobell's standards, Shaughnessy excelled. She had mastered the art of telephone networking and she acknowledged no hierarchical authority. She was loyal to the cabinet ministers who had won her respect, but she regarded ministers, backbenchers, and staff as equally entitled to that respect.

This new-model Shaughnessy was so at odds with her life-of-the-party reputation that many people, watching at a distance, were perplexed. Was this the same woman? Yes, it was, but with rising esteem came the confidence to show her serious side, to leave behind the exhibitionist tricks that had won her membership in the boys' club.

Her partisanship, however, would never soften. In the early days of her time as chair of the Justice Committee, Shaughnessy's chief rival was the Reform committee member Jack Ramsay. She regarded his views of crime and punishment as old-fashioned, harsh, and intolerant, and she was not subtle about her disdain. Ramsay found Shaughnessy too partisan, too abrupt, even rude.

The breaking point came in early November 1996, after a series of intense wrangles between the Liberals and the Reform Party over the future of hearings on the Young Offenders Act. The youth justice issue had been at the centre of the committee's studies since Shaughnessy had taken the chair, and the MPs had travelled across Canada during the spring and fall. The tension between Shaughnessy and Ramsay was always present, sometimes showing up in curt rejoinders in committee, sometimes taking on almost farcical proportions outside the hearings.

On one occasion the committee was scheduled to hear testimony in Montreal, then fly to Iqaluit. After a late night in Montreal, during which Shaughnessy seriously overindulged, she boarded the airporter bus the next morning with an unsettled stomach. Ramsay was seated in the row ahead of her when the inevitable happened; the bottom of his pants bore the evidence. The episode became one of her favourite stories: "Did I ever tell you about the time I threw up on Jack Ramsay?"

Shaughnessy was intent on winding up the youth justice hearings with a final flourish: a televised forum in Ottawa, complete with witnesses flown in from all over the country. Ramsay and the Reformers balked at the idea. In their eyes, such theatrics were nothing more than wasteful grandstanding at the taxpayers' expense. Ramsay refused to cooperate, and Shaughnessy would find it harder to fund the event without consensus from her committee.

On November 7, the committee put aside youth justice to conduct hearings into Bill C-17, a grab bag of Criminal Code amendments dealing with everything from impaired driving to police rights of search and seizure. Shaughnessy was only half listening to the testimony, preoccupied with Reform's threat to scuttle her plans. Shaughnessy asked Ramsay to step outside to discuss the youth justice forum. Once in the corridor, she accused him of attempting to destroy the work of the committee. As Ramsay started to protest, she snapped, "Oh, fuck off." That was the final straw for Ramsay – he vowed to make her pay for her foul language.

Shaughnessy put on a tough front, but she walked away from the encounter knowing that she had crossed the line. Quickly, she asked Paddy Torsney to take over the chair while she tried to undo the damage. She went directly to Jerry Yanover's office to confess: "Well, I've done it," she said. "I told Jack Ramsay to fuck off." Yanover, a genius of procedural strategy, immediately looked for some loophole in this very unparliamentary breach of decorum.

"You didn't say it while you were sitting in the chair, did you?" Yanover asked.

The fact that the exchange occurred outside, in the corridor, Yanover told her, was her sole salvation. He advised her to just stick to that fact and get ready to brave Reform's furor.

In the House of Commons the next day, Jack Ramsay stood up and protested that his privileges as a member of Parliament had been violated. "Just yesterday the chair of the Standing Committee on Justice and Legal Affairs indicated that she wanted to speak to me outside the room," Ramsay said. "When I obliged and attended I was accosted with inaccurate accusations. Filthy language was directed at me in a manner that was far below the ethical standards of members of this House. What course do we have to deal with that?"

Shaughnessy responded with a classic, if overused, battle plan: the best defence is a good offence. She lashed out at her Reform colleagues, charging them with obstructionism. "In an absolutely unbelievable act yesterday, those members moved to try to prevent the Justice Committee from completing its deliberations by hearing from Canadians across the country . . . I can announce that the Justice Committee, on November 22, will spend a day with 40 experts and ordinary citizens from across the country trying to reconcile the different views on the issue of youth justice."

Ramsay chose not to attend the committee sessions for several weeks. On November 19, the Reform Party whip, Chuck Strahl, took Ramsay's place at the table and demanded that the committee confront the question of whether Shaughnessy was suited to the chair's job.

"I move that this committee consider, in a report to the House, the recent improper conduct of the chair of this committee," Strahl said. "Being the chair of a committee is an important responsibility. It's not given lightly, nor is it taken lightly, I suppose. The chair of a committee frequently sets the tone of the debate, sets the standard of the debate, and sets the demeanour of the committee . . . I'm not exactly sure how that is supposed to add to decorum and decency and respect for the chair when you get invited by the chair to step outside and are promptly told to 'f– off' if you don't like what she says."

Shaughnessy, of course, was neither the first nor the most famous politician to lose control of her language in a public place. Pierre Trudeau and Brian Mulroney were both accused during their tenure of uttering the f-word in the heat of debate. Judy LaMarsh, one of Shaughnessy's role models, was also known for salty language. She once described Trudeau as "that bastard" within range of CBC microphones.

Taking Yanover's advice, Shaughnessy simply stayed out of the fray, sticking to her contention that the words had been uttered outside the committee room and therefore were not within the disciplinary purview of the Speaker or Parliament. Ramsay eventually returned to the committee and Shaughnessy had her forum. She opened the proceedings on November 22.

"I want to call what I think is the largest meeting we've ever had of the House of Commons Justice Committee to order," Shaughnessy said, looking around a room filled with lawyers, judges, social workers, and political advocates. Windsor's Neil Jessop was there as president of the Canadian Police Association; Priscilla de Villiers was on hand to talk about the work of her victims' rights group, CAVEAT (Canadians Against Violence Everywhere Advocating Its Termination); respected justice experts such as Anthony Doob from the University of Toronto were among the more than 30 witnesses gathered for the youth justice forum.

"For the record and for those watching at 3 o'clock in the morning, when they can't sleep," Shaughnessy said, "we are conducting today a national forum on youth crime and justice. It is the last hurrah of the Justice Committee's review of the Young Offenders Act... One thing we have learned throughout the course of our study, and one thing I think we all share, is the belief that in many parts of the country there is a remarkable lack of accurate information about the state of the Canadian youth justice system. This is one format we can use for public education and also for political education... It's a real opportunity for us as parliamentarians to do something that, in my view, we should be doing, which is to foster and promote a national dialogue on subjects of interest to Canadians."

Shaughnessy told the participants that, in her role as chair of the session, she would be fair but tough. "I have a stopwatch and I'm vicious," she said, smiling and waving her gavel. "I also have a hammer and I like that."

In the following months and years, Shaughnessy became ever more expert in this tough-but-fair political style. Indeed, she came to be known for her skills at building consensus in a committee that was always in danger of being riven with controversy.

Of all the portfolios in government, justice is the richest treasure trove for the would-be novelist, a file laden with tales of crime, bravery, and misfortune. The woman who dreamed of writing whodunits was never happier than when her Justice Committee was uncovering such little-known stories. She was fascinated by the implications of DNA analysis in the law; she was riveted when victims of crime testified about their experiences.

Shaughnessy was no stranger to victims' issues, having worked in criminal prosecution and defence, and she had developed a sophisticated understanding of victims' concerns with the justice system. Lynn Kainz, who worked as a victim/witness coordinator in the provincial attorney general's office in Windsor, knew Shaughnessy through their work together in the courts. She watched Shaughnessy's expertise in this area grow with her career. "She became an advocate for victims' issues along the way. You have to have someone who is passionate, and she was starting to 'get it' – that's the only way I know how to put it. You either get it or you don't. She did."

Shaughnessy's contacts with victims' advocates stretched far beyond Windsor. Priscilla de Villiers had encountered plenty of politicians by the time Shaughnessy came to the Justice Committee in 1996. Her daughter, Nina, had been murdered in 1991 while jogging in Burlington, Ontario. Her attacker was a man with a long history of violent assaults, out on bail; he later killed himself. In the wake of her daughter's death, de Villiers had become an advocate for stronger representation of victims' rights in the judicial process. CAVEAT had presented a petition, signed by 2.5 million Canadians, to Allan Rock in February 1994.

CAVEAT had lobbied hard on Rock's side during the gun control debates. Shaughn was one of the crowd then in de Villiers's eyes – committed, yes, but partisan too. In the fall of 1996, however, de Villiers gave a talk in Windsor with Deborah Mahaffy, mother of one of the victims of the grisly crimes of Paul Bernardo. The event was sponsored by the local Victims Services office, and more than a thousand people turned out.

The crowd surprised de Villiers. Though Windsor was no stranger to crime, it had not seen a high-profile tragedy such as the Bernardo case. Watching Shaughnessy operate so comfortably in this milieu, obviously no stranger to victims' concerns, de Villiers was impressed. They began to talk regularly by telephone, their conversations touching on justice issues as well as the state of their lives and their families.

Another member of CAVEAT, closer to her Windsor home, also looked to Shaughnessy for connection between victims and the politicians in Ottawa. Angela Peters, a nurse, a mother and grandmother, had lived a normal, contented life in Windsor until a September day in 1987 when a 20-year-old man, out on parole after a prison term for a previous sexual assault, abducted and raped her as she was walking her dog on a residential street. In the years after her ordeal, she found a measure of personal healing in helping the healing of others. Shaughnessy became an ally in that mission. Shortly after she became chair of the Justice Committee, Shaughnessy arranged for Peters and Lynn Kainz to meet with Herb Gray, to present a series of 67 recommendations resulting from a conference titled "The Protection of Our Children."

Peters was also on stage at the September 1996 meeting when de Villiers spoke to the Windsor crowd. No seeker of the limelight, she had bravely taken the microphone to do the introductions that night. Shaughnessy sought her out afterwards to offer congratulations and to reiterate her personal commitment to Peters's work on behalf of victims' rights.

For Peters, the lasting impression of Shaughnessy was of a woman in almost constant motion. At events like this and countless others, she was gregarious, encouraging, and determined, connecting almost effortlessly with everyone in the room. Peters knew of no one else who made politics look like such fun.

I 2

Some of My Best Friends

Justice issues received enthusiastic attention in the first term of the Chrétien government. As Allan Rock had observed, they allowed the Liberals to be expansive and innovative without spending a lot of money. Shaughnessy's position as Justice Committee chair gave her an influential voice in these issues, whether or not they came before her committee. One such issue was the "gay rights" debate.

In the summer of 1993, the organization Equality for Gays and Lesbians Everywhere (EGALE) had sent out a pre-election question-naire to all parties, soliciting their platforms on gay rights issues. Jean Chrétien had replied: "Liberals have long agreed that discrimination on the basis of sexual orientation should be prohibited." Allan Rock had followed up this statement with an October 1994 letter to EGALE. "As you are aware, this government is committed to amend-ing the Canadian Human Rights Act to add the ground of sexual orientation. I want to table such legislation as soon as possible," the justice minister wrote. But by the spring of 1996, that phrase – "as soon as possible" – was starting to ring hollow.

A committed knot of Liberal MPs, including Shaughnessy and

Sheila Finestone, were intent on pushing for an amendment to the Human Rights Act that would explicitly forbid discrimination on the basis of sexual orientation. Finestone came to her awareness of discrimination against gays and lesbians in her days as a Montreal social activist, working with the Fédération des Femmes du Québec and the local YWCA, where there had been opposition to a gay and lesbian club within the organization. Shaughn's convictions were rooted in her feelings about tolerance. Like Finestone, she had been moved by stories of gays and lesbians forced to live secret lives or forge sham marriages, and she had her own "some of my best friends" story. On Pelee Island, her close friends Barry Wayman and Tom Brown had shown her the endurance and strength of a gay relationship. She loved "the boys," as everyone on Pelee called them, and considered them members of her extended family.

The Liberals were on the record as committed to amending the Human Rights Act, but the prime minister, always politically cautious, was in no hurry to fulfill the pledge. Provincial governments, such as those in Ontario and Alberta, had landed themselves in messy controversies when they tried to deal with issues surrounding same-sex couples. Simply opening the discussion set off storms of debate over "family values," morality, and the place of the government in the bedrooms of the nation. Chrétien didn't look forward to that kind of turmoil so soon after the gun control debates.

But a caucus group led by Bill Graham, a Toronto MP, was growing impatient. Graham, a tall, erudite lawyer, former law professor, and father of two, is a member of one of Canada's wealthier families. While Mary Clancy served as moderator of the series of five Liberal leadership debates held across the country in 1990, Graham had been the referee.

In March 1996, Graham and several other MPs met with the prime minister, hoping to persuade him to act on the Human Rights Act amendment. The delegation, deliberately composed of an eclectic band of MPs – including Geoff Regan from Nova Scotia, former Quebec cabinet minister Michel Dupuy, and Saskatchewan MP Georgette Sheridan – tried to impress upon the prime minister why this was so important to the party at this moment. They too promoted the concept of cost-effective Liberalism. "We were saying, 'Look, here's an opportunity for us to do something Liberal with a big L. We're not talking budget here, we're talking social policy,'" Graham said.

Allan Rock stirred up some momentum for the measure by saying publicly as he left a cabinet meeting one day that he needed a little help from the country to push the rest of his colleagues (meaning the prime minister) to fulfill the gay rights promise. Graham took the cue and gathered his ammunition for a campaign of persuasion. He armed himself with polls showing that 75 percent of Canadians were in favour of such a measure. He urged the prime minister to make it a matter of Liberal policy, as fundamental to the government's philosophy as gun control or the budget: those who voted against it would face party discipline, as had Warren Allmand for voting against the 1995 budget and the foes of gun control for opposing Rock's bill. Chrétien was noncommittal. For some, gay rights was so much a question of personal morality that it seemed heavy-handed to threaten party discipline.

One day in the caucus, Graham tried another tack, an argument designed to appeal to the PMO's fixation on Quebec. "This is a matter of *unité nationale*," Graham declared, pointing out that in its tolerance about sexual orientation, Quebec was far ahead of the rest of the country. "When Quebec gets to the left of us, it's not good for national unity," he said. Think of it, Graham said: if just 2 percent of Quebec's population were gay and voted according to which government was more progressive, they could prove to be decisive in another close referendum. Intergovernmental Affairs Minister Stéphane Dion congratulated Graham at the end of his speech, praising his understanding of Quebec's position on the issue.

Chrétien, though, appeared to be leaning towards a free vote. When Mary Clancy tried to argue that the amendment should be considered party policy, he disagreed.

"No," Chrétien told her. "You guys have got to trust your colleagues to do the right thing."

Over a lunch of sandwiches in Allan Rock's office, Graham, Shaughnessy, and the minister discussed a strategy to force the amendment onto the legislative agenda. The gun control debate had been instructive, at least in terms of tactics. They recognized the advantage of pressing the issue hard in caucus, as Nault and his fellow opponents of gun control had done the previous year. Numbers counted, and the more people who spoke in favour of the amendment, the better.

Rock had also learned that in dealing with tough, emotionally charged issues, it's best not to prolong the debate. Get the controversy out of the way as quickly and as cleanly as possible, with lots of noisy support up front. Though he had come into politics with the somewhat naive belief that people could be persuaded and cajoled onto the right path, Rock had discovered in the gun control fight that no amount of argument would change minds when the discussion was framed as a question of values or principles. This time, he was for the speedy and spirited solution.

It was recognized too that the opponents of any such initiative by the government would always have a louder voice than the proponents. Chrétien himself acknowledged the phenomenon: "When you have a controversial piece of legislation like this one, those who are in favour when you start, and know you are doing what they want, shut up," he said. "Those who oppose get very active." The trick in the caucus, then, Shaughnessy and the others agreed, was to encourage the proponents to be as vocal as possible, while shutting down or shutting out the opponents.

The most visible – and, to Shaughnessy, the most annoying – caucus opponent on the gay rights issue was Roseanne Skoke, a rookie MP from Nova Scotia. A devout Roman Catholic who had campaigned for the right to kneel for prayers at her local church before running for Parliament, Skoke believed abortion and homosexuality were sinful, even criminal. Once in the House, she made her position perfectly clear: "The reference to sexual orientation in the [Criminal] Code and its proposed inclusion in the human rights legislation gives recognition to a faction in our society which is undermining and destroying our Canadian values and Christian morality," she said. On another occasion she declared, "Homo-sexuality is not natural, it is immoral, and it is undermining the inherent right and values of our Canadian families, and it must not and should not be condoned." Homosexuality would "annihilate mankind," she argued.

It was statements such as these that prompted the NDP's Svend Robinson, the first openly gay MP in Ottawa, to write to Chrétien in September 1994, asking him to expel Skoke from the Liberal caucus for what he called "hate-mongering homophobia." Shaughnessy and Mary would have been entirely happy with her expulsion and never ceased to be appalled by her rhetoric.

Gay rights were not the only preoccupation of the Liberal gov-ernment in early 1996. Fallout from the Quebec referendum was still being felt; Bloc Québécois leader Lucien Bouchard had left Ottawa to succeed Jacques Parizeau as premier of the province. Former prime minister Brian Mulroney had launched a lawsuit against Allan Rock and the government of Canada, accusing them of libelling him during an RCMP investigation into alleged kickbacks paid in Air Canada's purchase of Airbus passenger planes. Mulroney's legal and communications strategists intended to turn the case into a crusade to restore the image of the hugely unpopular former prime minister. The fight promised to be nasty.

Miraculously, Chrétien continued to ride high in the polls, but his deputy prime minister, Sheila Copps, was not in the public's good graces. She was caught in the mess over the Liberals' 1993 electioneering against the hated goods and service tax.

From the moment the Liberals came to office, the GST was a ticking bomb. Chrétien had tried not to box himself in during the election campaign, saying vaguely that he didn't like the GST but adding, always parenthetically, that no government could afford to lose the revenue it generated. Copps had been less careful in her campaign rhetoric. In the heat of the 1993 battle, she had vowed to resign if the Liberals didn't abolish the GST.

Midway through the mandate, it was clear the Liberals weren't going to kill the GST. The government didn't like to be reminded of its pledges, though. John Nunziata, a maverick already on thin ice for voting against the 1995 budget cuts, got himself expelled from the Liberal caucus on April 22, 1996, after his public condemnation of his government for not doing away with the tax.

The next day, Finance Minister Paul Martin attempted to finesse the Liberals' reversal on the GST with an unusual press conference, at which he announced a *mea culpa* to Canadian voters: "We made a mistake," he said. "It was an honest mistake. It was a mistake in thinking we could bring in a completely different tax without undue economic distortion and within a reasonable time period."

Unfortunately, Prime Minister Chrétien was of the old school when it came to admitting mistakes. Voters don't like mistakes and view them as a sign of weakness, he thought. Before caucus the day following, Chrétien declared that Martin might have been a little too candid at his press conference. "Paul has caused us a problem," he said. One of his advisers, speaking anonymously to the media as usual, confessed that Martin's press conference might have been a tactical error. Indeed, some Liberals were scratching their heads, wondering why Nunziata had been ousted on Monday for making the same public acknowledgment that Martin did on Tuesday. (Not Shaughnessy. She saw a contrast in the way the two men had framed the debate – how and why they said what they did. "Nunziata is trying to make himself look good at our expense – like he's the only Liberal who's true to his convictions," Shaughnessy explained. "Paul is trying to help us get out of this. That's the difference.")

Meanwhile, Copps was being hammered in the media. Now that her old Rat Pack ally Nunziata had put his caucus membership where his mouth was, Copps was haunted by her 1993 promise to resign. The *Globe and Mail* ran an editorial every day for more than a week, sanctimoniously reminding Copps of her own words and demanding her resignation.

Pierre Trudeau liked to dismiss hypothetical questions with a quip: "If, if, if... If my grandmother had wheels, she'd be a bus." Chrétien picked up on this line and repeated it a few times to reporters when peppered with such questions. At this point in Chrétien's government, though, it was fair to say that if the Liberal caucus was a bus, the wheels were falling off.

In late April the federal party's Ontario wing was to stage its convention in Windsor. Shaughnessy was named co-host for the gathering, at first accepting only reluctantly. She had protested that she was too busy at the Justice Committee. But as the date neared, she decided that it might indeed be fun. She bought herself a new red dress and, along with Garry Fortune, set about to make the Windsor convention memorable and eventful.

The media didn't have to be persuaded to come to Windsor. Thanks to the GST controversy and the gay rights debate, journalists were riveted by every detail of Liberal caucus politics. Paul Martin, even though a Quebec MP, agreed to make an appearance to handle the thorny GST issue.

There was one notable absentee. Herb Gray had been diagnosed earlier that month with stomach cancer and was undergoing treatment at Ottawa's Civic Hospital. Shaughnessy's get-well gift was a copy of the bestselling political novel *Primary Colors*. (Gray loved the book, though he enjoyed the 1997 movie more.)

Shaughnessy was heartsick that Gray couldn't be at this convention in his hometown. So were her fellow Liberals. Chrétien spoke on Friday night and drew a neat line between the reputation of the esteemed Herb Gray and the now-disgraced John Nunziata – without ever mentioning the name of the MP he had ejected from caucus a week earlier.

"There has been a lot of talk this week about the role of the MP," the prime minister said. "How can an MP serve his country and be true to his own ideals? I have been thinking a lot about that this week... and I have been thinking about a particular MP – Herb Gray. He is the ideal MP. He is a team player of terrific integrity, not a grandstander interested in headlines."

It was yet another reminder that this prime minister valued the pragmatic will of the collective over the ideology of the individual. He expected every member of his caucus to understand this principle.

Shaughnessy got it; some other MPs did not. "He didn't name John Nunziata because it's not his style to name someone who is not here to defend himself," Shaughnessy told the *Windsor Star*. "But he had to put it to rest for the party's sake."

Shaughnessy's goal at the convention was to create some momentum for the issues she was pushing in Ottawa. The average citizen might find it unlikely that a weekend meeting of diehard partisans, who often spent more time in bars than in conference rooms, would have any effect on the workings of Parliament. But MPs who have attended dozens of these conventions know that party meetings can create the will for government change.

Graham was on hand in Windsor, busily working the corridors and hosting receptions to promote the Human Rights Act amendment. His Rosedale riding association had put forward a resolution for the policy discussions that weekend, and if it passed, he would have a significant show of support for his campaign to make this measure a matter of Liberal policy.

Shaughnessy was working the corridors too, touring the convention centre in her red dress, feeding tips to the local and national media. On Saturday she gathered up a contingent of reporters and party members to go to Brigantino's, where she had everyone dancing in a conga line by the end of the night. Her favourite tune at this Italian restaurant was the Spanish Christmas song "Feliz Navidad," and the musicians played it over and over again for the reigning queen of Windsor that weekend.

The schmoozing paid off. Alongside some great pictures of Shaughn, the *Windsor Star* summed up the meeting in its Monday-morning report with the headline "Windsor Delegates Set Party Priorities." The story went on to report: "Cutting the federal tax on spirits emerged as the No. 1 priority of the Ontario wing of the federal Liberal party over the weekend."

Even though Paul Martin had been in Windsor to deal with the GST issue, Sheila Copps had been there to talk about anything but her future, the prime minister was prepared to speak about the state of his caucus, and the new intergovernmental affairs minister,

Stéphane Dion, wanted to address the referendum fallout, the number one story out of the convention was indeed about liquor taxes. Somehow, in no small measure because of Shaughnessy's influence, and amid all the other national issues bubbling at the surface, her own campaign against liquor taxation became the focus of the weekend. The delegates started with 132 policy resolutions and ended with a priority list of 15. A reduction in federal liquor taxes was at the top.

Graham's resolution also passed, and Chrétien finally came forward with the legislation. Bill C-33 would be subject to a free vote. Graham had lost that strategic battle, but he had won the larger fight for the legislation.

But the war was far from over. There was opposition to Bill C-33 without and within, the former being the least troublesome. The pro-amendment forces were delighted by Reform's laughably inept response to the issue (Preston Manning was forced to suspend three MPs from his caucus: David Chatters and Robert Ringma for their anti-gay remarks and Jan Brown for expressing dismay over her caucus's hostility to gays generally) and were quick to try to silence Liberal critics with loud cries of outrage at the Reform spectacle.

The Commons Human Rights Committee held two days of hearings on the bill in early May. Finestone, now at peace with her ejection from the front bench, was chair of the committee and was determined that these hearings not become a platform for anti-gay sentiments. Several opponents of the amendment had their say, but the MPs who took part were a moderate, largely pro-amendment lot. However, the Liberal dissenters were busy beyond the committee's carefully controlled hearings. MPs such as Tom Wappel and Dan McTeague were not content simply to oppose the legislation by adding their voices to the nays when it came time for the free vote. They were furiously drafting amendments designed to gut the bill at the report stage, when the legislation is meant to be approved in principle.

On May 8, the Liberal caucus met in a tumultuous session. Chrétien was angry at those MPs who had been preparing amendments to put before the House later that day. The deal, he said, was that Liberals got a free vote on the final reading of Bill C-33. All this talk of amendments was tantamount to disloyalty.

"I've been betrayed here," the prime minister said, levelling an angry stare in the direction of Wappel and company. "You've got one leader and I'm it. Don't throw a stone at your leader. We're not the Reform Party. We're not going to unravel over this."

Still, when the bill came before the House that night for the report-stage vote, 14 Liberals, including Wappel, McTeague, and Skoke, voted against it. The next day, the bill passed its third and final reading by a vote of 156 to 76, with the Liberal naysayers numbering 27. Liberals and Reformers alike were happy to put this divisive item behind them.

Copps was having less luck dealing with her difficulties. After the Windsor convention, she realized she couldn't simply ride out the fuss over her GST promise. Less than two weeks after John Nunziata was kicked out of the caucus, Copps announced that she was resigning from the government and from her seat to run again. That silenced her critics, finally. And she won handily in the by-election in June. The Liberals once more went into summer retreat, bruised and battered after another difficult year.

The fall of 1996 was quieter for Shaughn. She buried herself in work at the Justice Committee, growing even more adept in the chair's role. The federal Liberals held their biennial meeting in Ottawa in October, and Shaughnessy enjoyed another chance to mix and mingle in the corridors and bars. But she wasn't paying attention to the state of her own political organization back in Windsor, and that would soon get her in trouble.

Early in 1997 the rumour mill started to buzz with election speculation and the possibility of a vote as early as May or June. At the same time another rumour circulated: Paul Martin was looking to leave his Montreal seat and run in a riding somewhere in Ontario. Leadership was the reason, it was said. Liberal leaders have traditionally alternated between Quebec and non-Quebec men. Martin would be flying in the face of that tradition if he tried to succeed Chrétien. Naturally, the rumour went, if Martin was to take any other seat in Canada, it would be the one that once belonged to his father, the one currently occupied by Shaughnessy.

Shaughnessy was aware of these stories and was inclined to have fun with them. She began to circulate the rumour that she was headed for the bench, opening the way for her pal Paul. Sometimes she could deliver this "news" with a straight face; more often she would have to leave the room, stifling giggles, if she found someone particularly gullible to believe the story. The truth was that she had no intention of vacating her seat.

Nonetheless, Shaughnessy wasn't entirely sure that spring was the best time for an election. Nor was she prepared at the riding level. Beyond her customary tendency to procrastinate on administrative matters, she was consumed by work at the Justice Committee. Two mammoth studies – a comprehensive review of the Young Offenders Act and an examination of a victims' bill of rights – had to be issued by April. The committee had held almost 40 meetings in the first few months of 1997.

Shaughn would return home to Windsor on the weekends exhausted by the week's demands and looking for rest. What she should have been doing was selling memberships, keeping her riding association active and campaign-ready. Once again, David Smith was in charge of the Liberals' election organization, and he was running a tight ship. All MPs were told to have 400 paid-up memberships in hand, as proof of their connection to their grass-roots support, if they wanted their nomination papers to be signed. No excuses.

In April, he got Shaughnessy on the telephone and asked if she had her 400 memberships.

"Got them right here!" she chirped.

"You've got them right there?" Smith said. "Then you won't mind if I send Sandra Leffler down to pick them up right away, will you?"

"Nope," Shaughnessy answered, and hung up.

Leffler had left Shaughnessy's employ a few months earlier, to take a job with the Liberal Party offices in Toronto. Shaughn had not been happy about Leffler's departure. Though she had encouraged John Ommaney to go on to better things – he won a job in Herb Gray's office – Shaughn seemed to have expected Leffler to stay with her through a full term in office. She had also hoped Leffler would serve as her campaign manager.

When Leffler arrived in Windsor later that evening, Shaughnessy's constituency office was dark. She wouldn't answer or return calls. Leffler knew something was wrong. She didn't know whether Shaughnessy was still miffed with her or hiding from the Liberal Party's checkup on the state of her organization.

Shaughnessy was certainly rattled. She was in tears when she told Garry Fortune about David Smith's phone call. Fortune gave her two pieces of advice: get on the phone and apologize to Smith, and get those memberships in. Shaughnessy snapped to it. She phoned Smith and told him she was sorry, then dragooned her friends into a mad scramble to find those 400 members. They made their headquarters the Victoria Tavern and completed the membership drive that weekend. Leffler was able to report to Smith that Shaughnessy had fulfilled the requirements to be a candidate in the coming election.

Her troubles weren't over, however. She was having a hard time finding someone to serve as her campaign manager. Brad Robitaille and Brian Ducharme were immersed in their legal careers and, truth be told, resentful over the Liberals' failure to give Brad a judicial appointment. Ron Doherty had been severely ill earlier in the year, and he was not up to the strain. Sandra Leffler had disappointed Shaughnessy by taking the party job in Toronto and becoming, however reluctantly, the taskmaster of her old boss. In stepped John Ommaney, eager to test his skills in the heat of a political contest. He agreed to pack up and head to Windsor to help Shaughnessy.

This scrambling, all necessary simply to keep her job, had left her shaken. She was in none too good a mood as the election loomed. Then, as she surveyed the scene in Windsor, she realized she had more reasons to be alarmed. Though the media had largely overlooked or missed the phenomenon, the New Democrats were rising as strong challengers to the Liberals. David Collenette had been warning of the NDP threat for months, but the left was being discounted by mainstream political analysts.

Chrétien visited the governor general in late April and the election was called for June 2. Most believed it would be an easy walk to victory for the Liberals. But not Shaughnessy, and not Mary Clancy either. Shaughnessy confessed to selected friends that with a resurgent NDP she was in trouble. Mary Clancy faced a race against NDP leader Alexa McDonough for her Halifax seat. They spent hours commiserating over those "goddamn Dippers" breathing down their necks.

Shaughnessy turned to a dependable saviour, Don Brown, when she began to feel vulnerable. "I might lose, you know," she'd say to Brown, who would try to reassure her. At one point in the campaign, Brown ran into Paul Martin passing through Toronto. He told Martin about Shaughnessy's anxiety and Martin promised to add a stop in Windsor to his schedule if it would make Shaughnessy feel better. It did. Martin paid a call on Windsor and glowingly praised his colleague as a dedicated worker for her city, in the spirit of his dear old dad.

Martin, meanwhile, was safe in his Montreal riding and his reputation had only been enhanced as he steered the government out of debt during the Liberals' first term in office. But in Atlantic Canada and the West the party was faring less well. Gun control had hurt its chances in the West and the Reform Party was barrelling ahead in the polls in the four western provinces. The Liberals' decision to campaign through the disastrous Manitoba floods in early May had also contributed to the perception that the Grits were insensitive to the region. In Atlantic Canada, lingering anger with Martin's budget cuts was channelled into anti-Liberal sentiment, and Maritimers, for the first time in their long history, were about to send a large contingent of New Democrats to Ottawa. In Quebec the Bloc Québécois still looked strong, despite having lost its popular leader, Lucien Bouchard. The decidedly less charismatic Gilles Duceppe now headed the BQ.

Only the Ontario Liberals seemed safe. Reform had failed to

make any inroads in the province, largely because of its ill-considered campaign ads against prime ministers from Quebec. Shaughnessy did feel the NDP's strength in Windsor–St. Clair, but she managed to hold her own. The size of her majority was reduced, but on June 2, Shaughnessy became a twice-elected MP. At her headquarters that night, she hugged John Ommaney, thanking him for a hard-won victory, and then ran around embracing Brad Robitaille, Brian Ducharme, and Ron Doherty – all the folks who had been loyal to her through the years. She expressed more relief than triumph, but she would enjoy the moment anyway.

Once the election was behind her, Shaughnessy was happy to take a short vacation, dividing her time between Windsor and Pelee Island and hanging out with Jerry and her two dogs, Brandy and Maggie, and Maggie's new puppy. Earlier that spring, Jerry and Shaughn had sent Maggie out to be professionally bred, to ensure another purebred Irish water spaniel. The match took, but Maggie had a litter of precisely one. Shaughnessy, as excited as a new parent, announced the new puppy within minutes of its birth. "It's loud, large, obnoxious, and wants its own way," she said. "If it's a male, I'm calling him Roger, and if it's a female, I'm calling her Mary." The puppy was duly named Maria.

As Shaughnessy relaxed with her menagerie over the summer, she experienced a moment of political déjà vu. Just as she was safely re-elected, another embarrassing personal story was reported in the *Windsor Star.*

"MP's Dog Quarantined for Biting Michigan Woman," read the July 25, 1997, headline on the "Windsor in Brief" column. "A dog which belongs to Windsor-St. Clair MP Shaughnessy Cohen has been quarantined because it bit a Michigan woman Monday." The story went on to explain, in Shaughnessy's words, how her dog Maggie had been under a bench on the Pelee Island ferry when another passenger walked by with a dog on a leash. "My dog thought her territory was being imposed on and she lunged out and bit the woman on the calf," Shaughnessy was quoted as saying. "We feel very, very badly about it."

In Herb Gray's constituency office, Garry Fortune happened to call up the *Windsor Star* story on his computer. He immediately captured it as a screensaver: the story free-floated across the monitor on his desktop. Then he telephoned Shaughnessy and asked her to come in to discuss "an important matter." Shaughnessy arrived at the office and Fortune started showing her some documents on his desk. Hovering above the documents was the floating image of the dog-bite story. Shaughnessy's eyes suddenly fastened on the screen. She was speechless, but only momentarily.

There was one justice issue that had preoccupied Shaughnessy well before she took the chair of the Justice Committee; indeed, it had attracted her attention long before she became an MP. As a law student, she had been in awe of Brian Ducharme's political connections through his position as an adviser to Eugene Whelan. His stature, at so early an age, was a clear demonstration of the connection between law, politics, and power. In 1983, she saw Ducharme at work in Ottawa, serving as Justice Minister Mark MacGuigan's eyes and ears in the realm that represented the ultimate power for any ambitious man or woman of the law: the appointment of judges.

That year Shaughnessy attended the People's Law Conference, one of the many Trudeau government initiatives aimed at offering citizens greater participation in reform of the law. (The patriation of the Constitution and the introduction of the Charter and Rights and Freedoms in 1982 were the centrepieces of this effort to "democratize" the laws of Canada.) Thanks to some artful lobbying on her behalf by Ducharme, she was chosen by MacGuigan as a Windsor delegate. There she met the former dean of Windsor's law school and learned how those coveted appointments to the bench were secured.

The federal government has the power to appoint a substantial number of judges in Canada, from the nine justices of the Supreme Court of Canada, to the dozens of judges on various federal courts (such as the Federal Court of Canada and the Tax Court of Canada), to the hundreds of judges on the provincial and territorial superior courts and courts of appeal. The total is about a thousand appointees. One of the preoccupations of the justice minister is to help sort out who will be chosen.

In MacGuigan's time in the post, from 1982 to 1984, judicial appointments were made almost entirely at the discretion of the justice minister. Ducharme spent three days a week in Ottawa, advising the minister on every federal judicial appointment made in Canada, except those in the province of Quebec. Technically, this amounted to Ducharme "consulting broadly" with lawyers across the country and recording their opinions and his observations in a notebook, which he kept under lock and key. It became a standing joke between Ducharme and his old law school friend – Shaughnessy would wheedle and beg for a glimpse of the notebook. Ducharme never obliged.

On one occasion, Ducharme had to see Brian Dickson, the chief justice of Canada, to discuss a vacancy on the Supreme Court, the highest court in the land. Ducharme was only too happy to answer Shaughnessy's breathless questions about the atmosphere of the court building, the wood-panelled office decor, and Dickson himself. But he maintained a stony silence on the substance of their discussion.

"Come on," she'd plead. "Just give me a scrap, just a tidbit!"

It was a fascination that sprang from Shaughnessy's boarding school and small-town roots, where gossip was currency. The judicial appointments process, as she first knew it, was in fact an institutionalized system built on village gossip within the legal community. To have the inside track on who was up and who was down in the race for judgeship made Shaughnessy a player. Later she would tell Ducharme and Brad Robitaille that if she ever succeeded in winning elected office, she intended to be right in the middle of this action. She knew plenty of men and women in Windsor who would make excellent judges.

Some wondered if Shaughnessy's intense interest was fuelled by her own desire to be a judge. Bruce Murray believed that's why his daughter had first entered politics; she had once told him that one needed political connections to make the leap from the counsel table to the bench. Certainly, it was a common enough ambition among lawyers, even more so in the last decade. According to Harvey Strosberg, a man close to the process of selecting judges in Ontario through most of the 1990s, the legal profession has been inundated in recent years with applications from would-be judges.

Burnout among lawyers is one reason: it's often said that law is a business that people are dying to get into when they're young, and dying to escape when they're at mid-career. Strosberg, who observed Shaughnessy's struggling law practice in Windsor, said that many lawyers came out of school thinking they were guaranteed a good living for the rest of their days. But tell that to someone who was specializing in real estate law when the recession hit in the early 1990s or to someone whose practice revolved around motor vehicle injury suits when no-fault insurance was introduced in Ontario (or to a criminal lawyer with an aversion to paperwork and a thirst for politics). The practice of law grew highly competitive, and the speed of technology – the fax machine and e-mail – made it even more high pressured. There was as well, Strosberg remarked, plain, old-fashioned boredom with doing the same thing, day in, day out, the endless paperwork and the mundane administrative detail – all very far removed from television's depiction of the law as a stage for life-and-death drama.

Some lawyers want to be judges for the chance to recapture the noble ideals they held as students, to take their experience to a more cerebral, considered level, and to immerse themselves in issues they might never encounter as practising lawyers. It's an opportunity to give back to the profession, sometimes at considerable sacrifice. In the 1990s, federally appointed judges earned more than $170,000 a year and enjoyed decent pension benefits. It sounds like a lot of money, but for some lawyers, especially corporate litigators in big cities, it would represent a major pay cut. Still, for small-town lawyers, or those like Shaughnessy, Ducharme, or Robitaille who would earn nowhere close to the six-figure salary plus pension that a judgeship would give them, bench appointments were appealing for all the reasons cited by Strosberg and more.

Shaughnessy arrived in Ottawa with a list of lawyer friends she wanted to see placed on the bench. It included a significant number of female candidates, but the name at the top of her list was Brad Robitaille's. He had helped her win the nomination in Windsor–St. Clair in 1988, and he was the friend to whom she turned for everything from staff recruitment to reorganization of her finances. There was also, of course, his considerable talent as a lawyer, an organizer, and an observer of human nature. She told everyone who would listen that Robitaille would make a superb judge.

The role of political patronage in judicial appointments has been a subject of debate in legal circles for decades. It was Liberal justice minister Otto Lang, in that portfolio from 1972 to 1975, who established the job of "special adviser" on judicial appointments – the job that Ducharme performed for MacGuigan. But in the seventies and eighties, organizations such as the Canadian Bar Association and the Canadian Association of Law Teachers called for a process that operated at greater distance from the minister's office. The CBA established a national committee that became an unofficial part of the consultation process, but the government was not obliged to follow its advice. In 1984, during the wave of Trudeau/Turner patronage appointments, the CBA committee was bypassed completely on at least one appointment.

It wasn't until 1988 that Justice Minister Ramon Hnatyshyn (later appointed governor general) installed a formal committee structure to vet judicial appointments. Permanent committees were established in every province and territory, each with five members – judges, lawyers, and members of the public. For the first time, individuals were allowed to apply for judgeships. The committee's job was to review applicants and determine which of two categories they fell into: "qualified" or "not qualified." This system was modified a few years later and the categories changed to "recommended," "highly recommended," and "unable to recommend." Candidates would not be told of their classification, though they were informed of the date when they were assessed. Committees were also asked to provide summaries of the candidates' qualities if they made a positive recommendation.

In the fall of 1993, a few months before the election that would send Shaughnessy and Allan Rock to Ottawa, a story in the *Lawyers Weekly* newspaper featured the head of Nova Scotia's judicial appointments advisory committee protesting that the system was a sham – committees would put forward good candidates, but politicians would simply ignore the recommendations and install their friends. After the election, Allan Rock was given the justice portfolio and a chance to put his own imprimatur on the system of appointing judges; Shaughnessy had her list of worthies at the ready. Unfortunately, these two new MPs could not have been more different in their outlook: Rock wanted patronage removed from the system, Shaughnessy very much wanted it to remain.

Rock's views about legal patronage had been shaped by his long years as a corporate litigator and his exasperation at the inherent weaknesses of a process that could put cronyism before qualifications. Rock vowed that he would not preside over such a system, and in 1994 he made the commitment that no appointee would be named by the minister who did not have the endorsement of the appropriate advisory committee. He made other modest changes, increasing the number of judicial appointments advisory committees in Quebec and Ontario to three and the number of people on each committee by two, one more layperson and one more lawyer on every panel.

It wasn't political interference in the judicial appointments system alone that troubled Rock. There was a long tradition of patronage in the appointment of the federal government's legal agents, local lawyers hired to conduct cases on behalf of the government across Canada. Rock had seen legal agents replaced, even in mid-trial, on the whim of a new minister in the justice job. "These cases are important," Rock said. "You're prosecuting for drug offences, or dealing with sensitive fisheries issues, or constitutional questions."

Here too he wanted "a process that was arm's-length from the department."

Shaughnessy was not happy with this proposed reform. She wanted the legal agent work taken out of the hands of Tories in Windsor – namely, her old electoral foes, Tom Porter and Bruck Easton – and put in the hands of Liberals. As long as Rock fiddled with the system, she argued, Tories such as Easton and Porter were just laughing at the Liberals – laughing all the way to the bank. She wasn't the only Liberal MP disturbed to see Tories still holding those jobs at the end of 1993. Rock was summoned to a meeting with the prime minister and told that he couldn't remove politics completely from the process. The justice minister came up with a compromise solution: new legal agents would be appointed only if the department cleared them for competence, Rock decided.

But he would not replace Porter and Easton, as incoming justice ministers would routinely have done in the past. Shaughnessy became impatient as the months passed and looked for ways to generate a bit of heat on her side of the debate. A few conversational asides with reporters – and on May 21, 1994, a pointed story appeared in the *Windsor Star*, under the byline of the newspaper's Parliament Hill correspondent, Paul McKeague. "The jig could soon be up for two former Tory candidates whose Windsor law firms have received hundreds of thousands of dollars in business from the federal government... Lawyers Tom Porter and Bruck Easton are both resigned to the fact that they could lose a lot of their legal work now that the Liberals are reportedly preparing to axe hundreds of Crown agents appointed by the former Tory government."

The story had no discernible effect. Shaughnessy never managed to get Herb Gray, the regional boss, to make a decisive move against her old rivals. She made several attempts to persuade Gray over her years in Ottawa, but the two Windsor Tories kept their jobs. Rock was proving just as stubborn on the legal agents issue and on the role of the advisory committees in the appointment of judges.

The advisory committees were especially distasteful to Shaughnessy. The one that operated on her turf was dominated by Harvey Strosberg, the man she regarded as the usurper of the influence that rightfully belonged to her as the member of Parliament. Strosberg had three avenues of influence over the selection process. First and most important, he sat on the advisory committee for judicial appointments in the Windsor region from 1994 to 1997 (except for a six-month interruption). Second, he had long been a friend of Allan Rock, serving as a bencher at the Law Society of Upper Canada when Rock was the treasurer in the early 1990s. And third, Strosberg won the treasurer's job for himself in 1997, becoming in essence the chairman of the board and spokesman for the legal profession in Ontario. In that position he enjoyed regular and frequent contact with the justice ministers in Ottawa and at Queen's Park.

His relationship with Rock went deeper than their professional association. The two men respected and admired each other immensely. So highly did Rock prize Strosberg's skills that he turned to him for personal representation in the Airbus case. Despite the optics of the eventual $2-million settlement with Mulroney in January 1997, Strosberg could claim a small victory: the Canadian government reserved the right to continue the Airbus investigation – with Mulroney as a suspect – and the former prime minister was forced to concede that Allan Rock had played no vindictive or political role in the case.

When it came to judicial appointments, Strosberg portrayed his most recent role in humble terms. "Historically, the treasurer of the Law Society and the president of the Canadian Bar Association are generally consulted when it comes to judicial appointments. What you are expected to do is give your opinion. It is one of many opinions that the government takes and evaluates. I can't tell you the respective weight that anybody gives to any opinion. That's not my decision. My function is simply when asked to give an opinion. Nothing more. Nothing less."

Nonetheless, Strosberg was unabashed about the fact that his advice on judicial appointments weighed more heavily than Shaughnessy's. "Shaughnessy had a lot of wonderful qualities, but . . .

I think my ability to judge legal horseflesh was better than hers. And I think there would be a lot of people whose judgment as to what would make a good judge would be better than Shaughnessy's."

He hastened to add, though, that this wasn't intended as a slight against the people she wanted to put on the bench. "That's not to say that the people she was championing weren't good people... I'm not saying she wasn't right... When you get ten people and they're all qualified, and you have to put them in a list, honest people exercising good judgment can disagree."

Disagree politely over candidates and differ radically over the process itself. Shaughnessy's relations with Strosberg were always warm and friendly — they were frequent travelling companions between Windsor and Ottawa, and his daughter used her Ottawa apartment one summer — and their opposing views were never the subject of any confontation between them. But the process of which he was a part rankled her deeply.

Shaughnessy was convinced that the old cronyism of federal patronage had simply been replaced by new cronyism in the local legal community. The difference between the two, she pointed out, was that at least those responsible in Ottawa were elected by the people; the local lawyers (the likes of Harvey Strosberg) had no democratic authority. Applicants vigorously lobbied the committees, whose members were as susceptible to bias as anyone else: law society benchers favoured other benchers; bar association representatives smiled on their favourites. And a judge on the panel could enjoy enormous unwarranted authority. The advisory committees were no guarantee of better appointments, in Shaughnessy's view; Rock should have left them as advisory bodies only, without their virtual veto on the minister's appointments.

Shaughnessy had felt early on that Rock just needed to be educated on the realities. He signalled his appreciation for her advice on strategy and communications and freely admitted that he had lots to learn from Shaughnessy on this score. During one of his trips to Windsor, for instance, Rock was scheduled to meet the editorial board of the *Windsor Star*. Shaughnessy briefed him before the event.

"Listen," she said. "They're going to ask whether you're willing to legalize dice games." She knew Rock could not give a straight answer because no policy was yet in place.

"Here's what you say," she told Rock. "Say you'd be happy to do something once Ontario moves in that direction. Throw it to Charlie Harnick," the Ontario attorney general. Rock followed her advice and Ottawa was allowed to skate away from the dice controversy. The *Star* duly reported that the pressure was on Ontario to make the next move on the dice issue.

By the end of 1995, after lending him her steady support on many files, including gun control, Shaughnessy believed that she was owed something from Rock. She mustered her arguments and made an appointment to see him. Presenting her best points, she ended by asking if there was any detour around the committee in Windsor. Rock bluntly refused to consider her question. He would not go around the committee process, he said, no matter how much Shaughnessy protested. He reminded her of the *Lawyers Weekly* article and of his commitment to ensure that advisory committees weren't a sham. The style of the lecture, as much as its substance, devastated Shaughnessy. She left his office feeling that she had been slapped down verbally, like an errant child.

Once she recovered from the humiliation of that encounter, her self-pity gave way to outright indignation. She insisted that Rock was abdicating his responsibility to ensure proper judicial appointments. He became another obstacle in her path, and she would not accept that his was the final word on the issue.

She had avoided putting her problems on the desk of the woman in the Prime Minister's Office officially charged with Liberal appointments – Penny Collenette – because she didn't want to be seen doing end runs around Gray or Rock. Collenette, a long-time friend of Chrétien, had been in charge of patronage appointments for the prime minister since 1994. Judges' appointments were not one of her responsibilities, but since Shaughnessy was getting nowhere with the ministers, she decided to request a businesslike meeting with Collenette to simply discuss the appointments issue in the abstract. She armed herself with notes and briefs that she thought would be useful in conversation with another female lawyer.

They met in Collenette's office in early October 1996 and had just exchanged opening pleasantries when David Collenette, Penny's husband and then the minister of defence, burst through the door. His face was ashen. Penny was shocked – David had never come to her office in their three years together in government. She stood up, forgetting that Shaughnessy was there, and asked, "What's wrong?"

David looked at Shaughnessy. She was already gathering her files and preparing to exit. She didn't try to jolly up the Collenettes or joke with David, as she usually did. "Obviously this isn't a good time," she said. "I'll leave you two alone." She slipped out the door, leaving the Collenettes to discuss the reason for David's distress: he had been forced to step down from the cabinet, over a letter he had written to the Immigration and Refugee Board.

Shaughnessy decided to switch to another tactic: to treat the matter as a lawyer would – prepare a brief, research the arguments, and assemble a case to present to the minister. Who better to help her in this effort than Don Brown, her most powerful legal friend outside Ottawa. The author of a definitive text on administrative law, Brown believed Rock's procedures could be contested on the principles of administrative law: the justice minister had no right to delegate his decision-making authority so completely. "I wasn't sure it would necessarily be successful, but it certainly would not be laughed out of court," Brown said. Shaughnessy and Brown weren't alone: John Turner shared their views about the way federal politics had been replaced by committee politics.

The secrecy of the process was also a source of complaint. "The fact that there was no opportunity for a candidate to talk to the committee and to deal with any statements that were being made about him or her bothered Shaughnessy, particularly since the candidate was typically investigated in a most haphazard and ad hoc way," Brown said. "Primarily the committees rely on their own knowledge together with inquiries made by members of the committee." Shaughnessy dismissed this evidence as "a crock" in her rants to Brown. "Of course she was bugged... She could not even find out the outcome of the committee decisions, except occasionally in an underhanded way, and she felt it left MPs either unknowingly flogging a dead horse or having to be duplicitous in dealing with any candidate who sought her help." The brief was an ongoing project for Shaughnessy over the next two years.

This was Shaughnessy's crusade, said Brown, but she had to proceed cautiously. She kept up friendly contact with Harvey Strosberg, quietly biding her time until his term on the advisory committee was up at the end of 1997. She let it be known that Donna Miller, her colleague at Hiatus House, would be a fine Windsor candidate for the committee and Miller did indeed get the job, but Shaughn wasn't content. Once her roommate, Anne McLellan, replaced Rock as justice minister after the 1997 election, she had to be especially guarded. There were no more lengthy telephone conversations with Anne's partner, John Law, the respected legalist at the University of Alberta, on the subject of judicial appointments, and Shaughnessy was no longer free to vent her fury in the apartment.

On May 5, 1998, during what was supposed to be a routine Justice Committee meeting with the commissioner for federal judicial affairs, Shaughnessy snapped – in public. Commissioner Guy Goulard was in the midst of explaining the process for selection of judges – how candidates were first vetted by local committees – when Shaughn lashed out at him for the lack of confidentiality in the system.

"The fact of the matter is, you have a secret process here, or an allegedly secret process, and what I would suggest is an inherently unfair process to the applicant. I'm telling you that you have leaks all over the place. I can tell you – and I don't have this from the minister's office or from my political minister's office, I have it from the street – who's on the list in Windsor. I'll bet I can tell you every one and I'll bet I can tell you the comments [from the committee]. So much for the confidentiality, Mr. Goulard. I suggest to you, sir, that there's a serious problem."

The outburst was prompted by recent events in Windsor, where Brad Robitaille had learned through the grapevine that he had been rejected by the local committee. Shaughnessy was furious at her helplessness in the face of this humiliation to her friend. If she could do nothing to get him named a judge, she would at least condemn the way in which he found out about his rejection.

Shaughnessy was no fool, either. If Rock could cite an article in the *Lawyers Weekly* to justify his opinion, she might as well try for some coverage to mobilize contrary sentiment. She got in touch with the paper and flagged her very public complaint. "I don't particularly want to rock the boat," Shaughnessy told reporter Cristin Schmitz rather disingenuously, "but as a member of Parliament with an interest in justice issues, I want to make sure that we have got very good people on the bench. And I want to make sure that a person who entrusts his or her entire life and reputation to a committee gets a fair hearing.

"When I hear that the partner of a member of a committee is telling someone, while they are on vacation together, who is eligible for judicial appointments in the country, then I have concerns." Schmitz's story ran on the front page of the *Lawyers Weekly*.

Of course, anyone who knew Shaughnessy's history could not miss the irony of this call for discretion. As far back as the days when Ducharme was involved in the appointments, discretion was hardly Shaughnessy's first concern. It was precisely the leaky nature of the process, the chance to be "in the know" about new judgeships, that made this part of politics so interesting to her. No, Shaughnessy's real frustration was that the new system removed the MP from the inner circle of decision-makers.

The *Lawyers Weekly* article landed with a thump on Miller's desk at Hiatus House in Windsor. In one of her very few moments of anger with her friend Shaughnessy, Miller picked up the phone and demanded to know what was going on.

"What are you accusing me of?" Miller asked.

"It's not you," Shaughnessy said, and went on to explain how this had been a long feud between herself and Justice officials, including their ministers. It was an attack on the department, not on her friends. Miller was reassured.

"So. How are things at the apartment?" Miller wanted to know.

Things were fine at the apartment, as it happened. Shaughnessy and Anne had managed to compartmentalize their professional and after-hours personas so effectively that even open criticisms such as this didn't make a dent in their relationship. When Shaughnessy had a complaint to lodge with Anne, she most often did so by letter. It was not unusual for the two women to work in their apartment in the evenings, Anne reviewing cabinet briefing notes while Shaughnessy drafted letters to the minister sitting in the housecoat in the chair opposite. She followed up her outburst at the committee with one such letter: "Dear Minister," it began, and then went on to list Shaughnessy's many concerns about who was getting judicial appointments, where they came from, what gender they were.

Shaughnessy approached her on the day the *Lawyers Weekly* article appeared. "So, uh, did you read – ?"

Anne cut her off, laughing. "Yes, Shaughnessy, I read it," she replied.

"Shaughnessy had the right to say what she wanted to say, and I never doubted her motivations, even though some of those comments were not helpful," Anne said later. "There was never any malice intended. It was simply that she was, in a very straightforward way, telling me what she thought."

As always.

13

Unexpectedly Called Away

The fall of 1997 saw Shaughnessy begin her second term as a more mature politician and member of Parliament. Her caucus colleagues noticed a mellowing of her reputedly harsh character and fewer of the antics that had been her trademark. Many attributed the change in Shaughnessy to the absence of Mary.

Mary had lost her Halifax seat in a tough fight against the New Democratic Party leader, Alexa McDonough. It's difficult for any politician, no matter how high-profile, to defeat a party leader. The leaders are given media coverage every day of the campaign, and this one was capitalizing on the Atlantic region's distrust of government budget cuts. After two terms in Parliament, Mary's hopes for re-election were dashed on the rocks of circumstance and Liberal unpopularity.

Shaughn reacted to Mary's defeat with a mix of compassion and fear. There but for the grace of the Windsor electorate went Shaughnessy. Had she confronted a high-profile NDP adversary, she too would have been sunk. Unlike the Liberal Party at large, Mary and Shaughn were always more wary of the threat from the left than the right. Reform and other conservative elements were not factors in their ridings. Several weeks after her election defeat, Mary was named consul general to Boston. Shaughnessy was immediately on the phone to her circle: "Guess what? We've got a place to stay in Boston and a driver!" Nonetheless, Shaughn would miss Mary in the caucus and in the Commons. Heckling of the Reform benches fell by several decibels.

In this second term, Shaughnessy would also become clear-eyed about her unquestioning loyalty to cabinet ministers, viewing herself less as an appendage to the powerful, more as someone with power in her own right. Bob Nault saw the change in her almost immediately after the election. "She became the Shaughnessy we knew was there. She was more confident, less eager to please the ministers."

Despite Mary's advice to seek a parliamentary secretary position and the inevitable pressure to give up the chair of the Justice Committee (non-cabinet MPs were expected to move back and forth between chair and PS responsibilities), Shaughnessy fought hard to stay in the committee chair's job. Bill Graham shared her enthusiasm for committee work. "We both believed that the committees were where the action was. You can have a real debate about issues . . . You get real give and take . . . When we go into the House to debate the same thing, people get up, they point fingers, scream and yell, read set pieces, and end up with a non-productive shouting match. The committee permits a better exchange of views because it's more informed on the issues."

There was another potential obstacle to her retaining the justice chair: her living arrangements. It was hardly the norm for the justice minister and the chair of the Commons Justice Committee to share accommodations, and the optics were unfortunate. Cozying up to cabinet ministers was one thing, living with one of them was quite another. Yet largely on the strength of the laudatory reviews she had received for her past work on the committee, Shaughnessy's wish was granted. When the new assignments were announced in late September 1997, the Justice Committee's chair was hers. Any grumbling came from her own ranks. Derek

Lee, who knew only too well what Shaughnessy could do in the name of loyalty, was not happy to see her back in the chair.

"She had a lot of communication with Anne, for sure, and it pissed me off in the beginning," Lee said. "It was hurting Anne's image." Lee decided he would let the two women handle the issue of appearances. And if Shaughnessy showed any favouritism to the minister, others would grumble too. "If she didn't perform as a good chair, it was obvious she was going to become toast, and I didn't mind that either," he said.

Neither Anne nor Shaughnessy worried about appearances, though. Any talk of possible conflict ignored the reality of the relationship back at the apartment and the clear boundaries they both observed.

The new Parliament was very different from its predecessor, and so too was the Justice Committee. At the previous committee, only three of the political parties enjoyed official standing; the Tories and New Democrats had had too few members to justify more than a symbolic presence at Commons committees. However, with the Conservatives' and the New Democrats' numbers back up, committees were now five-party affairs, and Shaughnessy's conciliation skills would be tested as never before. She had no choice but to work with her political adversaries.

Shaughnessy found it easy to do so with the Conservative member, Peter MacKay, son of the former Tory cabinet minister Elmer MacKay. On the first day, Shaughnessy went out of her way to welcome him.

"You're the guy who beat Roseanne Skoke, aren't you?" she bellowed, enfolding him in a welcoming hug. The two became almost immediate friends, linked by their common experience as criminal lawyers and by the view that their legal and political careers went hand in hand. Just because you had political aspirations didn't mean you were a bad lawyer.

Shaughnessy was outraged on MacKay's behalf that he'd been fired from his job as a prosecutor when he sought the Tory nomination in his riding. He was suing Nova Scotia's Liberal government over the firing, and Shaughnessy promised to help. "I'll just talk to Russell [MacLellan, then the premier, her predecessor as chair of the Justice Committee before he left federal politics to return to his home province] and get him to settle that silly suit," she said. "Don't worry. We'll fix it."

The committee tackled its work with zeal that fall session. Its first task was to fill a hole left in the Criminal Code after the Supreme Court had struck down police powers of arrest without a warrant. It was a complicated, high-profile issue, and MacKay had some strong feelings about what should be done. He soon appreciated that Shaughnessy was a formidable but generous chair.

"Shaughnessy cut me a lot of slack on that particular debate and she allowed me to move some amendments to the government bill," MacKay said. "It was encouraging to see her wrestle with the party line. I think she had a really hard time with toeing the line, on occasion."

Shaughnessy was, in fact, being more discriminating with her loyalty now, less prone to knee-jerk partisan reactions. The greatest evidence of this was her response to the trouble that befell her old Reform nemesis, Jack Ramsay, soon after the 1997 election. Ramsay was charged for a sexual assault that was alleged to have taken place more than 20 years earlier, when he was serving as an RCMP officer on a native reserve. Shaughnessy had been expected to react with delight to this development. She didn't. One day, quietly, she went over and sat down with Ramsay in the House and asked how he was doing. Ramsay was so touched, so moved by the gesture – even some of his Reform colleagues had not been so generous – that the hatchet was buried, permanently. "I will never forget that – never," Ramsay said.

Shaughnessy, for her part, explained that if she had taken any glee in Ramsay's plight, she would have revealed herself to be no better than the most judgmental Reformers, those who saw the world in black and white and condemned people in the court of public opinion before they even arrived in a court of law. She knew the world was more complicated than that.

In January 1998, the Liberal MPs prepared to converge on Collingwood, Ontario, for a two-day retreat. Shaughnessy and Roger decided that they would drive to the meeting. The two MPs were seasoned road warriors by this point. In a cost-saving move during this Parliament, they had decided to drive back and forth from Ottawa whenever possible. Roger would generally set out from Sarnia and pick up Shaughnessy in Windsor, and the two would drive all day to the nation's capital, through southern and eastern Ontario.

Armed with cellphones, Roger and Shaughnessy filled the eight-to-ten-hour drive with call-in reports from the road. Any amusing incident, any witty insight would be immediately conveyed to a group of a half-dozen or more friends on the phone network. Immediately after the new year's ice storm in Ontario and Quebec, for instance, they followed a route that allowed maximum viewing of broken trees and downed power lines. Like children, they delighted in scenes of nature's devastation.

"There's lots of destruction on Highway 416," Shaughnessy announced, traffic-reporter-style, in her calls to friends. "If you're coming to Ottawa, you want to take the 16 to see real destruction."

When the time came a few weeks later for the Liberals to gather in Collingwood, Shaughnessy and Roger looked forward to a road trip – one that would include Anne McLellan. Their plan was to start out early from southwestern Ontario, drive to Pearson Airport in Toronto, pick up Anne, and then grab dinner in Toronto with friends before driving north to Collingwood.

As the pair barrelled down the 401 towards Toronto, they hatched a giddy plan. It revolved around rumours of the undeclared but simmering leadership race that were circulating in the wake of the 1997 Liberal election victory. Knowing Anne's extreme sensitivity to suggestions that she consider entering the contest to succeed Chrétien, Roger and Shaughn decided that a public embarrassment was in order. Just outside Cambridge, Ontario, about 50 kilometres from Pearson Airport, they stopped at a party shop and bought supplies: balloons with "Anne" printed on them, party hats, streamers, and little silver sheriff's badges (in recognition of Anne's position as the justice minister from the West). En route to the airport, Shaughn sketched out a placard: "Ontario Welcomes Anne McLellan." At Pearson, they decked themselves out in their Anne-for-leader suits and stood beaming in the arrivals area.

As Anne came down the escalator to the luggage area, she saw the reception party at once. Her eyes darted around in panic as she wondered who else might be witnessing this spectacle. Senator Anne Cools was in the crowd, but she hadn't yet noticed the ridiculously outfitted pair. Shaughnessy and Roger, meanwhile, having spotted their target, were hooting loudly, waving the balloons, and flashing their badges.

That night, the small group at dinner waited for Shaughnessy to leave the table before discussing another extravaganza, her surprise 50th-birthday party. Shaughnessy would be 50 on February 11, and she regarded the event as a big deal – the whole week, she proclaimed, would be her "jubilee celebration." A surprise party, organized in Ottawa by Anne and Roger, would be an entirely fitting kickoff.

The scramble began to send out invitations and book rooms without Shaughnessy finding out. Radio Shaughnessy was a transmitter and a receiver; not much happened on Parliament Hill without her picking up the signals. Mary planned to fly in from Boston; others were due from Toronto. A second event was in the works for Windsor.

On Wednesday evening of the jubilee week, Roger and Anne told Shaughnessy that they were all going out for a quiet dinner at a Chinese restaurant to mark her birthday. Shaughnessy, true to her reputation, had an inkling that more was up – a cab driver, of all people, had asked her a few days earlier whether she was attending the big birthday bash that week for "some woman MP." Ottawa is a very small town.

But she had no idea how big the party was to be. Almost every cabinet minister was waiting for her, as well as dozens of MPs, aides, and friends, in a cavernous private room upstairs at the restaurant.

When Shaughnessy walked in, her jaw dropped. Making a quick recovery, she cried, "Welcome to my jubilee celebration!" Then she toured the room to kiss and hug more than a hundred guests.

Oakville MP Bonnie Brown looked around and tried to articulate what it was that had brought these people together. Was it Shaughnessy's personality? The chance to mingle with ministers? The desperate need for a party in chilly Ottawa in February? "I know what it is," she said to the people at her table. "Every person in this room loves a good belly laugh."

At the midpoint in the evening, Roger and Anne wheeled out a huge cake, adorned with 50 candles.

"Speech! Speech!" the politicians demanded.

Shaughnessy seemed almost reticent, saying only that she wanted to thank everyone sincerely for being there. Then, cranking herself up, she turned attention away from herself and towards the hot topic of the hour – namely, leadership politics.

"The prime minister isn't here, right?" she said, casting her eyes about the room. "Okay then. So we can admit it: there's a leadership campaign coming, isn't there?"

A few nervous laughs and coughs. John Manley shifted in his seat; Jane Stewart's eyes flashed. Paul Martin stared at his plate.

"You know how I know there's a leadership race on? It's *my* birthday, but everyone wants to sit with Paul Martin!" Shaughnessy said. The considerable mob at Paul Martin's table burst out laughing; Martin blushed and wagged his finger at Shaughnessy.

"Well, Paul," she said, "I have some disappointing news for you. I was with you last time, but I'm not going to be with you the next time – at least not on the first ballot. Right, Anne?"

Standing primly beside Shaughn, her hands folded in front of her, Anne nodded. "That's right, Shaughnessy," she said.

"You see, Paul, Anne and I have decided that she should run . . . We have a platform. Tell them what it is, Anne."

Anne piped up: "Save the Seals."

"That's right," Shaughnessy said. "It's perfect. Given that Anne's from out west, with all those hunters and sportsmen, she'll almost certainly be one of the candidates to be dropped after the first ballot, and that means we'll have to cross the floor – to you, of course. You know what this means – we'll be on TV. We'll have to buy ourselves nice outfits for our parade across the hall. What better reason for a leadership campaign than an excuse to get a nice outfit? Right, Anne?"

Anne nodded obediently.

"Now what's that slogan again, Anne?"

"Save the Seals," Anne replied.

"So that's my announcement. Oh, one other thing," Shaughnessy said. "I'm sorry to have to tell you all this, but Anne's leadership campaign may require Roger and me to dress up in seal costumes. Thank you again for coming to my birthday party!"

In reality, Shaughnessy had eyes for only one candidate – Paul Martin – as a leadership race began to be discussed in earnest. One day early in 1998, Shaughnessy had a phone call from an Ottawa lobbyist who explained to her that the Martin team was now assembling and wondered if she wanted a role in it. Shaughnessy readily agreed to do whatever she could, then hung up. "Wait a minute," she thought. "If I want to work on Paul's leadership campaign, I don't need to be recruited by some lobbyist! If I want to get on board, I can talk to Paul Martin whenever I want." Shaughnessy promptly called Martin's office and warned that this kind of shadowy campaigning, carried on by people trying to hang their ambitions on Martin, could prove extremely dangerous to his chances. "Paul doesn't need this kind of freelancing," she advised. It wouldn't be the last time that Martin's people heard these complaints.

Shaughnessy had no anxiety about the prospect of entering her 50s. It seemed everyone in her political world was turning 50 that year: Mary had already hit that milestone; Roger would pass his in May. It was business as usual for Shaughnessy Cohen at the half-century mark in her life. But one March morning as she prepared to go to her office, there came a shocking reminder of everyone's mortality. The news announced the sudden death of Yves Landry, president of Chrysler Canada, felled by a heart attack while taking a rare vacation in Florida with his wife. He was just 60 years old and his passing was a blow to many.

Yves Landry was an important individual, not just to Shaughnessy's Windsor riding but to the country as a whole. A few weeks before, Landry had been asked to serve as chairman of the Liberals' new $2-million Millennium Scholarship Fund. Shaughnessy was proud that someone she knew, someone from the heart of Windsor and the auto industry, was a significant player in this government initiative.

Landry's funeral was a major event in Windsor, one of several such sad ceremonies that the city would witness before the year was out. (Mark MacGuigan had died weeks earlier.) Prime Minister Jean Chrétien arranged for a Challenger to fly a group to Landry's funeral on the cold morning of March 18.

On the way down to Windsor, Shaughnessy sat with John Manley, Paul Martin, and Bruce Hartley, the prime minister's aide. As Shaughn and John shared breakfast, they talked freely about the tragedy of Landry's death. Here was a man with so much to contribute, so busy with work and civic duties, who was denied the chance to relax at the end of his life, to slow down and enjoy his family and the simpler pleasures. They grappled with the truth that life has no guarantees.

"We had a mutual understanding of the lesson of Landry's funeral," Manley said. "That was: you've got to take life in its context; life is finite."

When Shaughnessy returned to Ottawa, she took the unusual step of cancelling all her appointments for the rest of the week. She fled home to Windsor. "I've just realized how stupid it is to be away from Jerry so much," she explained. "I've just realized that life is too precious to spend far away from the people you love."

Her conversation with Manley prompted a restless period of soul-searching about what was really important to her. She dreaded the idea of losing Jerry or anyone else close to her while she was preoccupied with politics. She was also shaken by the end of Jane

Stewart's marriage that year. Shaughnessy had developed a special fondness for Stewart back in the days when the Brantford MP was chair of the national caucus. The Stewarts and the Cohens had travelled together on a parliamentary junket to Israel and the two couples had become close. Shaughnessy fretted that Jane's marriage had crumbled under the pressure of her absences from home. She told Jerry that she intended to be more assertive about controlling her time, even if that meant sometimes saying no to Herb Gray.

With equal parts sarcasm and sincerity, Jerry insisted that their marriage was fine and that life as a political spouse was grand. "I told her I didn't mind us not having as much of a private life as we might want and that I was, strange as it might seem, beginning to enjoy those banquets and those folk dances. I was beginning to see that there were actually differences in the steps between them. I enjoyed waiting four or five hours to see some guy who donated a ton of money to charity being awarded citizen of the year and receiving all the plaques and scrolls from the important officials of the community including the MP, MPP, mayor, police chief, you name it."

While Shaughnessy worked to ensure that she had enough time with Jerry, she also seemed to have an increased capacity in these months to take an active interest in her friends and their well-being. Priscilla de Villiers, impressed with Shaughnessy as a committee chair, came to see her as a confidante too. When de Villiers realized her 27-year marriage was in trouble in 1997, it was Shaughnessy to whom she turned for advice and support. Shaughnessy, in turn, sought out de Villiers for guidance on how to make the Justice Committee's work even more relevant in this second term.

One day, during one of their regular telephone conversations, de Villiers mentioned to Shaughnessy how impressed she had been with the committee's hearings on youth justice in the previous mandate. The two women wondered aloud whether the same type of hearings would be useful for victims' rights, an issue of particular importance to them both and one on which Shaughnessy believed the government should show leadership.

The public arena seemed ready for such a debate. Statistics Canada had released results of the 1996 International Crime Victimization Survey, which was carried out in Canada and ten other Western industrialized nations. In general, the survey showed, crimes against the person were less likely to be reported to police than property crimes. Recent Canadian statistics confirmed that assault and sexual assault were the least frequently reported of all. As a report of the Justice Committee later characterized the meaning of the numbers, they "spoke to the mentality of the victim – the sense that property crimes were random, but that people 'deserved' in some way the personal hurts they suffered." Shaughnessy was angered by what these findings signalled about the way victims saw themselves. As she had in the controversy over gay rights, she spoke intensely about her abhorrence of a world where people are made to feel ashamed for things that are beyond their control.

Shaughnessy's initiative and Priscilla de Villiers's support resulted in the staging of the National Forum on Victims on June 15 and 16, 1998. As de Villiers walked to the Railway Committee Room, down that same corridor where Shaughn had been overcome on her first day as an MP on Parliament Hill, the victims' rights advocate was herself overwhelmed by the moment. "There really was a sense of history in the room, when you looked around and saw all these people, their voices formally being heard," de Villiers said.

Derek Lee was similarly impressed. After his long years working on justice issues in Parliament, this was a chance to see their debates in a new light. "It allowed the MPs to wear the shoes of the victims for more than just two minutes," he said.

Both days of hearings were televised and Shaughnessy was her irrepressible self, flashing a warm smile at the camera and listening, rapt, as victims told their stories to the committee. For the committee and the participants, it was a job well done. Parliamentarians were asked to deal with some tough, emotional issues and challenged to make the justice system more responsive. The MPs promised to put victims' rights near the top of the minister's agenda.

This success under her belt, Shaughnessy began to make plans for the summer. Unlike other summers, spent attending to constituency work and relaxing on Pelee Island, Shaughnessy would make this a working holiday, as long as Jerry could be part of it.

She wanted to explore the North. Her previous visits, all too brief, had allowed glimpses of this part of Canada through the windows of planes or taxicabs. Now a huge expanse of the eastern Arctic – bigger than any one of Canada's provinces – was about to become the country's newest territory. This would be the summer to see Nunavut in the making.

Along with Paddy Torsney, she hatched a plan for the "Northern Lights Tour," which would take a group of parliamentarians through the soon-to-be-declared territory of Nunavut, as well as through the western Arctic and Yukon. She enlisted the help of Peter Adams, parliamentary secretary to the House leader. In his previous life as an academic and scientist, Adams had spent years in the North studying the nature of ice. Before he knew what was happening, he found himself advising Shaughnessy on the itinerary, helping her to understand the immense distances that must be travelled in the North and the relative difficulty of hopping from place to place. Adams then squirmed out of Shaughnessy's clutches before she could delegate any tasks to him.

His avoidance plan lasted precisely one week. At the next informal meeting of the Northern Lights brigade, held at Shaughn's usual place in the government lobby, Adams found himself drawn into the circle, talking about how "we" could go here and there. "I was hooked," he said. "She had a way of doing that."

Other MPs hooked into the trip included Roger, of course, Paddy Torsney, Sheila Finestone, Hamilton MP Stan Keyes (one of Roger's friends in the True Grit Band), Carolyn Bennett, and Susan Whelan. Shaughnessy and Nunavut MP Nancy Karetak-Lindell were the tour's team leaders. Shaughnessy also managed to get two staff members, Kate Archer from her office and Farah Mohamed from Torsney's office, included in the party. These young women handled much of the organizational detail.

The itinerary mapped out by Adams would take the group

from Resolute Bay to Pond Inlet on Baffin Island, over to Grise
Fiord on Ellesmere Island, then back to Iqaluit, Pangnirtung, and
Cape Dorset on Baffin. As the time for the trip neared, Shaughnessy and her pals locked themselves in briefing sessions with
bureaucrats from Justice, Finance, and Indian Affairs. Tending to
more mundane preparations, Shaughnessy made a flying visit to
Mountain Equipment Co-op in Toronto, to buy accessories for
herself and Jerry.

On July 21, 1998, the Northern Lights Tour piled into its
charter and headed to Resolute Bay, where the MPs held meetings
with some of the Inuit who had been sent to the area in the 1950s
as part of the federal government's relocation program. They also
inspected the base of the Polar Continental Shelf Project, which
serves as the centre of logistical and aircraft support for researchers
in the Arctic, and listened as the scientists there explained how the
project had been undermined by budget cuts in recent years. The
MPs promised to do what they could to restore funding. (Their
later lobbying efforts did bear fruit: the project was given an additional $1 million by the federal government, largely as a result of
the report from the Northern Lights Tour.)

In Pond Inlet, the group was entertained by throat singers. At
Grise Fiord, they heard complaints about damaging transportation
costs and inadequate services. The schedule was gruelling, the
issues were complex, but it was an experience none of the MPs
would ever forget.

As soon as they returned, Shaughn and Jerry prepared to hit the
road again, this time on a foreign trip to Malaysia and Thailand.
One of the purposes of the mission was to encourage Asian governments to approve the international land-mines treaty that Lloyd
Axworthy had been instrumental in framing earlier in the year.
Jerry watched one evening as Sheila Finestone, never a shrinking
violet, pressed her hosts aggressively on why the treaty had not
moved through the Malaysian Parliament. Shaughnessy quickly
moved in to defuse the tension that he could see building as
Finestone lectured. Almost imperceptibly, Shaughnessy guided the

conversation to safer ground, asking questions about the structure of the Malaysian government. If the discussion became too charged in matters of substance, she would instinctively reach for a point about process to neutralize the situation. The question of "why" could be softened by the question of "how."

When she returned to Canada, Shaughnessy started to experience intense stomach pain. It felt like heartburn but lasted for days and then weeks. She was downing bottles of milk of magnesia or Pepto-Bismol and crunching antacid tablets constantly. Finally, she went to see a doctor. The diagnosis? Her gallbladder was acting up. For now, Shaughnessy was to watch her diet, avoid alcohol, and prepare for surgery that might be necessary if the problem didn't clear itself.

In the meantime, Shaughnessy's sister Judi had been on a diet. When Shaughnessy had her first gallbladder attack, her sister was already boasting a 30-pound weight loss. Shaughn decided to make it a contest, and what better time, now that she had to watch what she was eating anyway? With a minimum amount of effort and restraint, the pounds started to melt away. Shaughnessy was delighted with herself and paid even closer attention to portion size and calorie counts.

"I can cross my legs again. So in my mind, I'm a size 6," she reported to friends.

Though the gallbladder problem gave her pain, and despite headaches and sore eyes that plagued her with disturbing frequency, Shaughnessy was still capable of high spirits. Everyone had noticed her relatively subdued demeanour in this second mandate, but she could be counted upon for the occasional flash of outrageousness and indiscretion.

In the fall of 1998, Jean Chrétien was in hot water over the 1997 APEC conference. There were accusations that he had influenced the actions of the RCMP against protestors at the Vancouver meeting of Pacific Rim leaders. At one point during the controversy, Shaughnessy read aloud to a reporter some of the negative mail she was receiving about Chrétien – an indiscretion that few, if

any, Liberal MPs would risk. She was equally candid in her assessment of Andy Scott, then the solicitor general. Scott was in trouble
for announcing his views on the RCMP's role in the affair to a fellow
airplane passenger. He didn't realize that NDP MP Dick Proctor was
sitting within earshot, noting every word. Proctor reported the
conversation to the House at the first opportunity. Scott's Liberal
colleagues, including Shaughnessy, made a public show of outrage
at Proctor's attack on the solicitor general but grumbled privately
that the minister had committed a serious faux pas.

As Scott was sinking in a quagmire of his own making, Shaughnessy ran into Harvey Strosberg on a Monday-morning flight from
Windsor. The two sat together and gossiped about Scott's travails.

"He's gone," Shaughnessy said. "He can't last in cabinet. What
he did was stupid."

Strosberg was amazed. Surely Chrétien wouldn't let Scott
resign – his government had prided itself on a record of relatively
few resignations. But Shaughnessy was adamant. "He's gone," she
repeated.

Then Shaughnessy and Strosberg turned to matters related to
the Justice Committee. She began to reveal behind-the-scenes
developments within the justice file. Strosberg was again amazed –
not five minutes after castigating Andy Scott for airplane indiscretion, she was doing the same thing herself.

"Shaughnessy!" he said. "What's the difference between this
and what Andy Scott did?

"Oh," she replied, lowering her volume to a loud whisper. "I'll
keep my voice down."

The slightly mellower Shaughnessy could not resist a round of
fun with Roger either, especially if it involved making political
sport with someone in the "we don't like" category. The newest
member of that castigated group was Liberal Senator Colin Kenny.
Roger had developed a deep antipathy to the Senate after its defeat
of his cable bill, and his anger had given rise to his Senate-abolition
campaign over the previous year. Roger was one of those MPs who
immersed themselves in constituency work; he saw his relationship

with Sarnia citizens as the very basis of his job as a legislator. Kenny, appointed to the Senate when he was just 41 and thus assured of 34 years of support at the taxpayers' expense without ever having to face an election or talk to a constituent, offended Roger's sensibilities.

Kenny touched a raw nerve with Shaughnessy for different reasons. He had championed a bill in the Senate, S-13, which sought to levy a special tax on cigarette manufacturers; the revenue would fund anti-smoking programs for youth. On the face of it, this shouldn't have aggravated anyone. But senators, primarily because they're unelected, are not permitted to introduce money bills. No taxation without representation, after all. Kenny's special tax definitely fell into that forbidden zone as far as Roger was concerned. Shaughnessy thought so too, but she was doubly intent on killing Kenny's bill because it represented dedicated taxation – levying taxes for a specific government program. Paul Martin had impressed upon her the danger of this use of government spending power.

Broadly speaking, taxpayers decide what's good for themselves, and governments decide what's good for the larger nation. Taxpayers think about the individual, governments think about the group. If Ontario decided, for instance, that all its taxes should be dedicated to programs that helped Ontario, the have-not provinces such as Newfoundland and Manitoba would quickly go broke. That's the deal of the federation, and dedicated taxation would break the deal.

As was their custom, Shaughnessy and Roger began to snipe privately at Kenny and ridicule him behind his back. They joked that Kenny, the owner of several tanning salons, was promoting a product dangerous to people's health. Suntanning causes skin cancer, doesn't it? Roger had the media-savvy team in his Ottawa office put together a file of statistics about the health hazards of tanning and its links to melanoma. The intention was to use this information to heckle Kenny in Liberal caucus gatherings.

But Shaughnessy was too delighted with the joke to keep it contained. Down in the lobby one November day after Question

Period, Shaughnessy and Roger huddled at the computer and drafted a hoax press statement.

"Cohen and Gallaway Fight Melanoma! Will Propose Amendment to Bill S-13," read the headline on the obviously bogus news release. "The science on this is clear," Roger was quoted as saying in the release. "Melanoma is caused by exposure to the ultra violet rays of the sun and of artificial light sources such as those emitted by devices used in tanning salons."

"Melatonin costs our health system . . ." Shaughnessy started to type.

"It's melanoma, not melatonin," Roger chided her.

"Melanoma costs our health system millions every year," she wrote. "There is no reason for us to continue to let business operation [*sic*] like tanning salons operate free of any responsibility for this scourge."

Pleased with their handiwork, Shaughnessy smugly pressed "print" on the computer. She then walked over to the photocopy machine and printed off several copies. The joke couldn't end there. She waded into the Commons foyer, where she regularly trolled for media contacts, and said to no one in particular: "Get out your wide-angle lenses. Roger and I are holding a press conference."

A horde of reporters descended on them. To Shaughnessy and Roger's growing unease, however, none of the reporters recognized the humour in the press release. The hot camera lights shone on their faces. Journalists demanded to know whether this was indeed a plan, who thought it up, and why it had been planted in the backbench. No, no, Shaughnessy protested, it was a joke.

"You think cancer is funny?" they were asked.

At that moment, Shaughnessy looked at Roger and saw him sweating under the lights. She was feeling none too cool herself; the prospect of Herb Gray's and Paul Martin's reactions to this little prank was distinctly unappealing. "I am in big trouble when this is all over," she said, as much to herself as to anyone there. But there was nothing else to do but ⚊ in Shaughnessy's time-honoured fashion ⚊ brazen it out.

Once the worst of the "press conference" died down, Shaughnessy was pulled aside by the CBC's Jason Moscovitz, host of one of her favourite programs, *The House*. He asked if she was willing to be interviewed about her prank. "Of course," she said. During the interview, Moscovitz challenged her on whether she had gone too far, whether she had badly overplayed the class-clown routine. It was a sobering reminder that the media were not simply her audience or her laugh track. But she would not admit defeat. When Moscovitz asked whether she wished she could take back the prank, she answered: "But then I wouldn't have been asked on your show, would I?"

Later that month, Jerry was to attend a conference in Dallas, and Shaughnessy decided to accompany him. Many of the world's leading animal behaviourists would be there, including, to Shaughnessy's delight, Stanley Coren, the author of a bestselling book on dog intelligence. Here was an opportunity for a true moment of celebrity worship. Her mission was to secure his definitive verdict on the value and intelligence of all her canine friends.

Returning to Ottawa after the conference, she arrived at the apartment to find the place dark and her roommate in bed. The news from Dallas couldn't wait, though. She slipped into Anne's room, Coren's book in hand, ready to reveal all she had learned about spaniels.

The spaniel debate was a running rivalry between Shaughn and Anne. Anne owned a Clumber spaniel named Susie, whose grace and dignity she constantly praised: "She's so dainty!" Shaughnessy owned Irish water spaniels, a breed she regarded as far superior to Clumbers.

Shaughnessy impatiently roused Anne. "I met Stanley Coren and I spoke to him about spaniels. He says Clumber spaniels are lazy, stupid, and sleep a lot."

"Shaughnessy, I'm not going to get into a fight with you about this."

"Well, it's right in here," Shaughn said, dropping Coren's book on Anne's bed and breezily bidding her goodnight.

Anne sat up and started thumbing furiously through the book for the reference to Clumber spaniels. It said that her breed of dog was docile and pleasant. Not a word about lazy. Not a word about Clumbers' sleep habits.

"Shaughnessy!" she yelled. "You liar!"

"Gotcha!" Shaughnessy called back.

In early December Anne hosted a dinner at the elegant Café Henry Burger in Hull, just across the road from the Museum of Civilization. It was a working affair at which MPs involved in justice issues would establish their goals and priorities for the coming year. Among the guests was Derek Lee, Shaughnessy's caucus and committee adversary since the early days of the first Chrétien government.

That night Lee saw a side of Shaughnessy he had not glimpsed before and witnessed the very positive depth and warmth of the relationship between the justice minister and the Justice Committee chair. The conversation that night alternated between business and personal life; Shaughnessy spoke of her family, her dogs, and Jerry.

"For the first time, I had good feelings about her," Lee said. "If she had turned on that staircase, I would have smiled. If she had needed help with her coat, I might have thrown it over her shoulders." He left the restaurant shaking his head. Who was this woman who had seemed so generous and so friendly that night? Could it be Anne's influence?

In hindsight, it seems uncanny that Shaughn happened to make contact in those December days with people who had given her trouble – and whom she had troubled – during her five years as an MP. On the plane from Windsor to Ottawa on the morning of December 7, Shaughnessy once again met up with Harvey Strosberg. She spoke of her recent trip to Dallas with Jerry and about how she liked to be with her husband, how she was seizing every opportunity to spend time in his company. She was happy to have missed her flight to Ottawa the night before because it had allowed her to spend an extra evening at home with Jerry. Even so, she looked forward to the week's pre-Christmas festivities. Then she uncharacteristically excused herself, moving a few seats back to spend the rest of the flight reading. Strosberg found this odd, but he knew he'd probably see her again at the end of the week when they both returned to Windsor. It often happened that way.

At noon on December 9, 1998, Shaughnessy walked through the lobby and down the Centre Block corridor where David Iftody, her old foe from the gun control debate, was waiting for the elevator to the parliamentary restaurant. The night before, at the caucus party, Iftody had decided to sit for a while with Shaughnessy and her friends. Carolyn Bennett was there; so was Bonnie Brown, whose husband, Ron, suffering from a rare and fatal degenerative disease, had been marched to the dance floor by Shaughnessy. For the first time in many months, he laughed in pure joy at the fun he was having. Bonnie marvelled at Ron's smile; it had been so long since she had seen him happy.

Sitting with these women, Iftody too had relaxed and had ended up talking about his life, about how he had put himself through university and how much he loved politics, even after all the hard knocks it had administered through the gun control controversy.

The next day he watched Shaughnessy approach, neither scowling nor ignoring him, as she normally did. Her eyes were shining, her face was bright, and she paused to say hello. As Iftody introduced his guest, Shaughnessy stepped close and began to straighten his scarf and his collar. It was a warm and tender gesture that caught Iftody off guard. When she finished with a kiss and a hug, he was speechless.

At 3:17 p.m. proceedings in the House of Commons were halted with Shaughnessy's drop to the floor. Colleagues who had seen her alive and bubbly just minutes or hours before were shocked by her abrupt exit from this world. Ambassador Gordon Giffin was leaving the U.S. embassy, directly across the street from Parliament, when he noticed the ambulances racing up the Hill. "I wonder what this is," he said aloud. One of his staff replied, "It's Shaughnessy Cohen. She's collapsed." Giffin refused to believe it could be anything serious. Barely 36 hours earlier, she had been sitting in his library, laughing and entertaining him as the night threatened to turn into day.

Reform MP Jack Ramsay was at a reception in the Speaker's lobby. When the television in the Speaker's office showed that the proceedings had been suspended, he ran into the chamber. There he saw the MPs with medical training working on Shaughnessy, now unconscious, and as he took in the expressions on their faces, he knew his long-time adversary was gone. "All the differences we had weren't worth a darn hoot compared to her life," Ramsay said later. "I didn't want her to go."

In those hours between her collapse that afternoon and her death shortly before 9 o'clock that night, many people would recoil at the suggestion that Shaughnessy was not indestructible. People kept shaking their heads. Surely that much energy couldn't be extinguished so quickly?

Bonnie Brown paced the streets around Parliament Hill, reluctant to return to her apartment and tell Ron that the woman who had made him so carefree the night before had succumbed to the fate that he knew awaited him.

Giffin, who ended up at the *Globe and Mail*'s Christmas cocktail party while Shaughnessy lay in the hospital, watched as the reporters left the function to write her obituary. No one, not the reporters or the guests, could believe that an obituary would be necessary. "It's too soon," people mumbled. Too soon to declare her dead, too soon for her to be gone – it meant the same thing.

Coincidentally, Giffin's predecessor, James Blanchard, was planning to have lunch with Shaughnessy that very week. He had just published a book about his experiences as ambassador to Canada, and his publicity tour would take him to Windsor on Friday, December 11. He thought of calling Shaughnessy on Wednesday, but he got too busy. Early on Thursday morning he called Giffin's office for Shaughnessy's number in Amherstburg. "Haven't you heard?" his former secretary asked. "Shaughnessy Cohen died last night!"

Instead of meeting Shaughnessy in Windsor that Friday after

his last radio interview, Blanchard walked sadly up the street to the Janisse and Brothers Funeral Home to pay his respects to one of his favourite members of Parliament.

The funeral was organized by Brad Robitaille and Garry Fortune, who were guided by instinct and knowledge. First, they felt certain that Shaughnessy herself would have wanted an elaborate affair; second, and strangely, Shaughn had spoken to Robitaille just a few weeks earlier about how she'd like her funeral to be handled. Her wishes were fulfilled. The memorial was a healthy combination of the sad and the comic; speeches and sermons were interrupted by applause and chuckles. The whole event, like Shaughnessy's life, ranged from pomp and ceremony at the Tecumseh church (the largest in her riding, though not one she had regularly attended) to the raucous wake at the Legion Hall in Walkerville, a stone's throw from the Victoria Tavern. The diehards, including Margaret Atwood, went to the Vic later in the evening to raise a glass in Shaughnessy's honour.

The master of ceremonies for the funeral service was Father Paul Charbonneau, who punched the air, told off-colour jokes, and reduced the crowd to tears of sadness and laughter, almost within the same breath. He praised Shaughnessy's irreverence and her ability to see life with the wonder of a child. It was a bravura performance.

The communion segment resembled a massive cocktail party, with all of Ottawa's VIPs mixing and mingling at the front of the church. The seating had been loosely organized with the numerous Murrays on one side and her political and legal families on the other. The first rows on the left-hand side of the church were filled by the prime minister, the lead cabinet ministers, and senior representatives of Windsor, including Senator Eugene Whelan. Jerry and Dena, Betty and Bruce sat in the first row on the right. On both sides, in the rows behind those organized according to protocol and relation, women predominated. Shaughn's sisters and nieces filled the second, third, and fourth rows on the family side; her closest women friends, Mary Clancy, Anne McLellan, Sheila Finestone, and Paddy Torsney, were placed immediately behind the prime minister. Roger, with his wife, Jane, at his side, was the only man in that row of friends.

The women in this pew sat through more than 90 minutes of ceremony, clutching hands and desperately trying to believe this wasn't happening. All of them had learned to be a little bit stronger, a little less afraid, a little more willing to accept their vulnerabilities, because of Shaughnessy. She had never portrayed herself as a flag-waving feminist, and yet it was clear that the people in the closest circles of her life were women. One of Shaughn's oft-repeated refrains to her female friends was: "Don't forget you're strong. You can survive anything." Somehow, the fact that Shaughnessy believed this was enough to convince them it was true. And that they, like her, were very, very important.

Charbonneau turned the podium over to the VIPs. The prime minister gave a reading from the Bible. Deputy Prime Minister Herb Gray delivered a tribute that was laced with humour, affection, and careful attention to all her accomplishments as a teacher, a lawyer, a politician, but, most important, as a friend. Brian Ducharme spoke of his closeness to Shaughnessy since law school and how she had been possessed by the ambition to be an MP as far back as the 1984 Liberal leadership convention, when she had crossed the floor to the Chrétien camp. Cathy Roberts, her sister, reminding people far too much of Shaughnessy, bravely fought the impulse to break down and cry so that she could speak for the Murray family. Paul Martin gave his eulogy, in which he evoked the memory of his parents and what Shaughnessy had meant to them. He suggested that Shaughnessy and Paul Sr. had shared a trait in common: their great pleasure in the spotlight.

"I couldn't help but think about what was going on in Heaven at that point," Martin said, imagining that his departed friend and his father might have been listening to the tributes in the House of Commons a few days earlier. "I can see my dad hearing all these tributes being paid to the member from Windsor. He must have called Shaughn over and said: 'Shaughnessy. Hear what they're saying after all these years. See what they're saying about me.' And

Shaughn at that point would look over at my father, and then she would get that great grin we all know so well, and she would say: 'It's not about you, Paul. It's about me.'"

As the funeral service drew to its conclusion, Charbonneau announced a final speaker, one not listed on the program. More than a few in that huge church dared to think: "Could it be Shaughnessy? Could this all have been an elaborate practical joke?"

It was Jerry who stood up and walked to the front of the church. Friends and relatives braced themselves for this poignant show of strength in the face of loss.

"Hello, I'm Jerry Cohen, Shaughnessy's husband," he said, intending to show that this was one more occasion on which he was happy to serve as backup to his famous, much-loved wife.

"Shaughnessy wishes to tell you that she regrets she could not be here in person today to hear your kind words of love and respect, but she was unexpectedly called away." The crowd laughed with relief and appreciation.

"She knows we are all very sad about this and may weep over this state of affairs. It's all right. Don't be ashamed to show your feelings. Goodness, if the finance minister who had the strength to tell us we couldn't spend more than we had, could cry before you, surely this is no sign of weakness.

"She asks, though, that you do not let your sorrow turn into despair, but rather remember the joy and fun we had working together to solve our problems. And while we can be proud that we build the best cars, make the best whisky, and have the most exciting games of chance, we should not forget that above all we care for each other. We have and maintained such organizations as Brentwood, Hiatus House, and the Hospice. We still have lots to do to help heal those of us who have been wounded in life. Even though she will no longer be here to help us in these endeavours, she asks us to continue to struggle for justice in the same spirit of humour and joy."

Jerry then addressed his own fears about life without Shaughn with a heartfelt appeal to her friends. "Now that she is no longer here, Jerry, her husband, will have lots of time on his hands. Please keep him involved in our community efforts and be patient with him, for he tends to give lots of advice, which is not always good. Being a university professor, he thinks he knows more than he really does. Finally, love one another and especially your dogs. But remember that the Irish water spaniel is the best breed going."

It was a perfect speech, which could well have been written by Shaughnessy. But it was also a hint of the epilogue to be written in the days and months after her death. Jerry wasn't finished speaking for her – at least not yet.

Epilogue

Shaughnessy's departure was so unexpected, so improbable, that many of those closest to her were desolated by her sudden absence from their lives. Who would fill that early-morning silence when the phone would normally ring? Who would suddenly appear to offer a spur-of-the-moment escape from the routine? Who would replace her?

For Jerry Cohen, all these questions were writ large. Shaughnessy had brought excitement, politics, interesting friends, and welcome chaos into his world. Without Shaughnessy, his life revolved more tightly around his much-loved laboratory, the dogs, and the empty homes in Amherstburg and on Pelee Island. Jerry had completely embraced Shaughn's priorities and shared her sense of political mission; he kept his ear to the ground in Windsor while Shaughn did the job in Ottawa. So it wasn't inconceivable that Jerry should contemplate the idea of filling Shaughnessy's shoes. He talked it over with Brad Robitaille, Brian Ducharme, and Ron Doherty. They were worried that it might be too soon for him to make such a decision, but they acknowledged the obvious benefits.

Jerry knew the local file and would honour Shaughnessy's memory by carrying on in the same spirit, and political activity would help fill that terrible void in his personal life.

These facts persuaded Shaughnessy's widower, still in mourning, to seek the nomination for the by-election necessitated by her untimely death. In Windsor's small community, the word inevitably got out. On December 23, a story appeared in the *Windsor Star*, under the headline "Widower Touted as Successor: Insiders Want Cohen to Consider Political Career." The opening paragraphs declared: "Jerry Cohen could now hold the key to the Liberal nomination for the seat vacated because of the sudden death of his wife, Shaughnessy. While friends and supporters still mourn the politician who truly loved her job, the reality of filling her very popular shoes has insiders looking to the future."

Two weeks later, though, Windsor councillor Rick Limoges announced his intention to seek the Liberal nomination and the seat – meaning that if Jerry ran, he would have a true contest on his hands. "Many potential candidates are beating the bushes, and I would like people to know I plan to be part of it," Limoges told reporters on January 6, 1999.

Limoges's declaration prompted Jerry's supporters in Windsor to redouble their efforts on his behalf. But among Shaughnessy's circle in Ottawa, the idea of Jerry's candidacy aroused concern. Would Jerry get hurt? Nothing could be assumed as long as the leadership question hung in the air. In the first place, he would be seen, thanks to Shaughnessy's well-known loyalties, as the Paul Martin candidate; the "anybody but Paul" contingent would try to defeat him just to prove a point.

Shaughn's detractors were still active, as evidenced by a *Frank* magazine article early in January, which insisted that Shaughn's debts had followed her beyond the grave and that Jerry was in imminent danger of losing the family's property. Once again, the story wasn't true – Shaughn's life insurance settlement and mortgage insurance had paid for everything – but what it indicated was that Jerry would inherit the enmity that Shaughnessy had created among certain folks. Undeterred, Jerry made his intentions formal on January 12, insisting that he was looking for more than the "grief" vote. "Shaughnessy and I worked as a team," he told reporters. "We had the same ideas and the same commitment to the issues."

Unfortunately, the process and the result would prove painful. He placed a distant third in the nomination race, despite a furious scramble to sell party memberships. Limoges emerged the winner; Jerry left the hall alone. Though he took it well, the sting of this defeat was almost unbearable for his friends, coming so soon after the tragedy of Shaughnessy's death. In the manner of a hardened political veteran, however, Jerry bounced back far more easily than those who had supported him. Within a few weeks, he was busily preoccupied with his laboratory rats and declaring his relief at not having to go to Ottawa. Who would have taken care of the dogs, after all?

The Windsor–St. Clair seat remained in Liberal hands, at least. Rick Limoges became the new MP in an April by-election. The former councillor and bank executive was chosen by the prime minister to move the Speech from the Throne in October 1999. Limoges took a moment in this maiden address to note the legacy of his predecessor.

"Shaughnessy had a heart of gold and an infectious personality," Limoges said. "She served her constituents well, and I intend to be just as enthusiastic as she was in representing the interests of my constituents."

In this chamber, where Shaughnessy literally lived and died, the business of politics and government marched on. Exactly one week after she died, her former roommate delivered the government's response to the report on victims' rights delivered by Shaughnessy's Justice Committee in June. On December 16, 1998, Justice Minister Anne McLellan vowed to embrace the report in its entirety, working with provinces and territories to make victims a more integral part of the justice system.

At the top of the official Justice Department response, these words appeared: "This Response is dedicated to the memory of

Shaughnessy Cohen, Member of Parliament for Windsor–St. Clair who, from March 12, 1996 to December 9, 1998, served as Chair of the Standing Committee on Justice and Human Rights... Ms. Cohen was instrumental in bringing about the broad consensus that is reflected in the Committee's report on victims, *Victims' Rights – A Voice, Not a Veto*, to which this document responds. She will be deeply missed."

Shaughnessy would have been equally delighted to know that Paul Martin came around to her way of thinking on the "banks bad" business. That same week, he announced that he was saying no to the mergers.

In March 1999, a remembrance of Shaughnessy was held on Parliament Hill, organized entirely by a group of female political staffers, including Kate Archer, Christina Smith, and Farah Mohamed. The enormous effort that these women dedicated to the event was tribute itself to Shaughnessy, who had always encouraged young women to go as far as their dreams would take them. Shaughnessy would have been proud. At this event, it was announced that Canadian auto industry interests, including dealers and the carmakers, had set up a scholarship in her name at the University of Windsor.

On April 7, craps games came to the Windsor Casino. The first roll of the dice was dedicated to Shaughnessy, and a plaque commemorates her efforts in making craps legal for Windsor. "Dedicated to Shaughnessy Cohen, MP. Thank you for making this happen," the brass plate reads.

In May, as Shaughnessy's family prepared to inter her ashes on Pelee Island, Agriculture Canada announced that a tree had been named in her honour. As a result of concerted lobbying by Paddy Torsney, Canada now has the "Shaughnessy Cohen Flowering Crabapple," a hardy tree which produces a huge, two-toned fuchsia blossom every spring. Nell Martin has her rose; Shaughnessy has her crabapple.

In July, the government announced that another of Shaughnessy's dreams had been fulfilled. Just south of Pelee Island lies a small, uninhabited piece of land known as Middle Island. It is Canada's southernmost spot. Shaughnessy had always been irritated that the island, though considered part of Canada as far as boundaries were concerned, was in the hands of private American owners. At an auction on July 28, 1999, Parks Canada, in partnership with the Nature Conservancy of Canada, was the successful bidder, buying the property for $1.3 million. Andy Mitchell, the secretary of state for parks (or, as Shaughnessy affectionately called him, the "minister of picnic tables"), told reporters that the late MP for Windsor–St. Clair had been one of those most dedicated to the cause of reclaiming Middle Island.

Members of Shaughnessy's family were less reverential about this part of the legacy. Said Shaughn's sister Patty: "It was kind of neat that she's being credited for the Canadian government's purchase of a hunk of rock covered in bird shit in the middle of the water. Shaughn works in mysterious ways."

In September, Health Minister Allan Rock announced that his department would begin to enforce Canadian-content regulations on whisky produced in the country. The campaign that Shaughnessy had so vigorously championed in the last weeks and days of her life found its target.

A few individuals who had known Shaughnessy back in her boarding school days were not sure whether they were more shocked by the way she had died or by the way she had lived. Until the news of her death hit the media in December 1998, many of these old friends were unaware that Shaughn Murray of the Mount had become Shaughnessy Cohen, MP for Windsor–St. Clair.

Isobel Plante, no longer a nun but still a confirmed smoker, realized that her former student had become an MP only when she picked up the December 21 issue of *Maclean's* and came across page 73. "Thank You for Sharing Her," the headline read, over a grinning photo of Shaughnessy leaning forward at her Justice Committee table. The pose, the smile took Plante back 35 years to the days when she watched Shaughn Murray take control of the yearbook committee. "That leadership. That confidence. It was always there," she said. One of Shaughnessy's old classmates, Rosemary Breault, is now a sculptor living in Quebec. She is creating a statue to honour the MP.

The "big hole" punched in the Murray family's heart will probably always be there, as Cathy said in her speech at the funeral. Without Shaughnessy, everyone is conscious of a subtle shift in their roles. Some of the sisters have had to assume more of the leadership that Shaughnessy naturally commanded in the family.

Bruce Murray comes downstairs every morning and sits in the foyer of the Thamesville house, where Shaughnessy's chair from the House of Commons is on display, next to a picture of his late daughter. He sits in the chair and thinks about her, remembering her mostly from her days as a child.

Over in nearby Ridgetown, Patty's son Liam and Richard's son, Brian, decided that Shaughnessy would be the subject of their public speaking assignment in Grade 6. Liam talked about the fun he'd had with his Aunt Shaughn at Cape Canaveral, at Universal Studios, and at the movies back home. "My aunt is the joy of my life," Liam said in the conclusion to his speech. "The reason I say 'is' is because she is not gone yet, and she will never be gone as long as people remember her by who she was, what she was like, and how she is missed."

Jerry has renovated the Amherstburg home with help from the men from Brentwood, and it now boasts glowing pine floors, a gleaming bathroom with a Jacuzzi, and a huge deck overlooking the river, complete with hot tub. The kitchen is big and open and finally, with dozens of brightly coloured Fiestaware jugs on display, looks just like the picture in her scrapbook of decorating ideas. One of her Fiestaware casserole dishes is no longer part of the collection, however. Shaughnessy's ashes were placed in the beloved dish and buried on Pelee Island, right near a water pump that carries the warning "Do Not Drink." Mary Clancy suggested the epitaph carved into the simple stone laid flat on the ground: "Age cannot wither her, nor custom stale her infinite variety," from Shakespeare's *Antony and Cleopatra*.

Garry Fortune still wheels his white van around Windsor on the weekends, keeping an eye on the city for Herb Gray and watching over the MPs in the area. Sometimes, when the weather is perfect or when he's tired of running from constituent to constituent, he will reach for his cellphone without thinking, instinctively hoping to find Shaughnessy and persuade her (it didn't take much) to knock off for the day and join him for a beer or two. "That's when it hits me that she's gone," says Fortune.

At the Vic, it's a little quieter on Friday afternoons. But tell the waitress that you're a friend of Shaughnessy Cohen, and you may get a free drink or two from Larry Burchell. The waitress will tell you, smiling, "She was a no-bullshit lady."

U.S. President Bill Clinton visited Ottawa again in October 1999. He would not have asked after Shaughnessy Cohen. But Clinton's representative in Canada, Gordon Giffin, misses that MP from Windsor–St. Clair. Shaughnessy, he says, is one of those politicians who actually did turn out to be irreplaceable. "There is nobody outside the formal part of the government, meaning the people who are assigned responsibility, who has replaced Shaughnessy as the informal chair of the Canada-U.S. caucus," Giffin says. "It takes an interest, first. It takes a level of energy. And it takes an insight for that to work."

Jane Stewart, now the human resources minister, still looks around the Ontario caucus on Wednesday mornings, half hoping to see that large woman from Windsor making an entrance. There is no one who can sashay into a room and show off a new outfit the way Shaughnessy did, says Stewart.

Anne McLellan has moved to a smaller apartment at the Queen Elizabeth Towers. All of Shaughnessy's furniture and belongings were shipped to Cathy, and Anne has made a new place for herself. Sometimes when she gets home and drops her heavy ministerial briefcase in the foyer, she is stopped for a moment by the quiet. No television news in the background; no group of MPs and pals gathered in the living room, raucously reviewing the day's events. When she stands before her bathroom mirror in the morning, the shelf littered with the trinkets that Shaughnessy brought back as gifts from her foreign trips, Anne wishes for the familiar figure in the doorway, entertaining her with tales from the night before.

Paul Martin feels Shaughnessy's absence every time he walks into the government lobby. The emptiest spot is that couch, where Shaughnessy used to sit. "What used to be a court is now just furniture," he says. "And you only have to look at Roger's face to see what's missing."

These days Roger Gallaway has a lot more time to pursue his various causes — his campaign to abolish the Senate, his crusade against the cable companies — without constant distractions from the member from Windsor–St. Clair in the office upstairs. The Can-Am Canteen posters lie rolled up beside the couch, the unused cases of beer sit untouched. Every now and then, as Roger lights yet another cigarette, a faint smile will dance across his face, as he remembers Shaughnessy's constant nagging on the smoking issue. "It will kill you," she used to say. As Roger takes a puff, he jokes: "I'm here. She's not. I guess I win!"

Sometimes on a beautiful Saturday afternoon or right in the middle of an absorbing task, the phone will ring. Before I know it, I've said: "Goddamn it, Shaughnessy! Don't you ever get off that phone?"

And then I realize that of course it isn't her. There are no more annoying interruptions at deadline time. I can finish whole articles, book chapters, or interviews without once having to grab the receiver and bark "What?" when that singsong voice comes on the line, saying, "Hi there. Just checking in!"

But I wouldn't mind hearing that voice again on the phone, wouldn't mind being told yet again how important she was. In her absence, then, let me say it for her: Shaughnessy Cohen was very, very important — to a lot of us.

Index

The text in this book is set in Bembo, a typeface produced
by Stanley Morison of Monotype in 1929. Bembo is based on
a roman typeface cut by Francesco Griffo in 1495;
the companion italic is based on a font designed by
Giovanni Tagliente in the 1520s.

Typesetting by Marie Jircik